ADAM MICKIEWICZ

ADAM
MICKIEWICZ

1798   1855

IN COMMEMORATION

OF THE

CENTENARY OF HIS DEATH

UNESCO

Published in 1955 by the United Nations
Educational, Scientific and Cultural Organization
19, avenue Kléber, Paris-16e
Printed by Buchdruckerei Berichthaus, Zurich

© Unesco 1955
Printed in Switzerland
CUA 55 D 16 A

Cover: 'Adam Mickiewicz.' Pencil portrait by Eugène Delacroix (1798–1863), 11×7.5 cm. (Paris, 1841). Album of Helen Hryniewicka. Mickiewicz Museum, Paris.   Photograph by W. Slawny.

Frontispiece: 'Adam Mickiewicz.' Charcoal drawing, oval, 12×15 cm. (Vilna, 1821). Original destroyed during the fire at the Krasiński Library, Warsaw, in 1944.   Photograph by L. Sempoliński.

To speak of Mickiewicz is to speak of beauty, justice and truth; of righteousness, of which he was the soldier, of duty, of which he was the hero, of freedom, of which he was the apostle and of liberation, of which he is the precursor. . . .

VICTOR HUGO

(Letter addressed to Władislas Mickiewicz, 17 May 1867)

PREFACE

At its eighth session, held in Montevideo in November and December 1954, Unesco's General Conference decided to publish a work honouring the memory of Adam Mickiewicz. In thus paying honour, on the centenary of his death, to the poet who wrote *Pan Tadeusz* and *Forefathers' Eve*, Unesco wishes to join in the celebration of a poet who has brought honour not only to Poland but to all mankind.

Though his song was weighed down by the sufferings of his country, it resounded throughout the world, as if coming from the very heart of the last century, with a message of hope and an assertion of faith in freedom. Even today this song has still retained its whole power and its noble example.

The present collection of writings is due to the co-operation of authors from countries which in a peculiar degree shared in the life and work of Adam Mickiewicz, or which were particularly responsive to the spreading influence of his genius. It is neither a work of erudition in literary history, nor a compilation of factual information. But the essays here collected and the selections from

Mickiewicz' poems which accompany them, will, we confidently hope, serve to introduce to a general public—which we trust will be considerable—works not only inaccessible to most readers in their original tongue but whose translations into French or English are often out of print.

Other volumes are being published in connexion with this centenary celebration, and Unesco is gratified to know that these publications will supplement the present collection of essays and selections, and will in a measure amend its shortcomings.

Unesco is grateful to all who have worked on this volume, especially to Professor Kazimierz Wyka, of the University of Cracow, whose enlightened counsel has been highly appreciated.

Tributes by contemporaries of Mickiewicz were collected by Adam Mauesberger.

The Biography was prepared by Mrs. Irena Kucharska, and the Bibliography by Mr. Piotr Grzegorczyk.

The illustrations were collected through the kindness of the Adam Mickiewicz Museum in Warsaw.

We are also grateful to the directors of the Adam Mickiewicz Museum of Paris who authorized the reproduction of several documents belonging to their collections.

CONTENTS

SELECTIONS FROM MICKIEWICZ' WRITINGS

TRIBUTES BY CONTEMPORARIES OF MICKIEWICZ

A BRIEF SKETCH

OF THE

LIFE OF ADAM MICKIEWICZ

dam Mickiewicz was born on 24 December 1798 in the village of Zaosia near Novogrodek, in Byelorussia, which at that time was under the domination of the Tsars. He came of an impecunious family of the lesser Polish nobility; his father, Nicholas, was a barrister at the police court in Novogrodek. After the death of his father in 1812, the financial situation of the widow and five children became more precarious. From then on, during his whole life, Mickiewicz had to struggle against money difficulties. From the moment his first volume of verse appeared, it was his pen that guaranteed him a livelihood.

Between 1807 and 1815, he attended the local Dominican school in Novogrodek. He left it in September 1815, to enter the University of Vilna, the best in Poland at the time, as the holder of a government scholarship. Eminent scholars like Joachim Lelewel, Jan and Jedrzej Sniadecki, were among the professors who taught there. In November 1817, with some fellow students, he founded a secret society for young people, known as the Philomats, with aims that were at once ethical, scientific and political.

The membership of that association, somewhat restricted at the outset, grew, and it became a much more important organization, which took the name of the Philarets. Mickiewicz was the prime mover.

In 1819, the poet left the university with the degree of Candidate in Philosophy.[1] During the vacation which followed, he made the acquaintance of Maryla Wereszczakowna, his romantic love, who was to play an important part in his work. In September of the same year, he taught literature, history and law at the secondary school in Kovno. Along with his teaching activities, he wrote occasional verse for his friends and began work on his *Ballads*. He also continued his studies and in 1822 received the degree of Magister Philosophia, on presentation of a thesis entitled *De criticae usu atque praestantia*. His thorough linguistic training enabled him, many years later, to occupy the Chair of Romance Literature at the University of Lausanne and that of Slavonic Literature at the Collège de France.

In June 1822 Mickiewicz published his first volume of poems, including *Ballads and Lyrics*—the most important manifesto of the romantic movement in Poland. During his second period in Kovno, in 1823, the second volume of his poems, containing the second and fourth parts of *Forefathers' Eve* and *Grazyna*, was published in Poland.

This period of Mickiewicz' life was to end in disaster, with the discovery of the secret youth societies by the Tsarist government. The poet was arrested on 23 October 1823. On 25 October 1824, Mickiewicz, condemned like most of the others to be deported to Russia, left his homeland for ever.

In November 1824 he arrived in St. Petersburg, where he made contact with Polish circles and with the Russian conspirators, later arrested in connexion with the Octobrist affair, and their relatives and friends.

In 1825, armed with letters of introduction to subversive circles in the south of Russia, he set off for Odessa, and visited the Crimea. The poetic fruits of this journey were two cycles

---

1. Equivalent to a bachelor's degree.

of sonnets—the *Sonnets of Love* and the *Crimean Sonnets*, published together in December 1826.

Mickiewicz was eventually attached to the Office of the Military Governor-General of Moscow, where he arrived in December 1825. Shortly after came the profoundly distressing news for the poet of the suppression of the Octobrist movement.

In Moscow, we find him making friends with Alexander Pushkin, writing for the *Moscow Telegraph* and planning to publish a Polish newspaper, the Iris, but permission for this was refused by the censorship authorities. At this time he met the famous Polish pianist Maria Szymanowska, whose daughter he was to marry some years later.

Konrad Wallenrod was published in February 1828, despite the censorship ban. During the poet's last period in St. Petersburg, in 1829, the two-volume edition of his poems appeared with a frankly polemical preface entitled 'On the Warsaw Critics and Essayists'.

After surmounting the many difficulties put in his way by the Tsarist authorities, Mickiewicz received permission to leave Russia. He set off in May 1829, carrying away with him a fund of valuable experience and unforgettable impressions.

He reached Berlin in June 1829, where he frequented Polish student circles and attended Hegel's lectures. He then went to Bohemia, and from there to Weimar, to visit Goethe on his eightieth birthday. In August, he continued his travels through Switzerland and Italy, where he stayed from October 1829 to July 1830, travelling constantly and making new contacts, while remaining in touch with Polish and Russian circles. In August and September 1830 he visited Switzerland.

In October 1830 Mickiewicz returned to Rome. There, in December, he received the news of the November insurrection in Poland directed against the Tsarist regime. He proceeded to Paris, where he hoped to obtain help for his compatriots in arms. When these hopes vanished, he set off in July 1831 for Poland, to Posen first of all, from where he tried unsuccessfully to cross the frontier beyond which the fighting continued. Already in September 1831, the insurrection was approaching its collapse. Mickiewicz remained in 'Great Poland'[1] until March 1832, when for the first time in his life he had an opportunity of really learning to know Poland. Until then he had known only Lithuania and Byelorussia, which were provinces of the former republic.

The failure of the November rising had a profound influence on the life and work of Mickiewicz. It marked the beginning, for the poet and fighter that he was, of a new period of long and generous service to his country, both in word and deed.

From March 1832, he linked his fate to that of the Polish exiles and set off for Dresden with what remained of the November rebels. They were enthusiastically welcomed by all the peoples of Europe who were struggling in the cause of freedom.

At Dresden, in April, Mickiewicz wrote the third part of *Forefathers' Eve*—a dramatic poem on the struggle for national freedom, against the background of the history of the Philomats movement. He arrived at the end of July 1832 in Paris, where he was received with some distrust by the French authorities, who kept him under police surveillance.

The third part of *Forefathers' Eve* was published in November of the same year. *The Book of the Polish Pilgrims* was published next, and translated as early as 1833 into French, English and German. This was a book dealing with current political problems.

Mickiewicz was already writing for the *Polish Pilgrim* in 1832, and in 1835 became its general editor for three months. At the same time he took an active part in the public and political

---

1. The name given to the part of Poland occupied by the Germans.

life of the Polish exiles. In December 1832, he began work on a great realist poem *Pan Tadeusz*, which he completed in February 1834. This poem was published in June of the same year. On 22 July 1834, Mickiewicz married Selina Szymanowska, whom he had known earlier in Moscow.

From 1835 to 1837, he turned away from his close connexions with Polish circles, since he did not share the political views of most of them. On the other hand, he established relations with French circles. The acquaintances that he made included Montalembert, and George Sand who, in 1839, wrote a celebrated article on him. He wrote for French papers, such as the *Revue du Nord* and the *Globe*, in which, after the death of Pushkin, he published his recollections of the great Russian poet.

Hearing that the Chair of Romance Literature was vacant at the University of Lausanne, Mickiewicz went to Switzerland on 11 June 1838, and was soon appointed professor there. The university authorities had the highest regard for his scholarship and teaching ability. During this period, he wrote a cycle of lyric poems, his last poetic work.

In 1840, the French Government invited Mickiewicz to the Chair of Slavonic Literature that had just been created at the Collège de France. He began his lectures there on 22 December 1840. These lectures, in the course of which he did not hesitate to raise political questions, aroused great interest on the part of the audiences, but at the same time gave rise to criticism, particularly in Polish emigrant circles.

At the end of 1841, Mickiewicz met Andrew Towiański—a mystic who was to have a certain influence on him. The poet joined the society of the followers of Towiański's doctrine, known as Le Cercle. After Towiański was driven out of France, Mickiewicz became its president. It was not until 1847 that Mickiewicz made a definite break with Towiański. Traces of the influence of the mysticism of the Cercle are to be found in the text of the Collège de France lectures. But Mickiewicz was

not willing to abandon his constant criticism of Western bourgeois society and the Papacy, and the violence of this criticism
caused his lectures to be suspended in May 1844.

After the events of February 1848, Mickiewicz left for
Italy, to organize a Polish Legion to fight against Austria; but
this move was opposed by a section of the Polish emigrants.
The poet tried in vain to interest Pope Pius IX in the cause.
On 1 May, the Polish Legion arrived in Milan, where it concluded an agreement with the Government of Lombardy, to
help the Italians in their struggle against Austria until such
time as revolution broke out in Poland. Mickiewicz returned
to Paris on 11 July 1848 to seek volunteers and financial support
for the Legion, which took part in revolutionary struggles in
various parts of Italy. After the failure of the revolution, it was
disarmed by the French and sent to Greece.

The path of the Legion did not bring the poet back to his
homeland. His desire to obtain a Chair at the Jagellonian
University in Cracow, as proposed by the Rector in January
1849, was not granted. On 15 March of the same year, in Paris,
Mickiewicz took over the French paper *La Tribune des peuples*,
founded by international political exiles. The aim of this paper
was to obtain support from the French Government for the
revolutionary movements in Europe. The poet was general
editor until its suspension on 13 June 1849. When it re-appeared
in September of that year he wrote for it clandestinely.
On 10 November, the French authorities put an end to the
Tribune.

In April 1852, Mickiewicz was suspended from his func-
tions as professor at the Collège de France, and deprived of
his modest salary. In October, he began work at the Library
of the Arsenal.

When the war in the Crimea between the European powers
and Russia raised a hope of bringing up the Polish question,
Mickiewicz set off on 11 September 1855 for Constantinople,

to organize a Polish Legion to fight against the Tsars. He died in Constantinople on 26 November 1855.

On 21 January, he was buried in the cemetery of Montmorency, near Paris. On 4 July 1890 his remains were taken to Poland and solemnly placed amongst the royal tombs in the Wawel—the Pantheon or Westminster Abbey of Poland.

ESSAYS

INTRODUCTION TO THE LIFE

AND WORK OF

ADAM MICKIEWICZ

Jan Parandowski

Veneration of great men is becoming an ever more powerful bond, uniting races and nations which are conscious of their common destinies, aspirations and ideals. Thus a world pantheon takes shape, to which each nation contributes its particular glories. But the time has passed when nations wished to introduce into it their former deities, fetishes of unreal power and authority, of false radiance—kings and warriors who represented nothing beyond a fleeting moment of history and partisan passion. Today they know that it is their great thinkers, the poets, the artists, the inventors, who confer on them their titles to nobility. It is they who honour them most eloquently, as well as the whole of humanity, for despite all the differences—of epoch, of environment, of language —a profound kinship unites them. The man who was once considered as no more than the spiritual leader of his own country is now seen to belong, by virtue of his genius and his humanitarian ideal, to the elect group of those who dominate the whole of humanity.

In this universal pantheon, Poland has more than one monument, but one finds constantly recurring these three

names: Copernicus, Chopin, Mickiewicz. Everyone knows
the first, so to speak, from his cradle; the second arrests
our attention at some time during our youth, through a
melody which we will never forget; the third, for the
majority of men throughout the world, is a nearly unpro-
nounceable collection of letters behind which no distinct
features are visible. Even those which Bourdelle carved in
his fine monument do not fix themselves in the memory,
for the statue is set high and the Place de l'Alma is so
crowded with traffic that it is impossible for the passer-by
to contemplate this pilgrim, as he stands above the bustle
of our times.

For Adam Mickiewicz was a pilgrim, literally and figur-
atively. A pilgrim of the soul, he moved towards liberty,
towards enlightenment, towards the future, inspired by
truth, goodness and beauty. In his earthly life he was a
wanderer whose every road took him farther from his
birthplace. Born at Novogrodek, in Poland's eastern
marches, he died at Constantinople, which he had never
thought to see. Yearning for his motherland had led him
there, and it was for her that he wished to fight by the side
of Turkey.

It was not the first time that Mickiewicz had drawn the
sword. He had already done so in 1848, during the thrilling
'Springtime of the Peoples' when he created the Polish
Legion in Italy, to fight, side by side with that country,
against Austria, one of the three oppressors of Poland.

He had visited Rome before, at that other great moment
of his life and of the history of Poland, after the defeat of
the November rising. He had not been able to take part
in the rising, and today we rejoice that his name was not

added to the list of victims, and that he was able later to
fulfil his great destiny. He had not taken part in the rising,
but his heart was with those who had captured the
Belvedere. Each one of them carried in his heart *Konrad
Wallenrod.*

It is a strange poem. It can no more be summarized or
retold than a stained-glass window can be described.
Konrad Wallenrod is complicated and obscure like the
stained-glass windows of old cathedrals, and just as over-
whelming in its manifold beauty. In it are the charm of
childhood, love, battle, the iridescent colours of the
familiar ancestral landscape, and each line is charged with
grief, hatred and vengeance. Captive Poland is represented
here by an allegory taken from the history of Lithuania and
her struggles against the Order of Teutonic Knights. The
hero of the poem is a Lithuanian whom the Teutonic
Knights have kidnapped as a child and brought up in a
language and in a spirit which are not his own. Through
his ability and courage he afterwards becomes their Grand
Master. He has not forgotten his country and, after attaining supreme power, he decides to use it for the ruin of the
Order, but when he has almost achieved his aim, he suc-
cumbs.

Above this poem hovers the spirit of Machiavelli, a
quotation from whom gives the keynote of the book; in
the figure of the hero, on the other hand, can be recognized
the features of some Byronic creation, such as Lara or the
Corsair. There is nothing surprising in this. No one at that
period could free himself from the influence of Byron, not
even the ageing Goethe. Along with the whole romantic
movement, Mickiewicz had undergone this influence; he

had translated the *Giaour* and extracts from *Childe Harold*. But Konrad Wallenrod far surpasses the Byronic heroes in the grandeur of his sentiments and aspirations, and his tragedy is more deeply moving than the incomprehensible sufferings of Lara or the Corsair.

Mickiewicz wrote *Konrad Wallenrod* in Russia. He was living there in enforced residence in 1824, after the trial of the Philomats. These were an association of university youth at Vilna, and the poet, who was about 20 at the time, was the soul of it. He had written the words of a few songs which were sung at meetings and on excursions by these enthusiastic young people, songs of rich gay rhythm, which spoke of brotherhood, of freedom, of social duty, of progress. The *Ode to Youth* was of an even higher inspiration; it was the poetical manifesto of a generation which captivity had not cast down, which on the contrary had drawn from that captivity faith in its own powers and the conviction that it was its task to change the order of a stagnant, dying world. The *Ode to Youth* could be the song of every nation and of every age, wherever consciousness of the struggle for progress and faith in the deathless springtime of the peoples is born again.

But Senator Novosiltsev, whom the Tsar had sent to Vilna 'to put order into the affairs of the university' did not desire such a spring. Like every satrap he had an unerring instinct and, in poems which spoke about flowers and young leaves, he was able to unearth evidence of a conspiracy against that order of things which had covered his chest with decorations and which, on the other hand, oppressed the unruly Polish nation. He immediately had the leading spirits of the movement imprisoned. Mickiewicz, shut up in a cell of the Basilian monastery, heard the November wind blowing and howling as a background to his lonely meditations.

Eternal stupidity of despots: Senator Novosiltsev, in confining Mickiewicz in this cell, felt sure of humiliating and breaking the prisoner; in fact, it was he himself who some years later was thrown into a prison which he was never to leave. In a scene of *Forefathers' Eve*, the Senator appears dancing, amusing himself, fighting against a nightmare, a prey to demons, conducting an inquiry or pronouncing a sentence, and revealing himself as a coward, a bully and a brute. As long as the Polish language endures, this scene will preserve for us an unforgettable vision of baseness and abjectness, a pitiless picture of oppression, all anathema, warning and menace. In this way the poet revenged himself on his tormentor—in return for a few weeks of confinement he bestowed centuries of ignominy upon him.

The trial of the young people took place. A number of them, including Mickiewicz, were charged with 'unreasonable Polish patriotism' and exiled to Russia. Mickiewicz was already a well-known poet. He had published two volumes of verse, including the *Ballads and Romances*, *Grażyna* and two parts of *Forefathers' Eve*. The appearance of this work marks the beginning of a Polish romanticism fully conscious of its ends and its means; it was an event of the same order as, for French poetry, the first night of *Hernani*, but it took place several years earlier. Romanticism had conquered all Poland almost without opposition and it was never to be renounced.

At the beginning of his book of ballads Mickiewicz had placed the word 'romanticism'. Everything about them is characteristic: the title, the introductory quotation from *Hamlet*, the text.

They formed a challenge to the 'classical' poets, to the men of the age of 'enlightenment' and to the principles of a classical, reasonable poetry which was faithful to the 'rules', not only of versification but of the various literary forms. Our ideas today are wider and we are catholic enough to reconcile the love of romanticism with an appreciation of the achievements of classical poetry. In the eyes of the romantics, the classics appeared as ludicrous, dried-up mummies, *des vieilles perruques*.

Mickiewicz was not one of those who could imagine no world but that of romanticism. He composed ballads full of ghosts and horror, but he also sang the praises of one of our 'enlightened poets' in whom he appreciated the formal excellence. His own background was a classical one, and his education had been thorough. His teacher, Groddeck, had been an eminent philologist of Vilna. He himself was not only an excellent latinist, capable of composing Latin verse, like the *Ode to the Glory of Napoleon III*, but also a hellenist to whom neither Homer nor Aeschylus nor Pindar presented any difficulties. He was in the line of the Polish humanist tradition, unbroken since the sixteenth century.

The action of *Forefathers' Eve* takes place in a township, among common people, almost peasants. In broad daylight a girl is walking, conversing with the spirit of her beloved; she can see him; she tries to draw near to the ghost, which disappears; she weeps. The people are touched and display their sympathy, but an eye-witness who happens to be there, clearly a learned man, speaks up against this sort of witchcraft and superstition. The poet sides with the girl and the common people against the reasoning of the scholar and, at the end, addresses to him these words which are a summary of his whole poetic philosophy: 'Open your own heart and look into the hearts of other people.'

At night, in a chapel in the graveyard, under the leadership of an old wizard, a group of peasants gathers and invokes the dead. The ghosts of children appear, as well as those of a girl who had died in early youth and of a cruel lord, the tyrant of the village. As each spirit appears, warnings and moral teachings are proclaimed. In an atmosphere of mystery the timid encounter of the living with the world of the dead takes place. At the end appears a strange phantom, on which no spell has any effect; a young woman steps forth from the crowd to follow it, passive and obedient.

This incident is a tranposition of the poet's own love drama. He had fallen in love with a girl of wealthy, noble family; as often happens in such cases, the poet, being poor, had been refused her hand, and the girl had been married to a count. This unhappy love affair was a godsend to Polish poetry. Never did a wounded heart express its feelings with the passion of Mickiewicz in the fourth part of *Forefathers' Eve*. It is a confession and, that it may sound the more probable, it takes place before a priest.

To the parish priest's house, at midnight on that night, comes a strange guest, half tramp, half madman, shaggy, oddly attired; and, amid the flood of his speech, we learn his name, his previous life and the tragedy of his love. His name is Gustav; he was once the priest's pupil; today

17

he is an outcast—if he can still be counted in the world of the living. The woman he loved was taken from him. No summary can convey the emotional effect of these dramatic scenes with their single character, or of the monologue composed like a symphony with its recurrent themes in which the tone, at times elegiac, at times plunges suddenly into a torrent of grief and despair and at others assumes a melancholy sincerity which recalls a stream flowing through a forest.

Gustav is a romantic hero who lacks the grotesquely exaggerated features characteristic of this type of character. He has not aged as have all the rest, those misty, gloomy, mysterious, satanic, ironical figures, bitter as poisoned flowers, who have converted dramas, poems and poetic novels into a mass of bric-à-brac into which no one now has the resolution to glance, save a few patient specialists who deserve our admiration. Every time the voice of Gustav rises from the page our hearts reply to it with an intensity of feeling which is worthy of this burning poetry.

It is astonishing that the poet should have been capable of writing, almost at the same period, the poem *Grazyna*, which is as epic as it is objective. Based, like the later work, *Konrad Wallenrod*, upon the history of Lithuania's long struggle against the Teutonic Order, this poem, more legendary than historical in character, is remarkable for its sense of measure, the purity of its composition and the monumental conception of the characters and scenes. The heroine is a woman who saves her husband's honour by taking his place in the fight against the Teutonic Knights at the moment when he, betraying his country, is about to ally himself with them. Prince Litawor's conversation during the night can stand comparison with the arrival of the messengers in Achilles' tent in the *Iliad*.

This, then, was the poetical baggage which preceded Mickiewicz when he set out for Russia after the sentence of the court. Literary circles in Russia had already heard his name; his reputation was enhanced by the charm which emanated from his person. With charm the young poet was well endowed; his superiority was revealed by the first words of his conversation. He dazzled his auditors by his gifts of improvisation. At such times they had the impression that the incarnate spirit of poetry had descended among them; some believed that they had before their eyes a magician, a man of supernatural gifts. His pallor, his flashing eyes, his whole striking figure, arrested the imagination and fixed itself in the memory.

He had made an easy conquest of the drawing-rooms of St. Petersburg and Moscow. He was welcomed everywhere with pleasure, particularly in progressive circles, where a Polish exile could be sure of encountering general sympathy. He had made friends among the Russian writers; he was intimately associated with Pushkin; the Russian poets translated his poems. The women also were ready to console him for his bitter memories of unhappy love. They inspired some ten sonnets which took their place beside those which he had translated or adapted from Petrarch; but, in making use of this intricate form, so dear to poets in love, Mickiewicz converted it into a magnificent instrument on which to express his feelings in a new way. A trip to the Crimea gave rise to the *Crimean Sonnets*, a cycle of poetic landscapes in which the emotion aroused by the beauty of nature is blended with meditation upon the world, upon man and upon the poet's own soul, the whole expressed in a style as concise as it is precise. Mickiewicz wrought his sonnets with great care. This was, without doubt, the only time in all his career when form, in the highest sense of the word, played so great a part in his work. He was like a Benvenuto Cellini who had exchanged the sculptor's tools for the delicate instruments of the goldsmith. The *Crimean Sonnets* sparkle like gems, so much colour and light has the poet concentrated in them: words and metaphors reflect the rays of the rainbow like iridescent diamonds.

The *Crimean Sonnets* and *Konrad Wallenrod* had appeared in Russia. In the latter work the censorship saw nothing more than a Byronic tale set in the past, and by the time its hidden meaning was detected it was too late! The poem was already in circulation and its author, equipped with a passport which he had long requested, was abroad and could safely laugh at all the senators and chiefs of police. He was free, with the freedom of an exile, an *émigré*, a wanderer, a pilgrim: these are the very terms which he was later to apply to himself in the successive stages of his wandering existence.

He did not know where he was going to settle down; the problem did not even occur to him. At the age of 30 he was surrounded by his nascent glory. He was thirsty for the world. Every door opened before him. Goethe welcomed him at Weimar and, in the course of a long conversation, had his draughtsman draw the portrait of the young poet, who had arrested his interest. He gave him as a keepsake a pen with these words:

Truveyser
1853

Photograph of Adam Mickiewicz, by M. Szweycer, Paris, 1853.

Dem Dichter widm' ich mich, der sich erprobt
Und unsre Freundin heiter gründlich lobt.[1]

The 'friend' referred to here was the celebrated pianist Maria Szymanowska, Goethe's last love and the mother of Mickiewicz' future wife.

Not only had he made his personal entry into the literary life of Europe, but his poems followed him: they were translated, read, discussed. These were happy years.

It was at Dresden that Polish poetry rose to its noblest heights. It was there that Mickiewicz wrote, during the spring of 1832, the third part of *Forefathers' Eve*, which is, along with *Pan Tadeusz*, his uncontested masterpiece.

Vain attempts have been made to trace the descent of this dramatic poem from *Faust*. Its only source is the soul of the poet amid the storms of his own life and of the nation's destiny. George Sand made no mistake when she set *Forefathers' Eve* above *Faust*.

In the entire history of European drama there is nothing equivalent to the scene in *Forefathers' Eve* where, alone in the silence of the night, Gustav, the unhappy lover, traces the following words with a piece of charcoal on the wall of his prison:

D. O. M.
Gustavus
obiit MDCCCXXIII
Calendis Novembris

1. 'I consecrate myself to the poet who proves himself
And who heartily praises our merry friend.'

and, on the other side:

Hic natus est
Conradus
MDCCCXXIII Calendis Novembris

The transformation of man is here accomplished not by an
act of witchcraft, not by a document signed with his
blood, but solely by an act of the will by which he frees
himself from the bonds of his personal failures to become
the spokesman of his people, the expression of its sorrow,
its despair and its hopes; finally, rising to a still higher
level, he incarnates the suffering of all mankind.

This epitaph bears the date of the period which
Mickiewicz spent in prison; the action is laid in the cell of
the Basilian monastery. Gustav Konrad is the poet himself,
regenerated by the baptism of national defeat. The culminating moment of the drama is Konrad's monologue,
known as 'the great improvisation', his dialogue and
struggle with God, which is charged with Aeschylean
tragic grandeur.

Prometheus is the poetical creation which is recalled by
these lines with their melody, which changes in character
as the conflicting principles of the soul change. Konrad
asks God to give him 'the power over souls'; like God,
he wishes to possess a power over men which shall be
capable of elevating them and freeing them; this son of an
oppressed, mortally wounded nation knew better than
anyone else what it is that men need. Sorrow gave him the
right to speak in the name of millions of men suffering in
silence. The idea of a Pole's mission to God and to the

world is combined in the poem with that of the mission of
Poland which, by her martyrdom, had won the right to
struggle not merely for herself but for all nations which are
bent beneath a political or social yoke. This thought is
expressed in the vision of Father Peter, the prison chaplain,
who sees Poland as Christ crucified, the innocent victim of
the whole world.

This idea was styled 'messianism', and for half a
century one section of the Poles accepted it while the other
rejected it. Mickiewicz was never to give it up. He had set
upon the brow of his martyred people a crown of lilies and
thorns, and this symbol recurs throughout his work as
well as in his political manifestos. Ten years later no one
was surprised to hear him speaking, from his Chair in the
Collège de France, more like an apostle than like a professor. This the government of Louis-Philippe was unable
to permit.

Mickiewicz had not found the subject of *Forefathers' Eve*
in past ages or in exotic lands, as the romantics were wont
to do; he had simply taken a recent event, still drenched in
reality as the roots of plants freshly torn from the ground
still remain moist; he had taken living characters and had
given them their real names. These characters were in
reality colourless and commonplace, as, in the history of
a great nation, the events from which the action of the
drama proceeds are insignificant. By the grandeur of his
inspiration, by the breadth of his thought, he had raised
this slice of life to the level of a myth. It was only a poetic
transfiguration of the facts of which he had been the witness
and the victim, of the trial of the Philomats; some of the
scenes, as for instance that of the Warsaw Drawing-Room,

begin with a sketch of the situation in Poland and awake
the echo of the persecutions in Lithuania, borne in a
frightened murmur from mouth to mouth, from heart to
heart, across the entire land.

The scenes succeed each other in a strange fashion.
Some, like the meetings of the prisoners in Konrad's cell,
are simple, everyday conversations expressed in admirable
verse, the rich and lively remarks of young men who are
always ready to blend laughter and tears. Others, like the
Improvisation or the Vision of Father Peter, attain a
sublime pathos. Others again take place in the Senator's
office or drawing-room. The ever-changing human soul
is revealed to us in nocturnal reveries. It is not necessary
to be a Pole in order to feel the horror of these prisons and
these punishments, where a man whose only crime is love
of country is sentenced by the usurper and by a law which
deprives him of the most sacred rights. In whatever part of
the world the words 'tyrant' and 'oppression' are known
these pages will be understood; and every mother will recognize herself in the old, blind Madame Rollison who, through
the thick prison walls, hears the cries of her tortured son.

In the same way, traitors, criminals, spies and informers,
whose living portraits attain symbolic grandeur in this
work, will recognize themselves. In brief scenes, in a few
lines, with Shakespearean clarity and realism, the poet
sketches unforgettable portraits, types of characters which
are known wherever the enemy has succeeded in finding
his servants and his collaborators inside the organization.
Mickiewicz is rich and prodigal like Shakespeare; after
relegating a character into a dark corner, he suddenly turns
a blinding light onto him, then leaves him again; another

would have made a whole drama or a comedy from the same material.

George Sand, seeking a point of comparison for *Forefathers' Eve*, rejected, one after another, *Manfred*, *Faust*, Dante. None of them was suitable. She even went much further: 'Since the tears and the imprecations of the prophets of Zion no voice has arisen with such power to sing so vast a subject as that of the fall of a nation.' And indeed, after *Forefathers' Eve*, Mickiewicz began work upon *The Book of the Polish Pilgrims*. Against the background of the history of the world he relates in Biblical verses the history and the martyrdom of Poland amid the decadence and abasement of the so-called happy communities. Written for the Polish *émigrés*, that human flotsam lost amid a foreign society, those men who still preserved a faint hope of which each passing day gnawed away a particle, *The Book of the Polish Pilgrims* was to bring these men consolation, to give them new courage, to raise these wanderers to the dignity of pilgrims; it compared them to Israel marching across the desert in search of the Promised Land. *The Book of the Polish Pilgrims* was adopted as their own by the peoples who were fighting for their independence, by the Italians in Mickiewicz' day, by Ireland and Israel in our own.

An unexpected period of calm occurred in his poetry, if not in his life, like a moment of serenity and appeasement. To it we owe *Pan Tadeusz*. At Berlin a few years before, Mickiewicz had attended Professor Gans' lecture on Napoleon. The Professor, catching sight of the poet among his students, suddenly interrupted his lecture and declared that Mickiewicz alone was capable of writing some day the Napoleonic epic. He must have read it in the stars, for

Mickiewicz had never thought of such a thing, and did not think of it even later, when he began to write *Pan Tadeusz*. It was only by a faint Napoleonic note, unexpected even for the poet himself, that he concluded this idyll at the end of the first canto. The chord continued to sound throughout this strange poetic symphony.

Mickiewicz, who was born in 1798, some years after the last partition of Poland, had been brought up among men who had personally experienced the loss of independence, but who could never adjust themselves to it; leading the same life amid the same surroundings, they could preserve the illusion that nothing had changed. But the year of Mickiewicz' birth was still close to those of the French Revolution, and he had seen with his own eyes Napoleon's expedition against Moscow. Hailing in his poem the memory of the spring of 1812, he concluded with this line: 'I have had only one such springtime in my life.'

Moved by his epic instinct, he chose the moment when the two worlds, the old and the new, meet and exist together before they are parted by the current of time. The work is impregnated with the melancholy of times gone by; the word 'last' recurs like a refrain in the mouths of the men of the old order; but at the same time the poem opens a window onto the vibrant contemporary period which in the last canto enters in the form of a colourful, turbulent throng of Napoleonic officers, unaware of the fact that they already have their place in the heart of legend. As he forged his theme, Mickiewicz gave way to his natural impulse to nourish his poetry from the fountainhead of the reality which he had himself known and lived.

Like Homer, he packed an action which lasted barely

a few days with such a wealth of facts, episodes and
characters, he opened so many windows upon the past and
the future, that we are lost in the calculation of the days
and nights, the sunrises and sunsets comprised in the
poet's calendar. For the romantic poet it was not enough
to say, 'when rosy-fingered Dawn appeared', to announce
the morning; in Mickiewicz the sun really rose, each day
in another way, amid an ever-different play of light and
cloud. All the other parts of day and night were described
by him in vast landscapes which foreshadow impressionism.

Nature, omnipresent, with her own unforgettable
features, reigns over this poem in equality with man. In it
are fields and gardens, undergrowth and ponds, animals
from the familiar birds to the lords of the forest, the wolf
and the bear, and the freshly-cut corn smells sweet. In the
same way as Homer immortalized the humblest of objects,
even the latches of the doors, so Mickiewicz tinged with
the glow of his poetic genius the whole of this life that was
past or passing, the life of a country gentleman's house
with its domestic concerns: food and drink, dress, arms,
amusements and quarrels, love and discord, intimate
conversations, gossip, legends, superstitions, fears and
hopes. He saved from oblivion an old ramshackle Jewish
wine-shop and preserved for ever the sound of a hunting
horn at the moment when it is dying 'at the gateway of
the sky'.

There are several themes in *Pan Tadeusz*: that of love,
which, after a series of developments, concludes with the
marriage of Tadeusz and Zosia, the incarnation of virginal
grace; that of the dispute between neighbours over an old
castle, a dispute which leads to an armed attack, and this

in turn to a clash with a Russian detachment; that of Jacek
Soplica who, beginning as an adventurer and murderer
becomes, first, a soldier of Napoleon, then a monk, an
emissary who plans the rising in Lithuania and who dies
reconciled with the world and with his own conscience.

Who is in reality the hero of the poem? Is he the man
who gave his name to it, but who is only a colourless
character in comparison with his father? Is it Jacek Soplica
who, notably in his death-bed confession, one of the most
beautiful passages in the whole epic, rises from a secondary
role to that of a hero? Perhaps the real hero is the soul of
Poland herself, which cannot be described in two words
and which every definition renders not clearer but more
obscure. What is tangible, concrete, comprehensible, is
the unity in the variety of the costumes and the character
of the people, in its virtues and its failings, in its land, its
flora, its fauna, under a sky which resembles in no respect
the skies which shine, each with its own sun and its own
stars, upon other nations. In the *Iliad*, too, one may hesitate
between Achilles and Hector and may in the end decide
that the hero is the very essence of the life and spirit of
Hellas, in which all the Greek peoples recognized themselves.

Pan Tadeusz is the only epic poem of the nineteenth
century, a century which did not have the gift of the epic.

Pan Tadeusz was received with admiration, enthusiasm,
veneration; but at once his people began to demand a new
work of Mickiewicz. The Poles were waiting for the next
portion of *Forefathers' Eve*; they wanted this national mystery
play to include the story of the rising. In the final scene of
the third part of *Forefathers' Eve* the crowd gathered in the

graveyard catches sight of a *kibitka*[1] speeding towards the east, bearing Konrad away. Everyone had the right to conclude from this scene that this was only the first act, as the title gave clearly to understand, and that the rest would soon follow. Mickiewicz himself thought of continuing the work.

But *Forefathers' Eve* remained a long fragment. Mickiewicz tried on several occasions to resume work on it. He outlined new scenes; he wrote a few dozen lines here and there; he scored through or tore up the scraps of paper on which he wrote, but he was unable to pick up the thread he had dropped. In the same way, *Faust* would have had no second part if Goethe's life had not been as long and as tranquil as it was. Mickiewicz' destiny was a different one. Being neither a lord, like Byron, nor a count, like Pushkin, nor a minister, like Goethe, he could be only a professor, like Schiller, and even that in another country and another language than his own.

The University of Lausanne offered him the Chair of Latin Literature and hailed him in the decree of appointment as 'one of the leading poetic geniuses of our time, an aureole of European glory'. He delivered his lectures in French, but he could equally well have employed Italian, English or German, if one of those countries had entrusted him with a professorship. However, after his mother tongue, French was the language he knew best; he wrote in French not only articles and studies but also dramas; but it was in his impromptu speeches that he expressed himself best, and Frenchmen often fell under the charm of

1. Carriage employed in Russia for the transport of prisoners.

his style, which was full of the delightful discoveries which
a foreigner makes in a language not his own, if the foreigner
happens to be a great poet.

Soon a Chair was created specially for him, that of
Slavonic Literatures at the Collège de France. It was impossible for him not to accept it and, although he enjoyed
the tranquillity of Lausanne and thought of Paris with
apprehension, he gave up everything to take up this new
appointment, which was so important to Poland and to
all the Slav nations. The Collège de France was attended
not only by students but by scholars and writers of all
nationalities. It had become the custom to look in there,
even if one was only passing through Paris. Every lecture
was discussed at length in Paris literary circles.

For the first time the Slavonic literatures had overcome
the indifference of Europe. For the first time they had at
their service an eloquent orator and a true scholar. At that
time the history of Polish literature was virtually non-
existent, and the same was true of the other Slavonic
literatures. In the case of some Slav peoples the situation
was even worse: they had no linguists, ethnographers or
historians of manners and culture, and even their history
still contained many gaps. Large numbers of literary
monuments were mouldering in old, incorrect editions.
Our admiration is aroused when we see Mickiewicz plunge
into this virgin forest, hastily gather his materials, rapidly
translate selections in verse and prose and draw bold,
vigorous historical pictures.

What stirred his listeners still more was the spirit of
liberty which gave wings to the professor's words. He let
slip no opportunity—and every century, every generation

in the history of the sorely-tried Slav peoples furnished
such opportunities—to proclaim the superiority of law
and justice to lawlessness and oppression. These ideas
united him to two other apostles of freedom, Quinet and
Michelet; we see them together on the celebrated medallion.
Soon the admirers who took down his lectures in short-
hand were joined by representatives of the secret police in
the guise of diligent students; their reports are known to
us today thanks to the researches of Edouard Herriot. In
the course of a few years these reports became so unfavourable that Mickiewicz was obliged, first, to terminate
his lectures and later to tender his resignation. 'He was
accused of going beyond his curriculum', cried Renan, in
his oration at Mickiewicz' grave. 'Ah! How difficult it is
to restrict oneself to the limits of a curriculum when one
is intoxicated with the infinite!'

Intoxicated with the infinite—it would be difficult to
find a better definition. Unfortunately, he had been given
a draught far more potent than the infinite, a decoction of
turbid theosophy. It was dispensed by a man who had the
reputation of a prophet, and Mickiewicz, by an incomprehensible freak of destiny, came to be among his most
fanatical adherents. It would serve no purpose to speak at
length on this subject, but the episodic attachment complicated Mickiewicz' life and helped to render it still more
difficult.

Married to Celina Szymanowska, the daughter of the
famous pianist, he was burdened by a household in which
a child was born every year; there were six in all. Neither
husband nor wife was capable of supporting them: the
poet's income was too small and too irregular, while his

wife was affected periodically by mental troubles which made it necessary for her to spend periods in various nursing homes. Stark poverty frequently reigned in the household. It was at such times that, in the quest for work which would provide a livelihood, he hastily compiled dramas intended to bring him success on the Parisian stage. They were never produced. The whole of Mickiewicz' literary output extends over some fifteen years, from his university days until his maturity. He was not yet 40 when he had already written all his works, apart from a few later fragments and those which the fire consumed. He never ceased to be a poet—as professor, politician, journalist and soldier he was still a poet. At every public appearance, and even in ordinary conversation (if his conversation could ever have been ordinary) he was enflamed by poetry, and it is this that explains the enthusiasm which he aroused even in those who had never read him: the Florentine crowd, dazzled by the flame which burst forth from the words of the leader of the Polish Legion, greeted him with the cry, 'Altissimo poeta!' In the records of the time we see a succession of men of every condition who felt, so to speak, transfigured in the presence of this prematurely lined face, with the shock of greying, dishevelled hair and the glance as burning as the poet's words. Mickiewicz was the incarnation of the romantic conception of the poet—*vates*, the seer—and he was to remain so in the memory and the veneration of the century.

After giving up poetry he became the apostle of a new faith, a journalist, a soldier. It was in the course of these manifold activities that he conceived the thirst for that 'domination over souls' which, through the mouth of Konrad, he demanded of God. He was not the only poet of the time who desired to attain power. At the same period when Mickiewicz was editor-in-chief of *Le Tribune des peuples* Lamartine became a member of the government. But, while Lamartine rejected the red flag, Mickiewicz unfurled it in his journal. This fact was to shorten the existence of the *Tribune* and even obliged Mickiewicz for some time to go into hiding.

The caustic sallies of his compatriots were more deeply wounding to him than the fact that he was persecuted as an *émigré* by a foreign government. Mickiewicz was spared no insult, no anathema. As today we walk in the shadow of his statues we find it hard to realize that this pilgrim was once the object of so much hatred, mockery and contempt. But his image had not yet been cast in bronze; he was merely a little middle-aged gentleman with a tendency to put on weight, in a threadbare frock-coat buttoned up to the throat—nothing more than an employee of the Arsenal library. This was the last post which he came to occupy, on one bitter day of his wandering life. It was from there that he set out on his last journey.

Byron's death at Missolonghi was still in every memory at the time when Mickiewicz conducted to Constantinople a detachment of Polish volunteers to fight the Russians side by side with Turkey. And, in the same way as the pestilential miasmas of the marshes had poisoned Byron in the prime of life, so the rough and wretched life of the camp exhausted the small store of strength which still remained to the weary pilgrim. So weak was he that he required a chair in order to lift himself into the saddle.

It is believed that he died of cholera. He breathed his last in a wretched room in an obscure corner of Pera, and it was only when his embalmed body was taken on board ship that Constantinople learnt that it had been the last stage in the life of the great poet. The entire polyglot throng of the Slav population of Constantinople in picturesque array attended the greatest singer of the Slavonic soul as he set out on his last voyage.

He was to rest only forty years in French soil. His remains were brought back to Cracow in 1890 and laid in a crypt among the tombs of the kings of Poland in the Wawel.

It was a symbolic act. The nation offered him the sceptre and the crown, it granted him the 'power over souls' which he had vainly sought during his lifetime as though he doubted whether he could win it by his poetry alone. No one denied him this right any longer. Mickiewicz is today the undisputed ruler of the kingdom of poetry which he created. There was not and there has not since been in our language a greater poet than he. He did not come like Dante at the time of the timid commencements of a national literature, or, like Shakespeare, at the threshold of a new era. He had behind him several centuries of poetry during which various literary forms and *genres* had been tried and perfected. His century could offer him only a new movement, romanticism, which was, no doubt, fruitful and stimulating, but which cannot be compared to those which, by their power, relegate the entire past into the shadows. Romanticism was not a revolution like the Renaissance. Mickiewicz, however, was a Renaissance phenomenon: he really did regenerate Polish poetry and fashion it anew. Goethe, I suppose, played a comparable part in the history of German poetry.

Mickiewicz invented a new form *(Forefathers' Eve)*, a new poetical tone, after which all that preceded it became outdated, while all that has come since derives from it. He brought a new conception of poetry. Before his time no one had loved his country to this degree, no one had expressed and sung this love and united its destiny to that of the world. In this sublime flight he joins the company of the greatest creators, those who before him had lifted man above the earth, as the Jehovah of the Sistine Chapel raises an Adam who is not yet free of the earthly slime.

'Adam Mickiewicz.' Bronze medallion, by Pierre-Jean David d'Angers (1788–1856), diameter 12.5 cm. (Weimar, 1829). Mickiewicz Museums in Paris and Warsaw. Photograph by L. Sempoliński.

ADAM MICKIEWICZ

AND EUROPEAN ROMANTICISM

Jean Fabre

'How', said Valéry, 'can people discuss the subject of "romanticism" rationally?' Is not the very word one of those 'abstract' and 'conventional' terms, the purpose of which seems to be 'to provide a pretext for an infinite series of disagreements'? Some of these 'disagreements' occur to the mind at once. Every critic in every country will be tempted to define romanticism in a different way according to the period and the atmosphere, the environment and the moment—according, above all, to his own fancy. There are such things as romantic art and the romantic soul: they do not always coincide. In characterizing the former, the books on the subject, particularly in France, tend to limit themselves to its most striking manifestations: the disdain of *genres* and rules, the combination of different styles, the fondness for the Middle Ages and for folklore, for historical or exotic colour, the primacy of lyricism, the flowering of drama. In the romantic soul there is an inextricable blend of profound exigencies and assumed attitudes—*spleen*, 'passion without object', *mal du siècle*, fondness for solitude, reverie and the idea of death; but also the will to power, the insistence upon heroism,

37

the primacy of action—this complex of often pretentious, arrogant egotism is susceptible of a thousand different combinations and nuances, from the purest narcissism to the most generous self-abnegation.

It is this that produces the effect of disorder and anarchy in which gloomy moralists have sought the explanation of the disequilibrium from which the modern world suffers. In fact, however, romanticism was not so much a cause as an effect. It revealed, rather than occasioned, the dislocation of the literary, religious, political, social and moral framework in which the civilization born in Europe of the compromise between the heritage of antiquity and the exigencies of Christianity had until then been enclosed. Amid this general wreck of values, one value alone seemed destined to escape the collapse of which it was the cause: what the philosophy of the Enlightenment termed 'natural individuality', and regarded as an inalienable appanage of individuals and nations alike, was to serve as the basis of romanticism. The latter is inseparable from an inner conviction of liberty, an urge for liberation. Literature gave this urge the opportunity of self-expression, but not of fulfilment. Romanticism restored to poetry its powers and its rights, only to offer it to man as a means of liberation, an instrument of action. It very soon ceased to find satisfaction in rhythms and phrases, if not in dreams. It strove to impose itself upon reality, upon the destiny of men and nations. It moved beyond literature into the field of politics and social change; it ceased to be elegiac and passive, and became heroic and militant. Renouncing their cherished anguish, poets aspired, and attempted, to place themselves at the service of their brothers and of life; they took their place in the front rank of that battle for a more humane society which, under various forms and with various changes of fortune, has been in progress ever since. In the end, therefore, romantic disorder served in the quest for a new order; its diversity makes manifest the unity, at once obvious and secret, which marks European civilization and everything in the world which derives from that civilization, at a decisive moment of its history.

That this view is not mere intellectual juggling is shown by the history of literature. Preoccupied by poetry in itself, Valéry did not observe that, unlike other terms, such as classicism and baroque, which were created after the event and which are indeed 'abstract and conventional', the word and the notion of romanticism were given their significance by the very people who participated in the movement. There was hardly a romantic writer who did not try to define his vocation and his art in terms of romanticism, even though the definition he gave might amount to a criticism and a rejection. This observation, which holds good for all, is verified in the most convincing manner in the case of Adam Mickiewicz. No one thought out the essence of romanticism more profoundly, no one lived it with more intense passion than he. It is this which confers on his destiny and his works their value as an example. It is he who more than any other writer enables one to comprehend the historical significance and, above all, the practical exigencies of the great movement which gave itself the name of romanticism.

The ballad with which, in 1822, Mickiewicz' first volume of verse opened, is entitled *Romantyczność* (Romanticism); it is prefaced by a vast 'Study of Romantic Poetry'.

In 1829 a further preface, in the form of a 'Reply to the Warsaw Critics', the obstinate adherents of a pseudo-classicism of the Baour-Lormian type, marks a new stage along the road to the liberation of poetry. Later, at a time when Mickiewicz had abandoned poetry, his lecture of 20 December 1842 at the Collège de France contained a profound study, one of the most penetrating which the subject ever inspired, on the origins and significance of European romanticism: Dante, Shakespeare, Byron and what Mickiewicz terms, somewhat vaguely, 'the German school', above all Goethe and Schiller, are adduced as witnesses. These three texts would suffice, at need, to furnish what might be called the charter of romanticism; but there are many more which naturally fall into place about them, as though stubborn meditation upon the subject of romanticism had lain at the origin, the heart and the summit of Mickiewicz' entire work.

This meditation is all the more instructive since for him romanticism was a discovery and a conquest, not a heritage or a datum. His education had been purely 'classical', in the sense in which a disciple of the *philosophes* and the *idéologues* would have understood the term. The philosophy of the Enlightenment had left a profound imprint upon Poland and had made it possible for an old State which was fated to disappear to acquire the means of survival and of rebirth as a nation. After Poland had disappeared, the task of public education, into which the Poles of the eighteenth century had put the best of their efforts, went on in the schools which they had founded, or at least in the shadow of those schools. The semi-academic, semi-secret societies of the Philomats and the Philarets in which

the young student of Vilna played an active part had at the
beginning no other object than to maintain this tradition.
Mickiewicz was never to forsake it. His ideal corresponds,
on the whole, to that which was expressed by Condorcet.
Like him, he believed in the 'progress of the human
spirit' and in the universal peace which would be its
consecration and its guarantee. The difference between
them was that he desired to give a more lyrical accent and
a more real content to that hope. The Man of the Enlightenment remained conventional and abstract; the 'Romantic
Man' appears more diverse and more complete, enriched
by all the virtualities of feeling and marked by the specific
characteristics of race and nation. A premature cosmopolitanism had not, indeed, authorized, but at least
tolerated so grave a crime against the real unity of the
human race as the partition of Poland. In the great
assemblage of the peoples to which romanticism aspired,
each one was to contribute intact its own natural individuality developed to the full under a regime of complete
sovereignty.

In demanding and foretelling this new order, the poet
remained in the line of the masters who had contributed
decisively to the moulding of his mind and, also, of his
taste. Mickiewicz began his poetical career with translations
from Voltaire and descriptive and didactic poems in the
manner of Delille, with the addition of colour. He composed Polish adaptations of the fables of La Fontaine with
no less love, and perhaps with more genuine pleasure, than
his adaptations of Byron. For, by taking La Fontaine as his
model and thereby entering into competition with his
compatriot Krasicki, the prince of the poetry of the

Enlightenment, he was following the genuine bent of his nature: common sense, good humour, sprightliness, subtle expression. These qualities were never to forsake him, even amid his raptures and ecstasies. Reason shines forth from amid his unreason. Herein lies one of the principal charms of a poet whom people tend to picture exclusively in the attitudes of prophet and seer, forgetting his qualities of simplicity and good nature—thus ignoring the sense of measure which led him to place literature at the service of an ideal which was higher than literature, and to refuse to poetry the quasi-religious devotion which was accorded to it by a certain type of romanticism, if never by his.

Indeed, purely literary considerations played only a very secondary part in Mickiewicz' literary conversion. He expressed the point with emphasis: if romanticism is nothing more than a pastime which consists of breaking the rules of art and 'putting devils everywhere', then it is not worth an hour's trouble. No doubt, romantic imagery blazes forth in all its strangeness in the *Romances and Ballads*, in the flowers, the ghosts and the watersprites which bewitch the lake of Świtez, as it does in the evocative sorcery of *Forefathers' Eve*. But their fantastic elements retain such a popular flavour and are enlivened with such humour that one never knows whether certain lines of Mickiewicz should be read in the tone of Goethe's *Fisherman* or in that of Marcel Aymé's *La Vouivre!* In plain terms, it should be observed that these feats of picturesqueness and rhythm were never, to him, any more than exercises, although on another level than that of mere virtuosity. 'People's hearts', he confessed one day to Marie d'Agoult, 'are more interesting to me than books.' Where so many other romantics sought only a masked ball of the imagination, Mickiewicz found an opportunity to link himself with the consciousness of his people and nation, the permanence of which it was the duty of poetry to make manifest. All this apparent fondness for what is fantastic and weird reveals the poet's quest for what he terms 'a living truth'. There is a palpitating life in the freshness of imagination, the ardour of feeling and the simplicity of faith which are peculiar to the Polish people. Before he could place himself at its service, the poet had to learn all that it could teach him. 'To have a heart oneself and to look into the hearts of other people'—the slogan launched by Mickiewicz at the conclusion of his *Romanticism*, far from being a romantic commonplace, expresses the most personal need, the prime condition of his vocation.

Already in the *Ode to Youth* this vocation has found its fire and vigour. To flee 'the skeleton peoples', to escape from the 'dead waters' of egoism, to attain the open sky of illusion is not necessarily to abandon reality. The poet summons his young companions to follow him: 'Ho there! Shoulder to shoulder! Let us encircle this wretched globe with our chain. . . . We will pull you out of your rut, old universe, and push you along new paths.' At a period when in France sensitive souls were melting over the languors of *L'Automne* or *Le Lac*, the voice of Mickiewicz was giving Polish romanticism an incomparably more manly accent. It uttered the first call to the revolution, the means and the purpose of which were as yet only half-glimpsed by the conspirator-poet: to liberate the peoples (in the first place, naturally, Poland), but to liberate them along with and through the common people.

It was a mighty undertaking. As he unfolds his sail, the mariner (Zeglarz), whom Mickiewicz chose as a symbol, is fully aware of the perils—rocks, darkness, storms— which will beset his voyage. But none of them is more insidious than the voice of the sirens. On more than one occasion the romantic poetry from which he drew his first fervour was to lure him with its spells, tempting him to abandon the struggle. Mickiewicz bears within him the melancholy of an unhappy love; in his hours of distress, death, dreams and art offer him a refuge. The sonnet *The New Year* which he wrote in the Vilna prison on the last day of 1823 on a theme recollected from Jean-Paul—a dangerous surety!—aspires to nothing more than the prison of a coffin wherein to sleep, to dream until the end of time. On more than one occasion, the romantic temptation was to bear him towards the man whom the genius of Poland had given him as a rival, as though to illustrate by this living contact the basic duality of romanticism.

There is no doubt that for Julius Stowacki poetry represented from the beginning and at all times the essential thing: a thrilling game, no doubt, but also 'the sleep of the soul', the means of fleeing from the world, the escape which his friend Louis Spitznagel had sought in suicide. Stowacki's heart, like that of his Greek insurgent Lambro, remains 'petrified' in its 'boredom' (*nuda*). To what, to whom can one dedicate oneself? 'I go among men', he says, 'as through an autumn forest. I crush the leaves beneath my feet; I disdain these leaves.' He has the world-weariness of René and the passion without object and the 'swallow's restlessness' which beset his tragic double, Kordjan; but he is fascinated, above all, by Byron and that for the very characteristics which Lamartine vainly conjured that false evil angel to discard: the contempt for mankind, the rebellion against the law and against God, the invectives, the sarcasms, the blasphemies.

Mickiewicz too will admit among the modern poets no other model than Byron—Byron, the hero of action, the great-hearted crusader. 'Lord Byron', he said in his *Course of Slavonic Literature*, 'opens the era of modern poetry. He was the first to make men feel the serious import of poetry. Men saw that they should live in accordance with what they wrote, that desires and words were not enough. . . . This deeply felt need to render life poetical, to bring together the ideal and the real, constitutes the entire poetic merit of Byron.' This paradoxical eulogy reveals the hyperbole to which Mickiewicz' genius tends: to make of poetry an act, in order then to sacrifice it to the imperative—or the mirage—of action. If Byron is for him much more than a poet—an intercessor, if he sees in him 'the mysterious link which attaches the great literature of the Slavs to that of the West', the reason is that 'the ray which kindled the poet's fire issued from the soul of Napoleon'. It is true that Byron depicted Napoleon as a corsair, but also as 'a soul ever at work'. This astonishing juxtaposition will not now be questioned; still less, the corollary which Mickiewicz boldly deduces from it: 'Napoleon created Lord Byron; Lord Byron's action and the very noise of his glory awakened Pushkin' and, with him, 'the provincial schools' of Poland and all the poetry which was latent in the Slavonic world. Mickiewicz' cult of the great emperor, the hero of the advancing revolution, became blind adoration and after 1848, was even directed to the other Napoleon in whom he thought he recognized 'the man of the age' announced by the prophecies of Towiański. These are the errors to which one is exposed when one endeavours to separate poetry from the poem in order to infuse it into the course of history and life.

The five years following his arrest, which Mickiewicz was to spend in Russia, not, indeed, in deportation, hardly even under police surveillance, gave him an opportunity to concentrate his powers and then to try them out. It would be a great error to interpret the splendid *Crimean Sonnets* as mock-oriental poetry, as mere sumptuous embroidery upon exotic themes. In the marvellous and poignant silence of *The Steppes of Akkerman*, in *The Silence of the Sea*, his nostalgia goes in pursuit not so much of images as of dreams. His poetry withdraws into itself before launching into the verbal exploits of *Farys*, in which the verse seems, like the hero's breast, to swell with the wind of the desert. One can understand the astonished admiration of Pushkin and the young poets who had given a fraternal welcome to their Polish guest. But their admiration was based on a misunderstanding, a disagreement as to the function of poetry. The poems which they hailed as an achievement were for Mickiewicz only a prelude and a diversion. Harshly, he sent his admirers back to their books and knick-knacks for happy people—local colour and the picturesque element in history. He said of Pushkin: 'At times he is Byron, at times Walter Scott; he is not yet himself.' And, according to Mickiewicz, grudging time was never to permit Pushkin to become himself.

To the luxury of personal problems and personal anguish, as also to the purely aesthetic traditionalism which aspires to offset them, Mickiewicz constantly counterposes his insistence upon the need for revolution and the consequent necessity for action, whether open or clandestine, against injustice and tyranny. His relations with the Decembrists show that he found in Russia inter-locutors who were capable of understanding him. The rest retained, from his ardent improvisations, only a sort of mirage. 'In the depth of his soul', Pushkin was to say in 1834, 'there was no hatred for us. And we too loved him. . . . He often spoke to us of the future, of the day when the peoples, forgetting their quarrels, will unite like one great family.' But one must work for this future before one sings it. *Konrad Wallenrod* makes plain how painful the birth of that future may be, and what total self-sacrifice it requires of those who work for it. Through the medium of the legendary Lithuanian hero, Mickiewicz boldly reveals to his Russian friends the only role which the fate of his country allowed him to play among them. Konrad has won the hearts of the fierce Teutonic Knights, the butchers of his race and country; he has become their Grand Master, but he exploits their total confidence only to lead them to their destruction. Certainly, he will pay with his remorse, his suicide and his damnation for the role of Grand Master which he was most reluctantly obliged to assume; but his country will be free.

A few years later, Musset treated the same theme in the context of a Florentine chronicle. The distance which separates *Lorenzaccio* from *Konrad*, both in inspiration and in artistic accomplishment, reveals the difference between

literary and militant romanticism. For *Konrad* was not
simply an heroic poem; it was an act; it created an abyss
between the destiny which Mickiewicz had chosen and
that which Russia's warm welcome offered him, that of a
poet laureate in receipt of all the goods of this world.

After Russia—alarmed but still generous—had chosen
to open the highways of Europe before the stubborn poet,
rather than continue to offer him a hospitality in which he
could see only the confinement of a prison, he was to meet
upon his road another poet, one who was to make possible
a dialogue such that no imagination can picture discussion
more lofty or more charged with significance. In August
1829 Goethe received Mickiewicz at Weimar. In their
persons classicism and romanticism seemed to have been
brought together in a sublime confrontation. The Pole
Odyniec was the witness, and endeavoured to be the re-
corder, of the meeting. What struck him in the first place
was the tone of the interlocutors. 'Goethe', he says, 'has
so profound, so mature, so lucid a mind, that to listen to
him is to learn; but, unlike Adam, he is not inspired to
say things which cut your breath short and halt the circulation of your blood.' The subject chosen was, naturally,
the only one which mattered—the future of Europe, the
reconciliation of the peoples, the hope of a fraternal world.
Goethe's reason does not exclude this hope, but it con-
ceives of its fulfilment only by the courses which it accepts
as reasonable. According to him, 'the duty of superior men
is to render international relations more humane, just as
it is to facilitate navigation and to open roads across the
mountains. The free exchange of ideas and sentiments
contributes to the well-being of mankind in the same way

as the free exchange of goods; if it is not practised yet, it is because international society has no fixed laws or moral principles. . . .' At the same time, Odyniec notes, Goethe did not indicate on what basis these principles and laws should be erected. How could he have done so, he who considered injustice to be a lesser evil than disorder? Mickiewicz, for his part, did try to indicate this basis or, at least, to lay down the conditions which must be fulfilled before one could speak without blasphemy of such principles and laws. In the face of the tragedy of man's state and of history, the only reasonable thing is the madness of poets, which plucks the world from its egoism, and conscience from its slumber. No one can read the verses *To a Polish Mother* without recognizing in them the accent of which Odyniec spoke and which awakens remorse in the soul of everyone who hears it.

Mickiewicz' mission was, at first, in the tragic years, to be 'The voice which says "Woe!"; the mouth which says "No!"' To compel him to accept this mission, destiny seems to have found obscure complicities in the poet's subconscious. One should beware of indulging in irony on the subject of the repeated concatenations of circumstances which prevented this singer of decisive acts from partaking in the risk and the intoxication of action. Mickiewicz was in Italy when, on 29 November 1830, the Warsaw insurrection broke out. It was eight months—and the material obstacles accumulated in his path do not suffice to explain the delay—before he reached the Polish frontier, just in time to be borne away on the flood which, as in the time of Kosciusko's wars, swept towards Dresden the survivors of a hopeless battle. 'God', he wrote to

Lelewel on 23 March 1832, 'did not permit me to partici-
pate in any way in that great work, so fruitful for the
future. I live only in the hope that my arms will not be
folded in the tomb before I have acted.' But this hope does
not compensate the shame or the remorse. Similarly,
Stowacki, who happened to be on the spot, left Warsaw
on the pretext of some diplomatic mission before the
hour of the last combats. Their very genius denied the two
poets the peaceful conscience and the self-satisfaction which
lie in wait for the veteran, even of a lost cause. Without
doubt, Mickiewicz' poetry required only this element of
irony amid tragedy to carry it to its highest pitch of
tension and to subject it to the unbearable force of
exaltation which breaks free—crushing the poet as it does
so—in the third part of *Forefathers' Eve*.

In this work romanticism reaches its loftiest peak, that
which it cannot hope to attain without the danger of
ridicule and to which it raises itself only at the price of
extravagance or death. Freed from his own suffering by a
suffering which was more real and more sublime, freed
from his past by his mission, from his heart by the grief
and despair which have broken it, Mickiewicz-Gustav,
transfigured into Konrad, symbolizes, without doubt, the
transition from elegiac to Promethean romanticism, but,
above all, endeavours to achieve that transmutation of the
human into the superhuman which is the most ancient
dream of the poets. Filled with the accumulated desire of
the Illuminati and the Magi who wished to crown the
demiurge in man, Konrad, from the depths of his prison,
extends his arms towards the sky, and 'his hands were set
upon the stars as upon crystal keys'. The only poets who

were to try to share his grotesque and mighty hallucination were the last, and the purest, adherents of the romantic creed: Lautréamont, who refers specifically to Konrad, and Rimbaud, who seems to be imitating his gestures and repeating his words in the last stammerings of *Les Illuminations*. Their example reveals clearly enough the price which their excessiveness is bound inevitably to pay: madness, silence, the desert of the soul where poetry has withered for ever. One thinks of Rimbaud's 'C'était mal'. But the forces which impelled Mickiewicz to blasphemy were suffering and love, not pride; and it is 'the voice of the Devil' which utters the final word of the challenge he has thrown to a Creator who is indifferent, or worse, to the misery of His creation, 'I shall cry that you are not the father of the world but—its Tsar!' Konrad has collapsed in the meantime like a corpse. Father Peter, bearing a message of pardon, comes in to speak words of exorcism and peace over the lifeless body. The man who rises at his words knows well that his destiny is not to perform miracles but to know 'the combat without glory', 'the martyrdom without resurrection' for which the poet once told 'a Polish mother' to prepare her child.

But he was always to bear within him, as a burden, not as a source of strength, the suffering which he had gathered to his arms: 'I hold in my embrace the whole nation, all of its generations past and future. . . . I feel their suffering as a mother feels the pain of the child which she carries in her womb.' After Mickiewicz and in imitation of him other poets in other tongues and other places gave voice to a similar claim. In the name of the whole body of French romanticism after 1830 a somewhat condescending generosity was to 'expand' the heart of Lamartine to admit 'the sorrows of his brothers':

And, like a great shroud unfolded by pity,
The soul of a single man, open to the groans of the crowd,
Will bewail all sorrows.

The nobility of the intention is beyond question—but it remains as abstract in its object as it is conventional in expression. In practice, the expansion of his heart will have no immediate consequence for the poet other than an electoral campaign to undertake or a banquet to preside over. One comprehends Mickiewicz' disdain for these apostles of human solidarity whom he sees swarming about him. The burden beneath which he bends does not resolve itself in dithyrambs and metaphors, however unbounded his pretensions may appear: 'My country and I are one thing: its name is Million.' The presumptuous formula describes with a kind of heartbreaking simplicity the real position in which the poet found himself when his poetry became the most real mode in which a nation reduced to the silence of the prison and the grave still manifested its existence. The aspiration of literary romanticism, to associate poetry with the profound life of the nation, received in the case of Poland its most magic and its most immediate significance. But it required as stout a heart and as robust a genius as that of Mickiewicz in order not to be crushed by it.

The humility which he represented as the prime virtue both for himself and for his people was, at bottom, only a counter to the lurking temptation of folly and pride.

'Zaosie', a village on the outskirts of Nowogródek where Mickiewicz was born on 24 December 1798. Drawing by Felix Brzozowski (ca. 1861). Photograph by L. Sempoliński.

The myth of the chosen people was common to the whole of European romanticism; but when Italy and Germany, in the course of their struggle for unity, put forward their claims to this title by the voice of their poets and thinkers, these claims marked the return of an ancient dream of power and domination. For Mickiewicz Poland was to be not the Winckelried but the Christ of the nations. In his messianism he does not hold out the promise of the Kingdom; he offers, first, regeneration through suffering, acceptance of the cross. In him, illuminism was freed from the pitiless harshness which alone inspires the thought of a de Maistre or a Gobineau. Similarly, the 'man of duty' whom he incarnates by identifying himself with the nation is at the opposite pole from Nietzsche's superman: he has received his consecration in order that he may love, not that he may scorn. The message which *Polish Pilgrims* was to bring to Europe was not the call of some new Moses charged with the task of leading the peoples on the march towards a Promised Land, but rather the cry of the prophet wandering through the streets of Nineveh to summon it to repent. The resurrection of his country, associated by him with the general liberation of the peoples, can take place only in a world that has been washed clean of sin; the last onslaught, which he ventures to prophesy, against the age-old forces of oppression and evil, will achieve victory only if it is inspired by brotherly love, not by hatred, only if each fighter has begun the revolution with himself, by killing the previous self in the depths of his heart. Taking one dream with another, this one is certainly as good as the myth of power, which romanticism was to accept under so many aberrant forms. Péguy's 'city of brotherhood' had no other foundation than the world of which Mickiewicz dreamed.

The voice of the prophet-poet could not hope to attain full resonance elsewhere than at the meeting point of all spiritual roads, the city of Paris, which was predestined by a poetic cliché to be 'the modern Babylon'. But the modern world has at its disposal more than one means of stifling the voices of its prophets, and none is more effective than the applause which it sometimes accords them. Among Mickiewicz' Parisian admirers even the most generous hearts, the best-intentioned minds—Lamennais and Montalembert, later Michelet and Quinet—at times made use of Mickiewicz in the service of causes which could not possibly be his; with the firm intention of amplifying his message, they gave only a distorted echo of it. Worse, in a world in which literature was queen, most people chose to see in his work nothing more than a heady kind of poetry—Balzac and de Vigny did not get beyond this misinterpretation; while the two women under whose influence he fell and who were soon to become jealous rivals, Marie d'Agoult and George Sand, had great difficulty in discovering, in the poet whom they called 'the great ecstatic', another personage than 'the new Byron' which they had at first hailed in him.

Mickiewicz suffered from this fundamental misunderstanding. Above all, he was stifled in the role which his celebrity obliged him to play. Crushed beneath the burden of his mission, harrowed by the quarrels of the *émigré* factions which strove to win his patronage or, at times, refused it, bewildered amid a political agitation of which he painfully realized the sterility, subjected to all the temptations of a mysticism which for him resembled an abdication rather than a fulfilment, agreeing for a moment to hand over his authority to Towiański, magician and no poet, and to be the Saint John of the new Messiah, then courageously breaking the spell which bound him, he could have only an infinitely painful, and at times disappointing, history. Fate possessed a hundred insidious means of exacting the price of his genius. He tried to escape, to be no more than a man among so many other men: he married, and had children. But banal worries assalied him from every side. Why could he not be a writer on the scale of Victor Hugo or, still better, Alexandre Dumas? The historical dramas which he strove to compose in French would have been better suited to the stage and would have been put on at the Porte St. Martin! Even when his professorships at Lausanne and later at the Collège de France made it possible for him to 'earn his living', the same uneasiness was gnawing at him, driving him from apartment to apartment in this Paris where he felt himself irremediably a stranger. Madness lurked in the shadow of his home; he felt that the dark contagion of insanity, into which his wife had several times sunk, was lying in wait for him.

But, by some particular grace, poetry offered itself to him for the last time, to aid him to live, to save him. The 'realism' which is so justly admired in *Pan Tadeusz* reveals primarily a victory of the poet over himself, a triumph of the instinct of self-preservation. After the terrible crisis which the events of 1830 and their sequel provoked in him, after his discouragement and disgust at the sight of an emigration painfully divided against itself, after the

long agony of his friend Garczyński, which he had followed
hour by hour throughout the summer of 1833—the
creation of his great poem, which was completed in
February 1834, marks for him a kind of reconciliation with
life. Fleeing from the nightmare reality which oppressed
him, he returned to the only reality which remained
associated in his memory with the notion of happiness.
Imagination here serves only to save this happiness from
vanishing in rapture and dreams: the construction of a
simple, picturesque story obliges him to become in the
first instance a story-teller like the ancient epic poet, to
forget his own personality in order to bring back to life
a world—and a particular piece of ground. But the woof
of *Pan Tadeusz* is made up of 'time recovered', of the
miracle which restores its fullness to every hour, its per-
fume to every blossom, and which draws from departed
pleasure an abiding joy. Freed from its illusions, preserved
by irony from excessiveness, poetry is here restored to its
original function of compelling the eyes to see, the ears to
hear and man to discover the beauty of things and the
wonder of the real. At last it can snap its fingers at poetry.
Romanticism finds its paradoxical fulfilment in this genial
parody in which it is diverted by itself, in this poem
which admits no other justification than the pleasure of
its creation.

But perhaps even the joy of which *Pan Tadeusz* was the
instrument and the pledge—'c'était mal'. The work seems
to have aroused in Mickiewicz a sort of confusion and
remorse. He nearly failed to finish. If, none the less, he did
publish it, it was doubtless because he did not feel himself
entitled to deny his companions in exile the viaticum

which he himself had found in it. *Pan Tadeusz*, the 'account-book' of the Polish nation, restored to every Polish exile the presence of his country. It remained, as it were, an ideal bond which brought them together, a place where all the sons of Poland could meet. No poet has ever performed a higher service to his country. With this poem, and with it alone, Mickiewicz, without being aware of it himself, had fulfilled his mission.

With this work done, he had no further part to play. In vain he strove to resume work upon his ever-unfinished drama, *Forefathers' Eve* and to expand it to gigantic proportions; one could almost say that the sublime inspiration had been degraded, dried up, by that of *Pan Tadeusz*. Mickiewicz could not now turn back. His poetry remained the prisoner of 'that land of childhood years . . . when he ran through the world as in a meadow', in the land of purity, trust and joy to which he was borne back by the unfinished epilogue of *Pan Tadeusz*, which stammers and breaks off because the lines in which the poet had hoped to express and excuse refused to be anything other than a song of happiness and love. The handful of 'last songs' did no more than express again and again this incurable yearning. 'It is only my body, a corpse, that is seated among you, looking into your eyes and chattering aloud. My soul is far off—ah! how far!—it strays and laments— ah! what a lament! . . . But within me I bear a country, the homeland of my thoughts. It is to it that I flee. I sit in the shelter of the fir-trees, I plunge in the lush, scented grass; I run after the sparrows, the butterflies. . . .' 'Gdy tu mój trup . . .' (while my corpse . . .). For twenty years more Mickiewicz was to live and struggle, with all the generosity of his heart, with all the chimeras of his mind, with all the remains of his genius. But of what avail were his acts and his words, since the poet in him was dead?

It is this silence which merits meditation. Does it not retain more power and significance than all the rest, that blend of greatness and wretchedness: Towiański and Rome, Lausanne and the Collège de France, Le Cercle and *La Tribune des peuples*, the Legion of Italy and the hero-pilgrim's death at Constantinople? The death of the poet twenty years before would remain a disconcerting mystery, if the destiny of at least one other poet, Rimbaud, did not serve as a warning that at a certain degree of intensity or of purity poetry can bear witness to itself only by dying, transforming him who had the gift of poetry into the 'corpse' of which Mickiewicz speaks. This too, one might say, is the extreme consequence of romanticism and reveals its inner meaning.

Mickiewicz tried to deceive himself. Certainly, his poetry was too generous to find its purpose within itself. He tried to forge of it a weapon, to place it at the service of an imperious duty. But poetry can derive its justification only from its own being; everything else that is given to it is subsidiary. The arguments with which Mickiewicz endeavours to justify such total renunciation after such total power are not valid, since it is no longer the poet in him but another man who invokes them. Are we now delivered from the mirage which subordinates artistic work to action, the poet to the fighter, and which defers poetry, that diversion of 'the most generous souls' to the happy days when, in the words of the lecture of 20 December 1842, 'the capital questions of humanity (but what are they?) are solved' and when man will be able without remorse to employ in art 'the creative fire' within him? Mickiewicz' example proves that a poet's action, 'the effect which he produces', has no other lever, no other secret, than his power as a poet. The 'literature of Europe', of which, like Goethe, Mazzini and Hugo, he spoke with such confidence in its unity and its future, should forget neither this great example nor this tragic lesson.

MICKIEWICZ IN RUSSIA

Serge Sovietov

On 25 October 1824, Mickiewicz, in the company of his friend Jan Sobolewski, crossed the border of the Province of Vilna. He reached St. Petersburg between 6 and 8 November 1824. St. Petersburg was subjected about this time to one of the worst floods in the history of the city, and the Polish poet saw its effects with his own eyes, the enormous damage it inflicted upon the Russian capital.

This flood left a profound and characteristic trace upon his consciousness.

It was not by chance that the description of this elemental catastrophe was associated in Mickiewicz' imagination with the figure of the celebrated Polish artist Józef Oleszkiewicz, who cursed the despotism of the Russian Tsar and undertook the defence of the 'little people' who, crushed by the autocracy, were apt at any moment to suffer the weight of the imperial displeasure: 'The poor in their hovels will be the first to be punished in obedience to his [the Tsar's] will. For lightning, when it strikes lifeless things, strikes first at the top, at the tower and the summit. But when its victim is man, it strikes first at the lowest, the humblest and the least protected.'[1]

In his description of the threatening flood the poet expressed the presentiment of revolution which took possession of him immediately upon his arrival in the Russian capital. He enunciated this, his first impression of Russia, in simple, sincere words: 'In this country, everyone is always, more or less, displeased with the government; they speak against it everywhere in private, and even in public it is attacked. . . . The foreigner, who is ill-informed as to the nature and significance of this internal opposition (which, though widespread, is nothing new and has never assumed a threatening aspect), who sees enemies of the existing system all around him, but no one ready to spring to its defence, concludes that *Russia is ripe for revolution*, that she only awaits the moment and the signal. This behaviour of the people and this revolutionary talk in society have ended by deceiving the Russians themselves including, unfortunately and more particularly, the noblest spirits among them. A small group of aristocrats and officers, devoted to the cause of freedom, have persuaded themselves that their own feelings are shared by all their compatriots without exception. Finally the moment arrives to crush despotism and set up in its place a constitutional monarchy or a republic. The plot is woven in the recesses of the clubs, and simultaneously it is sought to propagate liberal ideas abroad, by books and letters.'[2]

1. A. MICKIEWICZ. *Dzieła*. Wyd. narodowe (Works. National Edition). 1949,Vol.III, p. 302–3.
2. A. MICKIEWICZ. *Dzieła*. Wyd. narodowe. 1952, Vol. V, Part I, p. 289. In the article 'Puszkin i ruch literacki w Rosji' (Pushkin and the literary movement in Russia). (Author's italics.)

Some time later Mickiewicz spoke with even greater frankness: 'The conspirators had two centres—the first in southern Russia, which enabled them to establish links with Poland, and the second in St. Petersburg. They conspired openly, and what was astonishing was the integrity of one and all. Five hundred persons, and even more, were involved—persons varying widely in rank and in the posts they held, who for ten years banded together in a country controlled by a powerful and suspicious government; yet none betrayed the conspiracy. Officers and officials even met, at St. Petersburg, in apartments whose windows looked on to the street; yet no one ever succeeded in discovering the purpose of their meetings. Public opinion was stronger than the menaces proffered by the government.'[1]

These words of Mickiewicz are witness to the closeness of his relations with the revolutionary Decembrist circles of Russian society and the extent to which he adopted their attitude during his short stay in St. Petersburg. He at once made contact with the best representatives of progressive Russian opinion and, in the first instance, with the Decembrists. There he first met Kondraty Ryleyev and Alexander Bestuzhev, with whom he quickly made friends. The latter noted in his diary the date of their first meeting, 31 December 1824. Ryleyev lived in the same house as Bestuzhev, who shared an apartment with Alexander Odoyevsky.[2]

1. A. MICKIEWICZ. *Dzieła*. Wyd. narodowe. 1952, Vol. X, p. 338-9. Literatura słowianska. Kurs II, wykład XXVIII (Slavonic Literature. Second Course, 28th Lecture.)
2. LEON GOMOLICKI. *Mickiewicz wśrod Rosjan* (Mickiewicz among the Russians), Warsaw, Książka i Wiedza, 1950, p. 28.

What at that moment was the most progressive, the most characteristic and the most advanced trend of the Russian movement for social liberation? It was, of course, the movement of the Decembrists, who were conducting a struggle 'against serfdom and autocracy' and who 'represented an organic development of the whole course of the historical process in Russia'.[1] From his conversations with his new friends, Mickiewicz cannot have failed to learn what the Decembrists proposed to do: 'Poland would rise in revolt along with Russia and would carry out on her territory the same revolutionary changes as it was proposed to bring about in Russia, after which revolutionary Russia would grant Poland political independence. Poland would take her place as an independent, sovereign State and would enter into the closest alliance with her liberator, Russia.'[2] Mickiewicz was in communication, for the most part, with the representatives of the 'Northern Society' of the Decembrists. In the Northern Society there was a strong republican element, the leader of which was K. Ryleyev, a consistent republican, a passionate patriot, a freedom-loving poet and the inspirer of the revolutionary youth.

Mickiewicz' intimate contact with this group, who represented the most advanced political trend in Russia, and the extent to which he shared the revolutionary mood of the Decembrists are illustrated by a characteristic incident which took place at a gathering of Russian revolutionaries, and which Mickiewicz himself later (in

1. M. B. NECHKINA. 'Decembrists', *Great Soviet Encyclopaedia*, 2nd ed., 1952, Vol. 13, p. 574. (In Russian.)
2. ibid., p. 576.

1847) related to the publicist and historian, Leonard
Rettel. In the course of a discussion among the Decembrists, someone proposed the toast 'Death to the Tsar!'
Everyone but Mickiewicz enthusiastically seized his glass;
Mickiewicz set his glass down on the table and refused to
drink. At first everyone was surprised, then protests
resounded from every side; some of those present even
shouted to Mickiewicz that he was a coward and a traitor.
Mickiewicz calmly replied that such toasts were never
anything more than an expression of impotent, sterile
audacity and that those who drank them, imagining that
they had thereby proven their devotion to a great cause,
remained satisfied with this and so went home to bed. If
they really wanted the death of the Tsar, he said, then they
should immediately arm themselves and go out into the
street to seek him out; and, in that case he, Mickiewicz,
would go with them. After Mickiewicz had finished
speaking, *Bestuzhev* (Alexander) *rushed to embrace him.* The
fear of possible consequences sobered many of those
present, and they began to say that the idea was still
premature and that the people were not yet ready for
this.[1]

And so, after arriving at St. Petersburg and making
contact with the most progressive people in Russia at that
time, the revolutionary aristocrats, Mickiewicz beheld with
his own eyes a new, young Russia which was seeking its
path towards freedom, striving to break the fetters of
tsardom and to emancipate the people. It was during this
stay in St. Petersburg and in this circle of revolutionaries

1. A. MICKIEWICZ. *Dzieła wszystkie.* Wyd. sejmowe (Complete Works. Edition of
   the Sejm). Warsaw, 1933, Vol. XVI, p. 273. (Author's italics.)

that the Polish poet conceived the idea of a joint struggle 'for your freedom and for ours', on the plane not only of national liberation but of the social emancipation of the Polish people.

At the same time, however, the poet saw another Russia, the tsarist Russia of bureaucratic officials, which was stifling with its tentacles everything which possessed vitality, purity and independence of mind. His attitude to this Russia, the Russia of the Tsar, was one of revulsion. This feeling found vivid expression in his biting satire on the world of bureaucrat officials, which he entitled *Czyn* (The Act).

'In Russia,' Mickiewicz wrote, 'in order to avoid being a *moujik* or a merchant—to have, that is, the privilege of escaping from the possible lash of the knout—one must enter the service of the State and obtain what is known as a position in society, or else a position in the hierarchy, in the world of officials.'[1]

The satire *Czyn* was an impromptu, produced by Mickiewicz at a party in 1824 at the St. Petersburg home of the well-known artist Alexander Orlovsky. Mickiewicz made use for his purposes of a theme from a song by the gifted French democrat-poet Pierre Béranger. In this poem Mickiewicz spoke not as a romantic poet but as a realist, lashing the corruption and the bureaucratic regime of the autocracy. While maintaining the attitude of an inoffensive poet, he depicted the comical and piteous figure of the tsarist bureaucrat-official, whose main ambition in life is to receive the maximum number of decorations and to

---

1. A. MICKIEWICZ. *Dziela*. Wyd. narodowe. 1949, Vol. III, p. 309. Note by Mickiewicz for the third part of *Dziady* (Forefathers' Eve).

rise as high as he can on the ladder of promotion. The bureaucratic hierarchy is comically represented in the likeness of a Russian bath-house with all its characteristic features—the clients stewing in sweat on the topmost, hottest steps; the self-flagellation with bundles of twigs, and so forth. It is curious that the regime could be likened only to a bath-house. Nevertheless, this bureaucratic hierarchy will not save any careerist from retribution if he has *soiled* his conscience; do what he may, he will break his neck.

If the representatives of progressive Russian opinion from the very beginning gave Mickiewicz a warm welcome, the tsarist government, for its part, saw in him only a dangerous political exile whom it was undesirable to detain for long in the capital. Mickiewicz received instructions to leave St. Petersburg and to go into 'exile in the south'. In January 1825 the Polish poet, accompanied by his friends Jeżowski and Malewski, left for Odessa.[1] In taking leave of the Decembrists, Mickiewicz received from Ryleyev and A. Bestuzhev letters of introduction to the poet Vasily Tumansky, who was in intimate relations with the Decembrists and who was living at the time in Odessa. Ryleyev wrote: 'Dear Tumansky, *Be good to Mickiewicz* and his friends Malewski and Jeżowski. *They are good-hearted, splendid fellows.* Really I don't need to say anything in writing: *their feelings and their way of thinking make them*

1. Alexander I, indeed, was not pleased that Mickiewicz had received permission to live in Odessa, which at that time was a point of attraction for many political figures. In March 1825 Łozinski wrote to Petraszkiewicz from St. Petersburg: 'The Sovereign was displeased because the Minister had authorized Odessa.' (J. KLEINER, *A. Mickiewicz* (*National Library Series*, 1, No. 66). Vol. I, p. 474.)

friends of ours in advance, while *Mickiewicz,* on top of that, *is the favourite poet of his country.'*

Alexander Bestuzhev echoed Ryleyev: 'This is to introduce Mickiewicz, Malewski and Jeżowski. The first you know by repute, and I'll stand warrant for his character and gifts. His friend Malewski's a grand fellow, too. Introduce them to people and show them the way round; look after them, poor fellows.'[1]

These letters are vivid testimony to the consideration, friendliness and confidence which the Decembrist revolutionaries showed Mickiewicz, not only as a poet but also as one who shared their political aspirations.

The poet's mood was one of cheerfulness and vitality: 'I am well, and go from the north to the other end of Europe with a light heart,'[2] wrote Mickiewicz to Odyniec from Kiev in February 1825. Somewhat later he wrote to the same correspondent on his travel impressions:

'Here I am, having crossed the whole of Europe from north to south and, what is more miraculous, in a sledge— an unheard-of thing here. I crossed a steppe where almost nothing was visible, where from one stage-post to another I saw naught but the soil, and the sky not at all, over a distance of nearly two hundred miles. Then in the Province of Kiev I left the road to penetrate into the country, and for the first time saw rocks which were unknown to us except through books. For me it was altogether a novel and interesting sight. The giant *masses* of granite, with gloomy ravines between them opening out on to great

---

1. N. Shemshurin. 'Tumansky and Mickiewicz', *Kievskaya Starina*, 1899. Vol. XIV, No. 3, p. 300. (In Russian.) (Author's italics.)
2. A. Mickiewicz. *Dzieła*. Wyd. narodowe. 1953, Vol. XIV, Part I, p. 250.

, Mickiewicz and Pushkin in front of the memorial to Peter the Great.'
Bas-relief by Milberger (Moscow, 1947).

plains, made me regret that I had not beheld the scene in summer, when it would have been beautified by water, greenery and vines. If such pygmies are imposing, what a colossus the Caucasus must be! I have decided that I must see the Caucasus.'[1]

In February 1825 the Polish poet reached Odessa. He and his friends, however, were unable, for political reasons, to establish themselves there as teachers at the Lycée Richelieu, and were obliged to await the further instructions of the government. In Odessa the Polish poet saw a good deal of a number of people who were in close relations with the Decembrists. There, too, he met Count Peter Moszinski, who was later exiled to Siberia for his relations with the Decembrists, and a number of others who were among the most progressive members of the intelligentsia at that time.[2] These, however, were isolated encounters. Mickiewicz was in much more regular contact with a set of people who watched his every step and who saw in him a politically dangerous 'criminal'. In the course of the summer and autumn Mickiewicz undertook his journey through the Crimea. It was not by chance that, on his way there, General Witte (Jan Witte was the chief administrator of the southern provinces and curator of the Odessa Lycée) dispatched a special report on Mickiewicz' conduct to Alexander I.[3] On the basis of such facts, one can judge of the oppressive and suspicious environment in which the Polish poet found himself. It must be added that

1. A. MICKIEWICZ. *Dzieła*. Wyd. narodowe. 1953, Vol. XIV, Part I, p. 252–3.
2. L. PODHORSKI OKOŁÓW. 'Łudziłem despotę' (I have lured the despot), *Realia Mickiewiczowskie*. 1953, p. 210 et seq.
3. H. SZYPER. *Adam Mickiewicz, poeta; człowiek czyna. Zarys popularny* (Adam Mickiewicz, the poet and man of action. Popular biography). Czytelnik, 1950, p. 67.

now for the first time Mickiewicz came to know the real face of the aristocratic salons of Odessa, which were characterized not only by a singular refinement of manners but by 'the brilliant gloss of parasitic, amoral personalities'.

Mickiewicz composed, during his stay in Odessa and his journey through the Crimea, the *Sonnets of Love* and the *Crimean Sonnets*, which he subsequently retouched, collected into a single cycle and published in Moscow in 1826.[1]

The *Crimean Sonnets* were the sequel to the 'love poems' and the fruit of Mickiewicz' Crimean journey. At the end of July 1825 the poet wrote to Franciszek Malewski from Odessa: 'This evening we are to set forth on our projected journey. Yesterday there was a terrible squall, which so whipped up the sea that even now it is growling and foaming. For half-an-hour I thought that Odessa would be swept away.'[2]

Although composed at different times as independent cameos, they are arranged, as collected by the poet, in accordance with a coherent pattern of ideas and themes. Beginning with the fifth sonnet, the poet is in immediate contact with the oriental life of the Crimea, with the grandeur of its mountains and with the surviving monuments of past ages. This sonnet conveys the impression, consciously exaggerated by the poet, of the grandeur and majesty of the mountain landscape. In the stern majesty and grandeur of nature the poet sees the inexhaustible riches and beauty of life; for the poet this majestic scenery contains, as it were, the essential truth of life. In the next two sonnets, No. 6, *Bakhchisarai*, and No. 7, *Bakhchisarai*

1. *Sonety Adama Mickiewicza*, Moscow, 1826.
2. A. Mickiewicz. *Dzieła*. Wyd. narodowe. Vol. XIV, Part I, p. 257.

at Night, he depicts the ruins of the city as 'traced out'
by the hand of Belshazzar; they remain merely as the symbol of the might of the bygone rulers and kings of this
land and incarnate now only destruction and death. On
the other hand, against the background of the ruins the
poet gives us a glimpse of the fountain of Bakhchisarai,
from which the spring water still gushes, incarnating life,
which never perishes. The last line of the sixth sonnet,
'Oh shame! You are no longer, but the source remains',[1]
resounds with genuine civic passion. In this exclamation
of Mickiewicz' one cannot fail to discern a grim warning
of the inevitable downfall of Russian tsarism. As though
in reply to this, the poet, in the eighth sonnet, at the sight
of Potocka's tomb, abandons himself to memories of his
distant homeland and sadly reflects upon his loneliness and
the impossibility of his return to his own country, for
which the existence of tsarism is to blame. The lyrical
conclusion of this sonnet is penetrated with patriotic
feeling of unusual intensity, with profound love for the
land where he was born. This sonnet represents the culminating point of the development and expansion of the
homeland theme in the *Crimean Sonnets*.

One cannot but note the further significant fact that
these three last-mentioned sonnets of Mickiewicz are
associated with the name of the great Pushkin. Mickiewicz
felt the attraction of the folk themes, as well as of the
entrancing figure of Maria, in Pushkin's poem *The Fountain
of Bakhchisarai* (1823), which undoubtedly exercised an
influence on the Polish poet's mood. Like Mickiewicz'

1. *Sonety Adama Mickiewicza*, op. cit., p. 34.

Crimean Sonnets, The Fountain of Bakhchisarai 'was inspired
by Pushkin's immediate impressions of the Crimea'.[1]
In his notes to the sonnet *Potocka's Tomb*, Mickiewicz
observed, with profound respect for the Russian poet:
'The popular tale about the tomb of Bakhchisarai has
provided the Russian poet Alexander Pushkin with the
subject for a poem which he has written with all the talent
that distinguishes him; it is called *The Fountain of Bakhchisarai*.'[2]

Mickiewicz reveals the full depth of his human sympathy in the following, ninth, sonnet, *The Graves of the
Harem*, which is closely related by its subject, its mood
and the images which it employs, to the preceding sonnet.
In both we encounter the image of the rose as a symbol
of womanhood. The ruins preserve the memory of the
perished slave girls whose fate had lain in the hands of
tyrannical kings. There is a real parallel between the figure
of Maria, who in essence is just such another slave girl,
and those of these oriental slaves. The poet is filled with
deep sympathy for these 'little people', the victims of the
Khan's passions. But this feeling is expressed not by the
poet himself (and thereby he employs a genuinely realistic
technique in the transmission of the emotion), but by a
mirza in conversation with the traveller: 'He alone, of the
strangers, had tears in his eyes as he beheld the scene.'

In these deeply-felt words can be detected, though still
in embryo, that theme which is familiar to us in the work
of Mickiewicz and which was later to develop into a

1. D. D. BLAGOI. *Pushkin's Creative Development (1813–1826)*. Academy of Sciences
of the U.S.S.R., Moscow-Leningrad, 1950, p. 278. (In Russian.)
2. *Sonety Adama Mickiewicza*, op. cit., p. 47.

boundless sympathy with all oppressed peoples in Europe and beyond it.

With the tenth sonnet a change is to be observed in the poet's mood. He passes from contemplative meditation upon life and upon his personal sorrows as symbolized by the scenes of nature to active, positive acceptance of life itself. He forgets all his sufferings in the intoxication of a wild gallop upon his horse or under the inspiration of the beauty of Alushta by day (sonnet No. 11) and by night (No. 12); the Crimean town calls to his mind an oriental beauty, an odalisque, full of passion and love. In the latter sonnet the air, impregnated with the fragrance and *music* of the flowers, speaks to the poet's heart in a voice that is inaudible to the ear, as it did in the sonnet *The Steppes of Akkerman*, where, amid the silence, Mickiewicz could faintly detect the almost imperceptible voice of the steppe.[1] And now before the eyes of the Polish wanderer rose Chatyrdagh in all its natural majesty, and the poet was dazzled by the scene which opened before him. In sonnet No. 13 he actually exaggerates the grandeur of the mountain. He intentionally places the description in the mouth of a mirza. In Chatyrdagh the poet saw the incarnation of the majesty of life and of its ideals: 'Setting thy foot upon the earth, on men and on the lightning-flash, thou hearest but what God to nature sayeth.'[2]

By Mickiewicz' confession, it was on Chatyrdagh that the first of his sonnets was born: this sonnet is most

---

1. *Sonety Adama Mickiewicza*, op. cit., p. 40.
2. ibid., p. 41. Cf. the same feeling for truth and beauty in nature, expressed in the sonnet *Widok gór ze stepów Kozłowa* (The view of the mountains from the Kozlov steppes), which is also associated with Chatyrdagh.

remarkable for the brilliancy of its oriental colouring. It was not without reason that it was, in 1826, translated into Persian by Hafiz Topchi-Pasha. But love of country prevailed over the poet's passing passion for the beauty of a world which was foreign to him. He confesses that the forest of his native Lithuania sings a sweeter song to him than the nightingales of the village of Baidari. In his poetic consciousness took shape the figure of the beloved Maryla, fusing with that of his homeland (sonnet No. 14, *The Pilgrim*). This sonnet reflects more vividly than anything else the struggle which was proceeding in the poet's soul for the homeland which he had lost. Later, in the realistic poem *Pan Tadeusz*, this central idea of the sonnet *The Pilgrim* is developed into Tadeusz' appeal for a struggle for patriotic ideals against the cosmopolitanism of the Polish aristocracy. In the fifteenth and sixteenth sonnets, *The Path over the Precipice of Czufut-Kale* and *Mount Kikineis*, the poet's entire attention is again absorbed by the grandeur and majesty of nature, and his memories of the past forsake him. Yet, in the seventeenth sonnet, *Castle Ruins of Balaklava*, Mickiewicz again speaks of the inevitable downfall of rapacious tyrants and enslavers of foreign peoples, which is foreshadowed by the successive overthrow of Greek, Genoese and Tartar power in this same country in times past. His ardour for freedom leads him to issue a positive and fruitful call to poets to compose such songs as will reflect the storm and passion of life and remain immortal for all time. With this appeal, in the eighteenth and final sonnet, *Ajudah*, the poet put the finishing touch to both the ideological foundation and the artistic pattern of the entire cycle of *Crimean Sonnets*.

A brief analysis of the *Sonnets of Love* and the *Crimean Sonnets* makes it possible to establish a close relationship between them. The theme of his loneliness and nostalgia in a foreign land amid the spiritual strangers who surrounded him in Odessa and who accompanied him in the Crimea, the theme of love for his motherland and, above all, the theme of the fight against despotism, of passionate aspiration towards justice in human affairs—these are the main common elements which relate the *Sonnets of Love* to the *Crimean Sonnets*, not merely formally but spiritually. The difference lies only in the fact that in the earlier cycle the themes of political lyricism are carefully camouflaged beneath love themes and come to the foreground, essentially, in the last three sonnets, which served as a kind of transition to the *Crimean Sonnets*; whereas in the second cycle these themes played a leading, distinctive part in all the sonnets, in harmonious association with the descriptions of the landscapes among which the poet found himself.

A characteristic feature of the composition of the *Crimean Sonnets* is the realistic description of the scenes and phenomena of nature, followed—at least in the majority of cases—by a brief lyrical conclusion which, as it were, confirms or reveals the true significance of all these descriptions of nature; while the images of nature, in their turn, serve to render concrete the thoughts, feelings and experiences of the poet. As an example of the concrete rendering of an abstract notion one may take the passage in the sonnet *The Steppes of Akkerman* where the idea of 'an altitude beyond the reach of an ordinary eye' is rendered by the realistic description: 'Stay! What silence! I hear the flight of cranes, that pass beyond the range of falcons' eyes.'[1]

Take again the sonnet *Mount Kikineis*, where the idea of a profound abyss across which one can spring only with great difficulty is expressed in the following figure: 'We must cross the ravine with one bound of our horse. I go first; you, be ready with the spur and the whip. When you no longer see me, look to the end of those rocks.'[2]

If we recall the figures of Alcaeus, Niemcewicz, Belshazzar in Mickiewicz' sonnets, we are entitled to speak of a definite system by which the poet expresses his feelings on political and social subjects through the employment of these figures as a disguise for his real thoughts. If in the sonnet *Bakhchisarai* the name 'Belshazzar' and the ruins served as a symbol of the death of kings, so, later, in the kasida *Farys*, the poet was to resort to the same system of camouflage. In this case I have in mind the figure of the 'pyramid', which is used to symbolize the death of kings. In the course of a furious struggle, the bedouin's bitterest enemy, the tempest in the desert, is transformed into a pyramid, that is, into a tomb of kings: 'He roars and marches on me like a moving pyramid.'[3]

Finally, in the sonnet *Bajdary*, we observe how the dynamic of internal emotion is rendered by means of a consistent, dynamic description of the external activity of man and nature. The poet, plying his whip, drives his horse at full gallop. Beneath his feet forests, valleys, crags *float* (płyną) and *disappear* (giną) *in turn* like the waves of

1. *Sonety Adama Mickiewicza*, op. cit., p. 29.
2. ibid., p. 34.
3. A. MICKIEWICZ. *Dzieła*. Wyd. narodowe. Vol. I, p. 245.

a torrent, *piling up on top of one another*. In this realistic
fashion the swift gallop of the horse is described as seen
through the eyes of the rider; and this speed provides
release for the poet's pent-up feelings. An entirely different
picture presents itself to the horseman's eyes in the following stanza, when the tired horse begins to slacken step:
'in the inflamed eyes of the weary rider, as in a broken
mirror, *stretch out, one after another, the phantoms* of forests,
valleys and crags'.[1] These descriptions reflect with great
realism the different types of movement and the impressions they convey: at first the poet depicts the galloping
horseman as he speeds past forests, crags and valleys; he
feels that all these objects are themselves moving towards
him and are fusing, so to speak, into a single uninterrupted
chain; afterwards we are shown the horseman riding
slowly after an exhausting gallop, and then all the objects
of nature which he encounters on his path are indistinct
and create the impression of misty phantoms. This realistic
method of depicting natural phenomena was first employed
by Mickiewicz in his *Crimean Sonnets*; it was to attain a
still wider range of application and a still higher perfection
of execution in the long poems *Farys* and *Pan Tadeusz*.[2]
It is interesting to observe that the same method of depicting the mental processes of his characters was employed
also by Pushkin in his maturity. Thus, for example, in the

1. *Sonety Adama Mickiewicza*, op. cit., p. 38.
2. Stanislaw Windakiewicz observed with great perspicacity this artistic feature of
   Mickiewicz' poetic style: 'Mickiewicz uses nine verbs, infinitely plastic and of
   increasing strength (see the third sonnet: *Żegluga*). This intensification of effect
   by means of dynamic verbs, cast as it were upon the calm waters of "noun"
   concepts, is a very special feature of his poetry' (S. Windakiewicz. 'Sonety
   Krymskie' (Crimean Sonnets), *Przeglad polski*. Cracow, 1896, p. 626).

poem *The Gypsies*, 'Pushkin's characters, beginning with
Aleko, are presented in terms not so much of their emotional experiences as of their actions; these actions throw
a bright light on their emotional processes, which are not
directly revealed to us.'[1]

The immense labour which Mickiewicz expended on
the creation of the Polish sonnet-form is revealed by the
numerous variants which have survived. This is true in
particular of the sonnets *The Steppes of Akkerman* and
Mount Kikineis. Mickiewicz composed four different versions of the first line alone of *The Steppes of Akkerman*
before it received the classical form which is now
famous: 'Thus am I launched upon the spaces of a dry
ocean.'[2] The difficulty was how to equate the steppes
with the ocean.[3]

The *Crimean Sonnets* were, then, a new and higher
achievement, a turning point in Mickiewicz' poetical
development. They were at the same time an inappreciable
contribution to the treasury of world poetry. Pushkin's
estimate of the worth of Mickiewicz' *Crimean Sonnets* was
a high one. He placed the Polish poet—and he was the
first of the poets and critics of his time to do so—among
the greatest sonnet-writers of the world: Dante, Petrarch,
Shakespeare, Camoens, Wordsworth. In his famous
sonnet of 1830, *Stern Dante did not scorn the Sonnet*, Pushkin
wrote,

1. D. D. BLAGOI, op. cit., p. 352.
2. *Sonety Adama Mickiewicza*, op. cit., p. 29.
3. Variants: I (have) made the ocean voyage of the steppes; I (have) sailed the
   dry steppes of the ocean; I (have) sailed on the ocean of the dry steppe; I have
   been (*or* was) surrounded by steppes that seemed like oceans.—J. KLEINER, op.
   cit., Vol. II (2nd edition), p. 553.

Beneath the shade of distant Tauris' mountains
Lithuania's singer in its cramped frame
For a moment found room for his dreams.[1]

The sonnets attracted the attention of Russians and Poles alike. Critical appraisals of them, favourable and unfavourable, appeared in the press. One of Mickiewicz' Russian admirers, E. A. Baratynsky, in the February 1827 number of the *Moscow Telegraph*, published a playful poem of encouragement to Mickiewicz, which constituted, as it were, a reply to the hostile critical articles and observations on the Polish poet provoked by the unauthorized publication in Warsaw of his impromptus and *Crimean Sonnets*. Baratynsky wrote: 'Do not fear biting criticism, but rather intoxicating praise. More than once it has happened that a mighty genius, after absorbing its fumes, has fallen with languid slumber. . . . Forgive me: I utter aloud my indignation; forgive me, teacher and prophet; I point with reproach to your laurel wreath. When Pegasus' ribs are firmly gripped by the legs of a bold rider, it is no harm if he receives the lash of a critic's whip.'[2]

The enthusiasm which was provoked by the appearance of Mickiewicz' sonnets was fully shared by progressive Russian opinion. The Decembrist W. Küchelbecker wrote enthusiastically to his sister from his prison in Dvinsk: 'The latter [Mickiewicz] I know in translation. His Crimean

1. A. S. PUSHKIN. *Complete Works*. Academy of Sciences of the U.S.S.R., 1948, Vol. III, Part 1, p. 214. (In Russian.)
2. *Moscow Telegraph*, 1827, Part XIII, No. 3, p. 96. Cf. M. A. TSYAVLOVSKY, 'Mickiewicz and his Russian Friends', *New World*, 1940, No. 11-12, p. 306 et seq. (In Russian.)

sonnets are wonderfully fine, even in our prose versions. What must they be like in the original?'[1]

Mickiewicz, with justice, felt like a conqueror. He wrote on 22 March 1828, in a somewhat playful tone and with conscious exaggeration of the facts: 'My sonnets are appearing in nearly all the almanacs (a whole series of almanacs are published here), and there are even some translations *in extenso*. One of these, said to be the best, is by Kozlov (the author of *The Venetian Night*); it is being printed, and will appear shortly.'[2]

In 1827 P. A. Vyazemsky produced a complete prose translation of the *Crimean Sonnets* and published it in the April number of the *Moscow Telegraph*.[3] In the same number appeared the third of Mickiewicz' *Crimean Sonnets* in a translation by I. I. Dimitriev, under the title *The Voyage*. On 14 April 1827 Mickiewicz himself informed Odyniec of the fact: 'The celebrated poet, old Dimitriev, has done me the honour of himself translating one of the sonnets.'[4]

P. A. Vyazemsky prefaced his translations with a long introduction, in which he expressed his opinion of the sonnets and of Mickiewicz' work as a whole: 'Here we have an unusual and gratifying phenomenon', he wrote. 'A foreign poetical creation, the work of one of Poland's greatest poets, has been published in Moscow. . . . Mickiewicz belongs to the chosen few who have been accorded

1. *The Decembrists and Their Times, Materials and Communications*, edited by M. P. Alekseyev and B. S. Meilach. Academy of Sciences of the U.S.S.R., Institute of Russian Literature, Moscow-Leningrad, 1951, p. 37. (In Russian.)

2. A. MICKIEWICZ. *Dzieła*. Wyd. narodowe. Vol. XIV, Part I, p. 340.

3. *Moscow Telegraph*, 1827, Part XIV, No. 7, p. 191–222. See P. A. VYAZEMSKY, *Complete Works*. St. Petersburg, 1878, published by Count S. D. Sheremetyev. Vol. I (1810–27), p. 326–36, 337–48. (In Russian.)

4. A. MICKIEWICZ. *Dzieła*. Wyd. narodowe. Vol. XIV, Part I, p. 309.

the right to figure as the representatives of the literary
glory of their peoples. . . . He occupies a place of honour
among the poets of the present day. . . . I feel that, if one
overlooks the occasional lack of strict economy in the
employment of bold figures and tropes, the function of
criticism in his respect is only to extol the luxuriant wealth
of imagination, the strong and vivid poetic feeling which
everywhere reveals itself in the work of the Polish poet and
which, through its truthful and fresh expression, is trans-
mitted to the heart of the reader, and the extraordinary skill
with which he has succeeded in compressing into the restricted framework of the sonnet pictures which are diverse
in their rich beauty and which are not infrequently titanic.'[1]

Vyazemsky's was the first appreciation of the sonnets.
On the one hand it was a symbol of close Russo-Polish
friendship in the field of artistic creation, and, on the other,
it stimulated public interest in Mickiewicz' sonnets. The
consequences were soon to be seen. Already in 1828 a
much greater number of Russian translations of Mickiewicz' *Crimean Sonnets* saw the light. A. K. Ilichevsky, a
school-friend of Pushkin, translated *The Steppes of Akkerman, The Voyage, Bakhchisarai* (in *Flowers of the North*, p. 37–
39); Y. I. Poznansky, *The Steppes of Akkerman* (in *Moscow
Herald*, No. 6, p. 137 et seq.); V. Shchastny, *Calm at Sea,
Alushta by Night, Chatyrdagh* (in *The Album of the Northern
Muses*, p. 94 et seq., 113 et seq.); I. I. Kozlov, *Chatyrdagh*
(in *The Slav*, Part V, No. 4, p. 145) and *The View of the Mountains from the Kozlov Steppes* (in *The Album of the Northern
Muses*, p. 344). The following year saw the publication of

1. *Moscow Telegraph*, 1827, Part XIV, p. 191 et seq., 200. (In Russian.)

the volume *The Crimean Sonnets of Adam Mickiewicz, Translations and Imitations by Ivan Kozlov*[1] to which Mickiewicz had referred the year before. Also in 1829 appeared a separate volume of translations by V. I. Lyubich-Romanovich, *Poems of Adam Mickiewicz, translated from the Polish by L. R.*[2] The foregoing is a complete list of the translations made from the sonnet cycle during Mickiewicz' residence in Russia.[3] Not one of the sonnets was translated in 1830, after the poet's departure from Russia. It is a significant fact that it was only from 1831, i.e., after the Polish insurrection, that Russian translations of Mickiewicz' sonnets began again to appear, as they have continued to do, in increasing volume, to the present day. They testify to the undying renown of the Polish poet who had created these 'pearls of poetry' in the heart of Russia itself. V. G. Belinsky, in the course of a severe criticism of Benediktov's translations from Mickiewicz, expressed, as Pushkin had done, the highest appreciation of the Polish poet's sonnets, attributing to them world-wide significance and emphasizing their realistic character: '. . . Mickiewicz, one of the greatest poets in world literature, realized to the full the effectiveness of this use of hyperbole in description. For this reason, in his *Crimean Sonnets* he very judiciously assumed the personality of an orthodox Musulman; and, in fact, the hyperbolical expression of admiration for Chatyrdagh appears perfectly

---

1. Published in St. Petersburg, 1829.
2. A manuscript bibliography of the translations of Mickiewicz' *Crimean Sonnets* in Russia has been compiled by A. V. Kaupuzh.
3. WIKTOR CZERNOBAJEW. 'Mickiewicz w Rosji w latach 1820–1830' (Mickiewicz in Russia during the years 1820–30), *Pamietnik Literack*, Part XXXI, Sections 3–4, Lwów, 1934, p. 297–305.

natural in the mouth of an adherent of Mohammed, a son of the Orient.'[1]

While the opinion he expressed of I. I. Kozlov's translations of Mickiewicz' *Crimean Sonnets* was on the whole favourable, Belinsky at the same time recognized the inevitability of a divergence between the original and the translation. He wrote: 'His [I. I. Kozlov's] translation of Mickiewicz' *Crimean Sonnets* is equally remarkable; but its relationship to the original is exactly the same as that of the translation of *The Bride of Abydos* to its original. The very fact that Kozlov sometimes takes 16, 18 or 20 lines to translate Mickiewicz' 14 indicates that the contest was an unequal one.'[2]

In this admission on the part of Belinsky one feels the intensity of his love for Mickiewicz and the depth of his understanding of his poetic genius.

In the course of his stay in Odessa Mickiewicz also conceived the idea of the first version of his long poem *Konrad Wallenrod*. In planning *Konrad Wallenrod*, Mickiewicz was under the immediate influence of the Decembrist poets and, in particular, of Ryleyev's poem *Voinarovsky*, which, as was remarked above, the poet probably read in manuscript in the house of Vasily Tumansky.[3] The name of the

1. V. G. BELINSKY. 'The Poems of Vladimir Benediktov', *Complete Works*. Academy of Sciences of the U.S.S.R., Moscow, 1953, Vol. I, p. 363 et seq. (In Russian.)
2. 'The Collected Poems of Ivan Kozlov', ibid., 1954, Vol. V, p. 72. (In Russian.)
3. L. GOMOLICKI, op. cit., p. 54. The poet's son, Władyslaw Mickiewicz, long ago spoke of the influence of the Decembrists on the creation of *Konrad Wallenrod*. He wrote: 'The sight of these great lords (i.e. the Decembrists) disdaining wealth and honours derived from slavery and oppression, the sight of men wearing, of necessity, a false docility but evolving a plan for breaking the chains of obedience —this may well have inspired, in the bard, the idea of Konrad Wallenrod.' (WŁAD. MICKIEWICZ, *W. Poznaniu*, 1890, Vol. I, p. 191).

heroic Wallenrod fused, in the poet's creative consciousness, with the name of the author of *Voinarovsky*, his close
friend the Decembrist Kondraty Ryleyev.[1] It was in the
Crimea, as Malewski records, that 'a poem, which should
include local scenes, was conceived'.[2] The poet had returned to Odessa with Marchocki. He was in a good frame
of mind; he felt for a time that he was free. It was then
that the central idea of the new poem occurred to him.
On his return he at once began to jot down passages which
were to form part of *Konrad Wallenrod*. He read out these
passages as he wrote them at literary gatherings on Fridays
at the houses of the Zalesky and Shemet families.[3]

The writings of the Decembrists, with which Mickiewicz, in regular contact as he was with Ryleyev, Bestuzhev
and others, was certainly acquainted, as well as the works
of Pushkin, who had visited Odessa before Mickiewicz' arrival there, expressed ideas which were very close to his own.
'The central, guiding idea of the writings of the Decembrists was that of a passionate denunciation of despotism
and serfdom, combined with an equally passionate ad-
vocacy of national independence. The Decembrist writers
glorified revolt against those who held the people in thrall.
. . . The favourite figure of Decembrist writing was that
of the politically advanced representative of his people who
sacrifices himself and perishes for the liberation of his

1. L. GOMOLICKI, op. cit., p. 54. Juliusz Kleiner also directly associates the title
'Konrad Wallenrod' with Ryleyev's first name, Kondraty (J.KLEINER, op.cit., p.484).
2. A. MICKIEWICZ. *Dzieła wszystkie*. Wyd. sejmowe. Vol. XVI, p. 47 and 55.
3. L. GOMOLICKI, op. cit., p. 55. See A. DUBIECKI, 'Pierwszy rok wygnania Adama
Mickiewicza' (Adam Mickiewicz' first year of exile), *Kurjer Polski* (The Polish
Courier), 4 May 1890. Cf. L. GOMOLICKI, *Dziennik pobytu Adama Mickiewicza w
Rosji, 1824–29* (Adam Mickiewicz' stay in Russia, 1824–29), Warsaw, Książka
i Wiedza, 1949, p. 64.

Księga I.

Dzieje dawne.

Za czasów pogańskich ludzie czcili Boga jednego, a narobili sobie bałwanów i balamidził ich i radzili się ich czci? nowem ofiary ofiarowali na ona swoich bałwanów.

Przeto Bóg zesłał na pogan najsroższą karę to jest niewolę.

I stała się podzina ludzie niewolniczą,

I stała się połowa ludzi niewolnicą drugiej połowy, chociaż wszyscy pochodzili od jednego ojca, bo wywiedli jedni podniesienie z wyrwy sili sobie rodny bycia; jedni rzekli że pochodzi od niego, drugi że pochodzi od innego bałwana jego, wyrzeci się gdzybi, iny mowie że...

A gdy ich jedni drugich brali w niewolę, wpadli wszyscy razem w niewolę Imperatora Rzymskiego.

Imperator Rzymski nawet i sam Bogiem, i powiedł ogłosił, iż nie ma na świecie innego prawa, tylko iego wola; co on pochwali, to było nazwano cnota, a co on zgani, to było nazwano zbrodnią,

I imperatorowie litościowie narami, który dowidli iż imperatorów ma prawo tak czynić.

A Imperator Rzymski nie miał ani nad sobą, ani przed sobą nie coby szanował, ażeby coby szanował.

I była ziemia cała, i państwa niewolnicą, a nikt wolnej taniej niewali, I nigdy na świecie ani przed ani przatem, oprócz w Rossyi za dni naszych.

Bo i wszystkim, wola Imperatora jest prawem;

Bo i w Turków, Sułtan musi sobie szanować prawo Mahometa, a nie może go sam wykładać; ale go, mało ksią Turecy.

W Rossyi zaś Imperator jest głowa, wiary, i wie każde wierni, który wierzy musia. Panuje więc i nad sumnieniem Moscia skim.

I stało się gdy Imperator Rzymski wzmocnił się na świecie, nastało to pokuszenie; jako pospolite ciemności, w noc najdłuższą Rzymskiego, tak pokuszenie wielki, wczoraz niewolnictwa Rzymskiego.

Przyszedł na ziemie, syn Boży Jezus Chrystus nauczając ludzi, iż wszyscy są bracia, rodzona, dziecmi jednego Boga, nie tem jest wierny miedzy ludzmi, kto im starszy, i kto powierza się dla ich Dobra. A im kto lypszy tem więcej, pokuszeci powie niem. A Chrystus bóg będąc najlepszym, miał dla nich krew wylewisi im na najboleśniejsza, najbardzi oświecona,

Przeto, nie jest szanowana na ziemi, ani mądrość luksy ani urzd, ani bogactwo, ani korona, ale samo tylko jest szanowane

Manuscript of *The Book of the Polish Pilgrims*. In the collection of the Adam Mickiewicz Museum, Paris.

country.'[1] This figure was dear also to Mickiewicz. Ever more vividly took shape in his imagination the character of the avenging warrior who strives to set his people free. The romantic Gustav was reborn as Konrad; henceforth the name of Konrad was inseparably linked in the poet's mind with a strong thirst for vengeance upon the oppressors of the nation which had given birth to Konrad himself. It is true that the Gustav of the fourth part of *Forefathers' Eve* already resents social injustice and desires to punish the oppressors, but here these feelings are in the embryo stage. Now, however, under the influence of all that he has personally experienced and seen ever since the time when he was imprisoned in a cell of the Basilian monastery, Mickiewicz, concentrating his attention upon the real world instead of the fabulous, romantic, ideal world of the heroes of ballads and romances, enters new paths of realistic creation.

Two observations of Mickiewicz explain this point of view and reveal his real state of mind and his attitude towards the high society of Odessa. In a poem entitled *The Sailor* he wrote, on 14 April 1825: 'He prefers to feel himself among the wilder elements of nature, constantly inviting fresh struggles and adventures, rather than to remain on land, contemplating the sea and measuring its powers of destruction.'[2]

---

1. A. G. TSEITLIN. 'The Literary Production of the Decembrists,' *Great Soviet Encyclopaedia*, 2nd ed., Vol. 13, p. 587; see also V. G. BAZANOV's exhaustive work *The Decembrist Poets: K. F. Ryleyev, V. K. Küchelbecker, A. O. Odoyevsky*, Academy of Sciences of the U.S.S.R., Moscow-Leningrad 1950, and B. Meilach, *The Poetical Production of the Decembrists* (in the collection, *The Poetry of the Decembrists*, Leningrad, 1950). (In Russian.)

2. A. MICKIEWICZ. *Dzieła*. Wyd. narodowe. Vol. I, p. 141.

These words reflect the strong strain of optimism running through the poet, and sound his summons to the struggle for the liberation of the oppressed. But the struggle is now entering a new phase. It is no longer that of the Philomats of the Vilna and Kovno period; the movement has now gained experience, has become realistic, relies on the goodwill and friendship of the 'gentlemen' of the revolution—the Decembrists. After his first journey to St. Petersburg and the creative period of Odessa, Mickiewicz feels an extraordinary inflow of fresh moral energy. His year of wandering has increased his stature and matured him spiritually. Modestly but significantly, he writes in a letter to Odyniec, on 22 February 1826: 'My muse is silent; she has, indeed, begun to give some signs of life, but at this very moment I am ordered to leave.'

He is, in fact, ordered to quit his southern exile and proceed to Moscow. Leaving Odessa, with no regrets, he recalls, in a farewell epistle of 29 October 1826, the tears he shed on being parted, as a youth, from the cherished surroundings of his boyhood; he now realizes how 'alone' he is; no one, in Odessa society, will shed tears at his departure on hearing the postilion's bells, the only sound that will mark the 'poet's' leaving.

He had been in Moscow for a year and a half when on 3 August 1828, before removing to St. Petersburg, he wrote to Thomas Lan, in the latter's distant exile: 'My life proceeds on the even tenor of its way. . . . I hope that the summer will see the reawakening of my desire to work; but for the moment I am avidly lazy, though I continue to read or meditate. Each day passes uneventfully. Early in the morning I read, and sometimes, but rarely, I write;

towards two or three o'clock I dine, or prepare to go out
to do so; in the evening I go to a concert or some other
entertainment, and generally return home late. I am also
giving a few ladies lessons in Polish. . . . This sort of life
has made me calmer and better balanced.'[1]

It is impossible for us, as we read these words, to suspect Mickiewicz of insincerity, for this admission was made
to one of his closest and dearest friends, who was then far
away in exile, living in great hardship; he would have been
incapable of deceiving him. The admission is extremely
important not only for the understanding of the mutual
relations between the Polish poet and the representatives
of progressive Russian culture, but above all because this
serenity of mind marked a turning point in Mickiewicz'
outlook and literary production. He was coming to ever
closer grips with reality, was penetrating it more deeply
and was looking at life more simply and more realistically.
The above-quoted words and his other confessions during
the period of his stay in Moscow are so many individual
strokes which go to form a picture of the spiritual growth
of Mickiewicz who, in this favourable environment, could
not but be influenced beneficially by his Russian friends.
Mickiewicz' social environment in Moscow was completely different in inner content from that in which he
had lived in Odessa. Whereas there he had experienced
with peculiar intensity homesickness and utter loneliness,
here, on the contrary, he enjoyed tranquillity, elation, joy
in creation and a genuine spiritual association with the
leaders of Russian social and political thought, among
whom he lived.

1. A. MICKIEWICZ. *Dzieła*. Wyd. narodowe. Vol. XIV, Part I, p. 345.

ADAM MICKIEWICZ IN FRANCE

PROFESSOR AND

SOCIAL PHILOSOPHER

Maxime Leroy

> The European situation is such that henceforth it
> will be impossible for any single nation to advance
> alone along the path of progress, without destroy-
> ing itself by thus compromising the common cause.[1]

> Today, the West is dying of its doctrines.[2]

Three names, indissolubly linked together, stirred the
imagination of young students during the last years
of the reign of Louis-Philippe: Michelet, Mickiewicz,
Quinet. These three taught side by side at the Collège de
France, they were close friends, and they held similar ideas.
They were eloquent speakers, feverishly applauded by a
public representing many different trends of thought.
Appointed during the same period, although not on the
same day, they lost their Chairs at the same time, in the
political uproar that heralded February 1848.

On account of the circumstances uniting him to his
two French colleagues, as well as the glory and disgrace

1. A. MICKIEWICZ. *La Tribune des peuples.* 14 March 1849.
2. A. MICKIEWICZ. Lecture at the Collège de France. 1 April 1844.

he shared with them, Mickiewicz, a Polish exile, was destined to play in French history a political and literary role whose exact ramifications it is rather difficult to retrace after the lapse of a century. We are, indeed, far removed from the time when the political passions that inspired the activities and thoughts of the three friends—who might well be called prophets, missionaries, or even the victims of hallucinations, since they all thought themselves messengers and agents of Providence—ran high.

We shall devote our attention to Mickiewicz the prophet, who nevertheless saw with clear eyes the needs of his own country. He was not simply a lyrical poet and an eloquent speaker. His personality was composed of many different elements, but there can be no denying that it possessed a certain, rather chaotic, unity. He was an ardent patriot, whose thoughts and actions were centred on Poland. The diversity of his nature arose out of the circumstances in which he evolved. Two facts dominated his life: the prestige of Napoleon, and the martyrdom of his native land. What he wanted was the resurrection of Poland, which would lead to the deliverance of all the martyred peoples. Mickiewicz, the patriot, was also an internationalist. Pacifist as he was, his desire was for a war of liberation, but the liberation of which he dreamed was universal.

It was through his lectures at the Collège de France that Mickiewicz played a part in the history of French thought during the reign of Louis-Philippe.

The economist Léon Faucher, a distant relative of Mickiewicz' wife, was mainly instrumental in procuring the appointment of the poet to the Chair of Slavonic

Languages and Literature at the Collège de France in 1840.
The Minister of Education, Cousin, signed the order for
his appointment.[1] Cousin had been fairly quickly won
over to support his candidature, but the proposal to
establish a Chair, which involved certain financial commit-
ments, ran into opposition from the Prime Minister,
Thiers, and the King. The Bill was introduced in the
Chamber of Deputies on 21 April 1840, and debated on
18 June. There was only one dissenting voice, that of
Auguis, author of a history of Catherine II, who, in his
speech, maintained that the Slavonic languages included
Hungarian. In the Senate, Mickiewicz had the support of
Gérando, who was a famous philanthropist, an interesting
writer on the history of philosophy, and an ideologist of
the school of Maine de Biran.

Mickiewicz' first lecture at the Collège de France was
delivered on 22 December 1840. It was a great success.

It was noted at the time—and today we note with even
greater astonishment—that the professor expressed no
word of thanks, in the way of ordinary courtesy, to the
minister who had taken such pains to secure his appointment. He was, however, pleased with this opening.

'My first lecture, although not brilliant, was appropriate
to the occasion and listened to with interest. It is not a bad
beginning, but matters are by no means easy, and each
lecture is like making a journey across the pampas, surrounded by wild animals and Indians. . . . Providence has
called me to a difficult post. May it continue to help me!'

The three professors, Mickiewicz, Quinet and Michelet

1. The order indicated that he was 'provisionally' appointed to this Chair.

—so alike and yet so different—were linked together in the minds of the general public and have remained associated ever since. They resembled one another in their mysticism, although each was mystical in his own particular way. All three were violently anti-clerical; but, whereas Quinet and Michelet tended to aspire after the establishment of creeds without public worship—vague, lay creeds of a humanitarian nature, based on the moral principles of 1789—Mickiewicz was waiting for the proclamation of a new evangelical revelation, the founding of a universal religion, i.e. a new heresy that would triumph over Rome.

What did Michelet and Quinet think of Mickiewicz?

It was Léon Faucher, a future minister of Napoleon III, who introduced Mickiewicz, Michelet and Quinet to one another in 1837, i.e. a few years before the Return of the Ashes, which took place in 1840. The first impressions of the two French historians were very favourable: 'Saw Mickiewicz,' Michelet recorded, 'finely chiselled features, but rather wild-looking owing to the abundance of beard and hair; abrupt and jerky manner of speaking.' This is what Quinet said: 'Nobody could possibly look more pleasing and more savage at the same time. I think he is a little mystical, but with a mysticism befitting a great and beautiful personality. He looks young and completely unaffected, which is by no means common nowadays. We are to see each other often.'

Mickiewicz had more in common with Quinet than with Michelet, who made a point of putting on record the respects in which he differed from his Polish colleague, whom he called his 'illustrious friend'. It was a very small incident which led Michelet to do this. In 1845 a

medal was struck, bearing the effigies of the three friends
and stamped with this significant motto: *Ut omnes unum
sint*. This emblem displeased Michelet, because it lumped
together the three professors, their doctrines and activities
as though there were not the slightest difference between
them. He unbosomed himself to Mickiewicz with the
utmost frankness. It was a very delicate matter, he wrote:
'United in friendship and in our sincere search for a truly
moral way of life, we nevertheless differ, perhaps fundamentally, in methods and in principles. My last book,[1]
which you must have received, corresponds to the needs
and circumstances of this country; it is *rationalist*. Can we,
by associating our effigies on a medal, make future
generations believe that we have been unanimous on the
religious and social questions? It costs me something, in
more than one way, to raise this doubt. What could be a
greater source of joy and pride to me than to be thus
associated with your immortality? . . .'

The day after he received this letter, dated 11 March
1845, Mickiewicz sent the following reply to Michelet:
'I deeply regret to have been a cause of vexation to you.
I am no more responsible than you are for the idea of
uniting our effigies on the same medal. I recall that, a year
ago, Mr. Savon,[2] accompanied by a few students, spoke
to me of their plan to strike medals for you and for
Quinet, and suggested I should associate my name with
both yours. I asked them whether they had received your
permission, and they said they had. It would have been
false modesty on my part to refuse and I accepted with

1. *Le Prêtre*.
2. An Italian poet who sought asylum in Paris.

sincere pleasure this mark of esteem for what I represent at the Collège. I assure you that nothing personal entered into this pleasure. When I recently saw the simple medal, I thought it had been authorized by you. Whatever may be your reasons for disapproving the form of this medal, I cannot but respect them. Please believe that there can be nothing in your explanations to cause me pain, for it was never your intention to hurt me. I am just finishing my second volume. I shall then have much more free time and hope to be able to visit you more often.'

It is interesting to observe that Mickiewicz did not object to the motto any more than the criticism raised by Michelet, who felt much more different from Mickiewicz than Mickiewicz did from him. It does not seem, as Mr. Z. L. Zaleski points out in his remarkable article 'Michelet, Mickiewicz et la Pologne',[1] that those who attended the lectures given by the two professors were struck by the differences emphasized by Michelet, who later modified them to some extent in this note, found among his papers: 'I was the most rationalist; Mickiewicz, the most legendary and mystical; and Quinet, through his Napoleon, was our intermediary. These differences of method were as naught compared with our *unity of mind*. All three were opposed in one respect to the teaching of the Restoration: free from the chains of history, but *making history*.' And he added, abandoning his contrasts: 'We three, a perfect image of brotherhood.'

Later, in February 1845, he again analysed these differences: Mickiewicz 'is less opposed to us than akin and

---

1. *Revue de la littérature comparée*, 1928.

symmetrical. The difference in outlook is mainly due to the difference between the peoples and the civilizations to which he and we belong'.

What did Mickiewicz think of his two friends? Mr. Z. L. Zaleski quotes these lines from one of the poet's letters, written in 1843, which clearly answer this question: 'Michelet sees far ahead, but he is lacking in tone. Quinet is less farsighted, but he maintains tone better.'

What is the meaning of this word 'tone'? Mickiewicz' biographer gives this explanation of what the poet wanted to suggest. The word, taken from the vocabulary of the mystic, Towiański, 'here signifies an attitude of inner harmony with the general idea of the doctrine, a kind of spiritual attitude which is conformable to the master's teaching, and the purity and moral value of which increase or diminish according as its intensity diminishes or increases'.

It was not in emotional intensity that Mickiewicz was lacking. Imprudent to the extent of alarming Michelet, who was not particularly cautious himself, he would make political and religious statements which ended by worrying the Minister of the Interior and the Minister of Education, particularly from the moment when he fell under the influence of Towiański, a peculiar person, who was perhaps a Russian police spy—at any rate, that was the opinion of the Minister of the Interior, Count Duchâtel. It is possible to share this opinion and at the same time to believe, like certain historians, at least to some extent, in the sincerity of Towiański's mysticism.

What drew the three men towards one another and made it possible, apart from an examination of their doctrines, to think of them in unison, was that Mickiewicz felt he was French, although he dwelt on his Polish nationality. He spoke as a Polish patriot just as much as a French patriot. He never ceased asking France to go on being a spiritual guide and a political leader. 'France, which has marched at the head of the Christian nations for so long, cannot abandon them in the midst of a moral retreat.'[1]

Passionate words which—as the publisher of his lectures mentions 'were loudly and enthusiastically applauded by the audience'.[2] 'Yes,' the speaker added, rising to this spectacular evidence of support, 'the French genius can no longer stay at home. This genius has convulsed the moral world: upset all local ideas, all national opinions, pushing them before it or dragging them along in its wake. . . . These ideas and opinions have at last had time to find their direction and to act in concert; today they are looking for a guide, a leader; they are looking for the genius of France.'[3]

How is the French genius to be defined? 'For us, the French genius is not an abstract idea,' he declared; 'it is embodied in great men; it is Charlemagne and his paladins; above all, it is Napoleon and his glorious imperial eagles.'[4]

Poland vibrated intensely with the French genius during the 'Trois Glorieuses' of July 1830; and the insurrection against Charles X had revolutionary repercussions in Poland. The same thing happened in 1848.

What next? Mickiewicz asked during one of his

1. *L'Église officielle et le messianisme*, II, p. 271.
2. ibid., II. p. 271 et seq.
3. ibid., II. p. 271.
4. ibid., II. p. 272.

lectures. Was France going to live barrenly on the sentiment that had provoked the riots against the Crown? How
was it going to accomplish its destiny as a liberator?
'Where is the genius of July? The genius of France? Tell
me, where is your genius? Where is your leader? Show
him to us: we are ready to follow him.'[1]

No leader! It was a cry often heard in France after 1830.

In 1831, in his *Avertissement à la monarchie* (of 1830),
Quinet exclaimed: 'Our souls are bereft of hope.' In 1834,
Lamennais gave utterance to these distracted lamentations:
'France is rotting on its dunghill: no one can tell how
long the disgusting agony of this demi-corpse will last, as
it lies wallowing in the mud that stifles it.'[2]

In his *Essais de philosophie*, the doctrinaire, Charles de
Rémusat, was saying much the same thing: 'There are no
great men in our time.'[3]

The parties which had paved the way for the July
Revolution and faced its dangers had been rapidly disil-
lusioned by the policy of Louis-Philippe. The saying soon
ran, and was given currency by Cabet, in particular, that
the Revolution had been juggled away. Abroad, the
parties—corresponding to the French revolutionary
parties—felt the same disillusionment, which explains
their extreme irritation. Mickiewicz was their spokesman.

The Last Supper, image of the communion between
heaven and earth, had stirred his imagination, as it had
Towiański's, and inspired the concluding phrases of his
course of lectures at the Collège de France. A great man

1. *L'Église officielle et le messianisme*, p. 273.
2. LATREILLE, *Un Lamennais inconnu*, p. 154.
3. Vol. 1, p. 22.

was needed to spread this mystical gospel. A leader, a Messiah—that was what Mickiewicz hoped and prayed for.

With this mystical, other-wordly mind, Mickiewicz nevertheless rejected neither experience, nor reason, nor government by the people; but he subordinated these things to divine inspiration, to the prophetic flights of genius towards the future: 'now, if we are to guide our fellow-men, and, still more, a nation, we must first see where we are leading them and know how to get there; we must foresee the future; we must be prophets'.[1]

To the awaited prophet he assigned a specific mission: to work out a constructive synthesis appropriate to the period in its progress towards the future: 'there must be a man fitted to make such a synthesis. ... If our century declares itself incapable of synthesis, he who provides it can only have discovered it by methods unknown to the learned of our time'.[2]

A Messiah with a doctrine—not just any kind of doctrine, for Mickiewicz emphasized the word 'synthesis'. There is in this word the drift of the whole thought of that period, expressing as it does a tendency carried to its extreme length by the Saint-Simonists, particularly by Auguste Comte, not to mention Victor Cousin. Like Henri de Saint-Simon and Auguste Comte, Mickiewicz complained of the prevailing intellectual anarchy. The Polish poet was not the only one in search of a general doctrine capable of replacing or reforming Catholic dogmas disrupted in the fourteenth century. It was a question of

1. *L'Église officielle et le messianisme*, p. 261.
2. ibid., p. 261.

reorganizing the Church in accordance with principles, the
first of which, in the social field, in the nineteenth century,
had been passionately and eloquently proclaimed by
Lamennais, at the beginning of the French Restoration, in
his famous *Essai sur l'indifférence en matière religieuse*. Lamennais and Mickiewicz, in close association with each other,
were long inspired with the same enthusiasm for the
emancipation of man in the name of the Gospel, freely
interpreted by these two tribunes. Mickiewicz vainly
implored the Pope to assist in the liberation of Poland.
Lamennais, wrote Mickiewicz in 1832, 'is the only Frenchman who has sincerely wept for me: his tears are the only
ones I have seen in Paris':[1] tears for the outlaw, the
exile. . . .

Between Lamennais and Mickiewicz, there was
affinity of thought and feeling, affinity of temperament,
and also the tie of friendship. These two men had much
in common: passionate enthusiasm, lyricism and humanitarianism. Mickiewicz met Lamennais only after the latter's
break with the Church, that is to say, after that extremist
and emulator of Joseph de Maistre and Bonald had become
a tribune of the people. There was a poet in Lamennais
and a tribune in Mickiewicz. However, they were both
lyricists and prophets.

Failing the Pope and the monarchs, in whom Lamennais had at first put his trust, how could the transformation
desired by Mickiewicz be brought about—lasting peace
among men, the better future so eagerly awaited and

---

1. A. MICKIEWICZ. *Correspondance*, published by his son, p. 108. In the *Affaires de
Rome*, Lamennais recognized that Mickiewicz' *Book of the Polish Pilgrims* had
inspired the lyricism and parables of his *Paroles d'un croyant*.

predicted? Mickiewicz, whose ideas on this matter were very similar to Bonald's, replied: 'theories establish nothing. . . . Western philosophers believe that intellectual progress and the propagation of certain opinions must lead to a new and happy state of affairs; Poland, on the contrary, believes that results can be achieved only by living persons'; that is, by men of action inspiring action, by men of action visited by a revelation. He held, moreover, that this opinion was justified by history; 'all the great States of antiquity and modern times have been established by great men. What is a great man and why is he great? The answer is that all we little men recognize a part of ourselves in his greatness. Every Arab felt in Mohammed his own passions and spiritual transports'. Mickiewicz then reverts, as always, to Napoleon. Why was Napoleon so great? 'Because every Frenchman recognized, in the energy and spontaneity of that extraordinary man, the essence of French genius and his own individual, inner feelings.'[1]

The phrase about Napoleon's energy has a ring of Stendhal.

It is not easy for us today to imagine the superhuman prestige of Napoleon. It was a childhood memory that evoked this prestige in the mind of Mickiewicz. In one of his poems he gives an imperishable picture of Napoleon's army invading Russia in 1812. He had seen this army in Lithuania, his native province, under the command of the Emperor's brother, Jerome, King of Westphalia.

Mickiewicz never ceased to associate Napoleon, France

1. *La Politique du XIX* siècle*, p. 433.

PAN
TADEUSZ

CZYLI

OSTATNI ZAJAZD NA LITWIE.

Historja szlachecka

z r. 1811 i 1812,

WE DWUNASTU KSIĘGACH, WIERSZEM,

przez

ADAMA MICKIEWICZA.

TOM PIERWSZY.

Wydanie Alexandra Jełowickiego,

Z POPRAWKAMI AUTORA.

PARYŻ.
1834.

A. MICKIEWICZ.

Podług Medaljonu wykonanego w Weimarze 1829
przez P. Dawida Szkoła Instytutu Francyi.

Mazurem Wincklerowi

poznan główno-twórczym z przyjaciel

Autora Weszyńskiej.

Pan Tadeusz. Title page of first edition.

and the resurrection of Poland; and, with him, the whole reign of Louis-Philippe was to be tormented by that idea of a France assisting in the national rebirth of Poland, and not only of Poland, but of Italy and Germany as well. The concept of nationhood impassioned revolutionaries, socialists, communists and republicans. They all dreamed of a reconstituted Poland, and of a unified Germany and Italy. This was their guiding principle, dangerous in itself, and dangerously exalting.

The *coup d'état* of Louis Bonaparte was approved by Mickiewicz: 'France', he wrote, 'needs a dictatorship to get it out of chaos; the act of the Head of the State marks the beginning of the country's rebirth.' Rash words. Neither Quinet nor Michelet could approve such an attitude. The poet replied: 'You were about to have the proscriptions of Antony, Octavius and Lepidus; you have Octavius immediately; what are you complaining about?'[1]

Vain optimism: in 1852, even before the Imperial Crown had been set upon his head, this strange Messiah was to remove the three friends from their Chairs.

This short-lived enthusiasm for the new regime sprang not only from the poet's ardent Napoleonism, but also from the circumstances, the chaos he had denounced and the social and political ideas represented and championed by Louis Bonaparte.

Unlike the liberals of Louis-Philippe's reign, who clove to the principles proclaimed in 1789, Louis Bonaparte had social ideas. Under the *royauté citoyenne*, he had published

1. MARIE CZAPSKA. *La Vie de Mickiewicz*, p. 289.

pamphlets in which as a thoughtful reader of Fourier and Henri de Saint-Simon he had expounded revolutionary ideas: *Rêveries politiques, Idées napoléoniennes, Extinction du paupérisme*, of which the last, published in 1844, is the most significant. In Louis Bonaparte's version, his uncle Napoleon was a general who had fought for the cause of peace, a promoter of the union of peoples, so dear to Mickiewicz' heart. *Si vis pacem fac bellum*. He himself, the pretender to the throne, regarded himself as chosen by God, a priest like Balzac, a *vates* like Hugo or like Mickiewicz himself, a minister of destiny like Robespierre, a sword of Providence like the victor of Marengo and Austerlitz. He wrote that the masses, whose accession to power and victory over the caste system he prophesied, needed guides, a supreme guide. 'They must be organized so that they can make known their will; and they must be disciplined so that they can be guided and enlightened regarding their own interests.'

This idea of dictatorship was so widespread that even those liberal-minded men, Sainte-Beuve and Proudhon, were not uninfluenced by it: Mickiewicz' enthusiasm for Napoleonism cannot therefore be regarded as a sort of paradox, an exceptional case of eccentricity. Moreover, as Proudhon pointed out, the period was rank with despotism. However, like them, Mickiewicz finally saw Louis Bonaparte as he really was; like them, he turned his back on the man who had so cruelly disappointed their hopes of reform.

It was not only of Napoleon that Mickiewicz was thinking: he joined his name with Byron's: 'Both were conscious of a mission to be accomplished on behalf of

other men, in a society corrupted by the scepticism and
libertinism of the eighteenth century.'[1]

Although Mickiewicz was a Napoleonist, he was not a
Bonapartist in the narrow sense of the term, notwithstanding certain rash utterances; his admiration for the
Emperor was not partisan; he had attached himself to a
general concept, an idea divinely personified, one might
say, unconnected with the various parties and the contro-
versies about the Emperor's action in any given circumstances. The Napoleon of Mickiewicz was a Messiah,
whom he, as a religious poet, understood in his relationship
to a reformed Christianity, to the great European ideas
and the main national concepts, which he had defended
by associating them with the most illustrious name of the
time. In 1851, for Mickiewicz, as for Sainte-Beuve, Alfred
de Vigny, Mérimée and the Saint-Simonians, it was not so
much a question of rallying 'round a man as of supporting
a programme of salvation.

Mickiewicz' actions and thoughts had always been
inspired by a mixture of patriotism and religious feeling
and, until the day when he met the mystic Towiański, this
mixture was not without a certain sweetness. The appearance in his life of the famous mystic turned his former
appeals to God and the Messiah, and his memories of his
tortured fatherland, into a kind of fanaticism, and we must
not shrink from saying that from that time onwards the poet
sometimes appeared to be suffering from hallucinations.
He became more a tribune than a poet, more a prophet
than an historian. His Christian humanitarianism turned

---

1. EDOUARD KRAKOWSKI. *Adam Mickiewicz, philosophe mystique*, p. 110.

quarrelsome, combative. From that period, however, dates
the great political and sentimental influence of the magnificent poet of the *Pilgrims*. Like the poets and theorists of
that period, Mickiewicz became ever more convinced that
he was a messenger and spokesman of God. In this respect,
he differed from his contemporaries only by his excessive
prophesying, his verbal turbulence and his zeal as a
reformer. Hugo, Lamartine, Balzac, and even Vigny were
prophets, and, above all, Pierre Leroux, the most vigorous
humanitarian of that passionate age. Mickiewicz was, at
once, a nationalist and an internationalist, a Pan-Slavist
and a Pole.

There is the man-Messiah, Napoleon, another Napoleon was awaited; there is the nation-Messiah, the Polish
nation: 'nationhood, in the noblest acceptation of the
term, denotes the mission of a nation, and represents the
body of individuals whom God has called to accomplish
a common task—linked by community of interests and
bound by the law of life. . . . In Poland, the inspiration of
all action has been the idea of the motherland'.[1]

And this point must be emphasized: it is not by
political arrangements that the Slav question facing
Europe can be settled. The Slav race, which is 'the largest
and materially the strongest' must be treated according to
its propensities, virtues and moral constitution, by appeal-
ing to its 'domestic, communal and political virtues'. It
is a great race, inevitably to become conscious of its unity,
and, as such, 'Serbs and Bohemians must acknowledge
their brotherhood with Poles and Russians'.[2]

1. A. MICKIEWICZ. *La Politique du XIXᵉ siècle*, p. 407.
2. ibid., p. 433.

It is clear, then, that Mickiewicz was not concerned with a Slav unity which would have meant no more than ordinary racial syncretism: he dreamed of a mighty union of peoples, aware of the source of their unity and of its spirituality, who would know well whence their brotherhood was born.

The birthplace of that brotherhood—says the Polish poet—is Poland. 'It cannot be elsewhere than in the midst of the people that has suffered most of all the Slav peoples, that has been closest to Europe and has rendered the greatest service to Europe. All this is true of the Polish people.'[1]

What has the Slav world to bring to France and the West? Religious, political and social unity. But will the Slavs be strong enough to achieve this unity? Mickiewicz turns once more to France, assuring her that she will surmount her difficulty in understanding her own mission if she takes the Slav race into her hands and makes it the instrument of unification. 'There is a traditional belief among us that France is fated to influence the North and that this will lead to the uniting of the Western and Northern races in support of a Christian ideal, which must find its champion. . . . The empire which men call the "Colossus of the North" will then collapse. . . .'[2]

Christianity, as Mickiewicz understood it, was far removed from Rome. His Christianity was imbued with a divine enthusiasm, which he left undefined, urging humanity upwards and nearer to saintliness. 'After sanctifying families and corporations, Christianity is now moving

1. A. MICKIEWICZ. *La Politique du XIXe siècle*, p. 434.
2. ibid., p. 435.

towards the santification of political States and nations. It challenges the peoples to produce new saints, national saints, who will not only edify us by all the Christian virtues, but also fortify us by showing forth in their persons the ideal of strength and activity that is characteristic of the present time. The spirit is exhorted to produce its statesmen and its national heroes.'[1]

The Slav race has this mission to accomplish in the world. 'It may truly be said that this people, despite its misery and its poverty, is the most powerful instrument that God has destined for the achievement of good on earth in the future.'[2]

Elsewhere he says: 'the Slav countries are at present in a state of solemn expectation. Everyone is ready to receive a new idea. . . . Will the Slav race be swept along, in the wake of Russia, towards conquest? Or will the Poles succeed in carrying it along with them in their adventurous quest for a future which the Russians say is a dream and the Bohemians, a Utopia, but which is simply an ideal?'[3]

Mickiewicz' direct conclusion was that 'Poland was destined to incarnate the new revelation; France is destined to be the first to receive it'.[4]

The Slav peasants, Russian and Polish, the poet saw as they existed in his own mind and through the eyes of the national poets and singers: hospitable, religious, unlike all other peoples, patient, resigned and gentle.

1. A. MICKIEWICZ. *La Politique du XIX*e *siècle*, p. 461 et seq.
2. ibid., p. 429.
3. ibid., p. 428 et seq.
4. *L'Église officielle et le messianisme*, II, p. 269.

Those were the qualities that would equip them to
accomplish their mission. 'This people can never be
roused to action in the name of a death-dealing doctrine.
It cannot be armed by the promise of lands and blood.'[1]
Thus, to use his own expression, Mickiewicz walked in
'the celestial realm of illusion'.

Mickiewicz condensed his strictly political and social ideas
into the 15 articles of the charter, known as the Polish
Political Creed which was drawn up in Rome in March
1848. It was obviously influenced by the events in Paris in
the February of that year:

1. The Christian spirit, in the holy Roman Catholic faith,
   to show itself in free acts.
2. The word of God, proclaimed in the Gospel, becoming
   the law of the State—civil and social law.
3. The Church as the guardian of that word.
4. The motherland, wherein the word of God may have
   life on earth.
5. The spirit of Poland as the servant of the Gospel,
   embodied in the soil of Poland and its people; Poland
   resurrected with the body in which it suffered and was
   laid in the tomb a hundred years ago.
6. In Poland, freedom of worship and association.
7. Free speech, freely expressed, and judged, as regards
   its consequences, in accordance with the law.
8. Whoever belongs to the nation is a citizen; all citizens
   are equal in rights and before the law.
9. Elective magistracy, freely appointed, freely accepted.

1. *L'Eglise officielle et le messianisme*, II, p. 429.

10. To Israel, our elder brother, respect, fraternity and assistance in its progress towards eternal and earthly weal—full equality of political and civil rights.

11. To our life's partner, woman, fraternity, citizenship, full equality of rights.

12. To every Slav established in Poland, fraternity, citizenship, full equality of rights.

13. To every family, its own field, under the protection of the commune; to every commune, a common field, under the protection of the nation.

14. All existing property is placed intact, under the protection of the national government.

15. Political aid, as from a kinsman, is due from Poland to our Bohemian brethren and the kindred peoples of Bohemia, to our Russian brethren and the Russian peoples. Christian aid to every nation as to our neighbour.[1]

This mixture of religion and socialism—and this fact must never be forgotten—is to be found in the writings of most French socialists of that time. It is the preponderance of one or other of these elements that distinguishes them individually. Political equality, equality of the sexes, religious toleration and elective magistracy constitute the political tenets of the creed. The social side is merely sketched in as the extension of private property and the establishment of communal estates.

Mickiewicz hoped for the emancipation of the workers. If he was not a socialist, he was at least sympathetic to the socialistic trends of his time, refusing to agree with those

---

1. *Mémorial de la légion polonaise de 1848*, published by Władislas Mickiewicz, I, p. 69.

who maintained that socialism was nothing but a verbal protest against society, or, in other words, a 'negative force'.[1]

He defined socialism as a combination of desires and passions; 'and desire and passion are never negative'.[2]

The social hostility of *La Presse*, published by Girardin of the Académie des sciences morales, which centred in the famous Comité de la Rue de Poitiers, showed a dangerous failure to appreciate the deepest needs and tendencies of the period, which was indicative of a sordid greed of gain. Mickiewicz described the way in which the Rue de Poitiers treated the question as 'hoarding', 'concealment', and 'evasion'; had no hesitation in saying that, fundamentally, it had no real effect, as the discerning public must realize that it was simply self-interested advertising. His articles on this subject were extremely passionate, and he wrote indeed that 'the hangman would be a better propagandist' than the anti-socialist newspapers and the magistrates of the criminal courts, whom he dismisses as 'would-be preachers of morality'.

He was of the opinion that, upon the whole, the propaganda being carried on was harmful to the 'old European society'. 'The honourable representatives of the old world, having no other credentials than their titles as the royalists, legitimists, and procurators of the old system—titles represented by bank-notes . . . divided among themselves by religion and political opinion, have at last found a common doctrine, that of *self-interest*.'

1. *La Politique du XIX*e *siècle*, p. 231 et seq. (reprint of articles published in 1849, chiefly in *La Tribune des peuples*).
2. ibid., p. 430.

He concluded, 'this doctrine is all they have to set up against socialism'; and added contemptuously that the committee 'is signing on apostles'.[1]

In spite of these violent attacks, it was the committee that triumphed; it was thanks to it that the elections of May 1849 were a disaster for Mickiewicz' friends: out of the 750 members of the Legislative Assembly, approximately five hundred were monarchists, elected through the influence of the clergy and the middle classes that were favourable to the monarchy.[2] It was, to use one of the polemical poet's own expressions,[3] the victory of the 'adoration of capital'.

It was as an attentive and sympathetic witness that he followed the socialist movement; he was interested by what it did and what it taught and on occasion openly supported it. Ample evidence of his attention and interest is to be found in *La Tribune des peuples*.[4] He quoted Cabet, Pierre Leroux, Victor Considérant, Proudhon, Fourier, and Saint-Simon. On 30 March 1849 he protested against the judgment of the Assizes Court of the Seine, condemning Proudhon to three years' imprisonment and a fine of 3,000 francs for violation of the laws governing the press,[5] at which he said, he was saddened rather than surprised. A few days earlier he had protested against the two warn-

---

1. *La Politique du XIX⁰ siècle*, p. 220–1.
2. CH. SEIGNOBOS. *Histoire politique de l'Europe contemporaine*, p. 152.
3. ibid., p. 226.
4. See the articles reproduced in *La Politique du XIX⁰ siècle*, published by Władislas Mickiewicz, the poet's son.
5. For two articles published in *Le Peuple*, one being entitled 'La Guerre', and the other 'Le Président de la République est responsable'. 'As the situation is serious', said the Public Prosecutor (Meynard de Franc, Advocate General), 'the articles which are the subject of the charge are of great importance'.

ings (22 March) addressed to Pierre Leroux by the President of the National Assembly, Armand Marrast: 'Citizen Pierre Leroux', he said, 'is a man of good faith'; and he stressed that he 'spoke with deep conviction'. He denounced the survival of Orleanism in 'the mouths of the present public prosecutors'.

What surprised Mickiewicz in the attitude of the socialists was their moderation; Considérant, for instance, promised a peaceful transformation 'capable of satisfying all interests without injuring anyone'.[1] Mickiewicz, as a warrior Messiah, declared: 'Socialism is offering its enemies a shameful armistice', and added, making his meaning clearer: 'It is surrendering the field of action to them. It is resigning itself to suffering and preaching, and adapting the spirit and style of its preaching to the level of its audience. It claims to be a tremendous force in the intellectual sphere but has a negligible influence in the political world.'

He would have liked the socialists to commit themselves to action: 'Results are achieved in the political world by armies, by soldiers. . . . The socialists are trying to convert instead of inciting to action. . . . They are exhausting their eloquence in trying to convert bankers, wholesale merchants and Malthusians.'[2]

He was afraid that the workers might succumb to the temptation of the comforts offered by the philanthropists, for example, in workers' housing schemes, which would be bound to weaken in them what he called the spirit of the February uprisings. 'Let them never forget that it was

1. At the meeting on 14 April 1849.
2. *La Politique du XIXe siècle*, p. 242 et seq.

by taking up arms on behalf of suffering and poverty throughout the world, by shouting "Long live France, long live Italy, long live Poland!"[1] that they, who had no place to lay their heads, won the right to live in these workers' cities. It was only after they had shaken the powers of the whole of Europe that they compelled the powerful in France to give thought to their fate.'[2]

What exasperated the poet was the fact that the socialists, or rather their spokesman in the National Assembly, the Fourierist, Victor Considérant,[3] omitted to strike where their enemies stood—in Austria, Poland, Italy, wherever 'popery and monarchism' triumphed. As a social thinker, Mickiewicz still remained a nationalist thinker. 'The practical men in the Assembly,' he wrote, 'the party leaders, the most skilful enemies of socialism, rejoiced in their hearts. They left the socialist speaker entirely free to attack the principles of the old society, secure in the knowledge that they were enabling the old society to control the destinies of Italy, Hungary and Poland.' In short, Mickiewicz was of the opinion that socialism could succeed only if the foreign policy adopted was directed against the leaders of reaction in the various countries concerned.[4]

Mickiewicz' work is a long exaltation of Polish patriotism, wherein are reflected the sufferings and the

1. Particularly on 15 May 1848, when the people, led by Blanqui, burst into the National Assembly.
2. *La Politique du XIXe siècle*, p. 249 et seq.
3. Particularly at the meeting on 14 April 1849.
4. See the article in *La Tribune des peuples*, dated 15 April 1849. (The first number of this journal was published on 15 March 1849 with the following subtitles: 'Fraternal pact with Germany. Restoration of a free and independent Poland. Emancipation of Italy.'

demands of the Polish nation. 'Patriotism or sacred fire, this sentiment is, in fact, simply the product of a long spiritual life.' Not every group of people, however large it may be, has the right to the name of nation, but only the groups in which this sacred fire burns, kindled by their ancestors and kept alive, for eye and ear, throughout the ages, by their customs, language, festivals and ceremonies, and by their poetry. 'The greatness of a people is proportionate to the intensity of its patriotic ardour.'[1]

This idea of nationalism was so deeply rooted in him that he said, in his thirteenth lecture at the Collège de France, that his course of lectures 'could not and should not be other than an appeal by the national spirit of Poland to the spirit of the French nation'.[2]

The memory of an inspired national poet is united with that of a noble spiritual leader and a great humanist; it is to this many-sidedness that Mickiewicz owes his very special position in the history of the political and social ideas of the nineteenth century. His survival, to which this commemorative work bears glorious witness, is due to the continuing memory of his personal charm and his vigour in dialectics, much of which can be found in his writings. His people still cherish his memory and have kept it green for the last hundred years.

A richly varied personality, Mickiewicz can still charm and console us, for he was one of those who, with pen in hand, do not confine themselves to writing from their imagination; he wanted his work to reflect the life of his suffering country and to echo the lamentation of the

1. *L'Église officielle et le messianisme*, II, p. 254.
2. ibid., II, p. 253.

universe and its yearning for a better life, under a Providence at last appeased.

It is true that much of Mickiewicz' thinking is no longer applicable to the trends of the present day: but, in spite of the attacks of time, his work as a whole has preserved its national vitality, its poetic verve; hence the continuance of his moral and political influence on his compatriots today. Bourdelle showed his understanding of this dynamic quality in Mickiewicz' work by representing him as a tireless pilgrim; and thus posterity sees him, in the Place de l'Alma in Paris, with staff in hand and eyes uplifted to the sky.[1]

1. The monument was erected in 1929.

ADAM MICKIEWICZ

AND ITALY

G. Maver

'It was a still, calm night, with little snow and ice along the dry roadsides. The moon cast silvery reflections on the rippling waters of the lake, and to the right, beyond them, revealed the fantastic ridges of the distant Alps, silhouetted against the shadows of the night and the starry sky, with the white outlines of Mont Blanc towering above them; to the left, the brown chain of the Jura. Sublime splendours of nature, which inspired some of the finest passages of Byron's *Childe Harold*, and remind pilgrims far from their homeland of another great poet of suffering humanity, Mickiewicz, and of the host of exiles gathered together from the enslaved countries of Europe to recount their sorrows in the surroundings of these alpine solitudes.'

During that night of 1 March 1850, Aurelio Saffi—who has left us such a vivid account of it—together with Ernest Haug, 'a Viennese exile who in Rome had served the cause of the Republic with the devotion to be expected from such an excellent officer', accompanied Giuseppe Mazzini on the road along Lake Geneva leading from Geneva to Lausanne. Pursued even by the Swiss police, the great Italian 'outlaw' had decided to seek refuge, a second time, in England and, in order to carry out his plan in complete secrecy, he had arranged a meeting at Rolle, between Geneva and Lausanne, with Maria Dal Verme who, with her coach, was to help him flee from Switzerland.

The three 'pilgrims', inspired by the splendour of the landscape, whiled away the time and 'sought relief from the rigours of the road' by discussing Byron and Mickiewicz. The conversation was not, as Saffi's account of it seems to suggest, simply a series of 'literary recollections' evoked by the places passed through, but—as Saffi himself emphasizes in a note—a definite discussion that actually took place.[1]

It took place in these special circumstances and for that reason gives us, better than any formal document could do, an idea of Mazzini's faith in the high ethical values of poetry. If it was undoubtedly between all the three friends together, we shall certainly not be wrong in thinking that Mazzini was the moving spirit, and that in the end the discussion turned more upon Mickiewicz than upon Byron, although the memories of Byron, because of his associations with Lake Geneva, will have inspired it. Saffi himself, when he refers to 'suffering humanity' and the 'multitude of exiles', seems to suggest that Mickiewicz was uppermost in their minds; as for Mazzini, we know of his unfailing admiration for the Polish poet, which

1. This information, which has so far escaped the attention of those interested in the Polish poet, is given in Aurelio Saffi's preface to Vol. IX of Mazzini's *Scritti editi e inediti*, and was republished in Vol. IV of A. Saffi's *Ricordi e scritti (1849-57)*, Florence, 1899, p. 30 et seq.

was proof against any difference of opinion between the two.

What Mazzini said is lost to us. But what better evidence of his affection and admiration for Byron and Mickiewicz could there be than this conversation, held in full view of Mont Blanc, in the anxious moments before an appointment on which his whole future activity depended?

The first of Mickiewicz' works to attract Mazzini's attention was *The Book of the Polish Pilgrims* which, shortly after the appearance of the French edition issued by Montalembert and by B. Janski, was also published in Italy for the first time, in 1834, anonymously. On 6 July, writing to his mother, his main confidant, Mazzini said: 'I have read Mickiewicz' *The Book of the Polish Pilgrims*. It is written in the same style as Lamennais' *Paroles d'un croyant*—not so vigorous, but containing other beauties, perhaps of equal value. Lamennais has imitated the Prophets more; the other, rather, the New Testament.'[1] The somewhat transient impression of the first letter soon gave way to warm and complete approval: 'Have you read', wrote Mazzini in another letter to his mother, on 18 November, 'a little book by a Pole, entitled *The Book of the Polish Pilgrims*? It is a masterpiece, of which a very weak Italian translation is now being printed. It is written by Mickiewicz, a poet, in my opinion the greatest poet of our time. The Poles include a number of extremely intelligent and fairly cultivated people, perhaps a greater

---

1. Mazzini's letters are quoted from the national edition of his *Scritti*. Since they are set out in chronological order (in the series *Epistolario*), we have omitted references to volumes or pagination.

number than the Germans; I am speaking of the exiles. This book on the Polish pilgrims is similar to the French one you have seen; or rather, it is to some extent its source, as it was published first. Perhaps it will soon lead to a similar book by an Italian author, because all peoples have their own particular style and we must not always allow foreigners to monopolize the various styles: when I say similar, I mean of the same kind, because it would be difficult to produce something of equal merit.'

This idea of giving the Italians a work containing the same words of comfort and faith as the Poles had found in *The Book of the Polish Pilgrims* never came to fruition; nor was the intention, mooted in 1836, of publishing (obviously in French) a *Bibliothèque du proscrit*—containing in addition to other works Mickiewicz' *The Book of the Polish Pilgrims* and *Crimean Sonnets*—ever carried into effect.

However, these projects, the flattering opinion concerning the Polish exiles, and above all the designation of Mickiewicz as the greatest living poet, are so many proofs that Mazzini was discovering the first signs of a new literature among a people whose great misfortune had stimulated it to proceed to a thorough renewal of its own culture; and that for him the herald of that new literature was Adam Mickiewicz, who, particularly with his *Book of the Polish Pilgrims*, had constituted himself the spokesman and symbol of Poland's misfortunes. Mazzini was not completely certain about his discovery; but he always remained confident that he was on the right track, if only because he absolutely needed to be confident, since he had long been vainly searching, in Italy and elsewhere, for signs of a poetry corresponding to the ideals of that new world which was the ultimate object of all his thoughts and actions.

Mazzini's enthusiasm for *The Book of the Polish Pilgrims* was thus, to some extent, as it were, predestined. An exile himself, he at once felt that he had discovered the signs of the new poetry in the work of the greatest poet of the exiles. Though he did not share all Mickiewicz' opinions, and from time to time, as often happens between friends, even adopted an angry and hostile attitude towards him ('I admire the man; I know no one in Europe at present who reaches the same heights; but he has taken the wrong road. He could have been the poet of the future, but he is simply the poet of great ruins. The future will no more depend on him than it will on the Catholic Church'—letter to Lisette Mandrot, of 2 September 1838), Mazzini regarded Mickiewicz as one to whom a revelation had been vouchsafed.

What was bound to strike him in *The Book of the Polish Pilgrims* was the unshakeable faith, which admitted of not the slightest doubt; the deep 'religiousness' that sternly rejected every form of egoistic materialism; the categorical affirmation of the superiority of suffering *vis-à-vis* the temporary triumph of evil, and of the high reward due to it; and lastly, the idealization of the 'pilgrims', entrusted with the mission of founding the new world order and regenerating mankind—a mission to be carried out with resoluteness and purity of life and purpose.

However, these ideological affinities alone would not in themselves have accounted for Mazzini's designating Mickiewicz as the greatest living poet. Of equal importance was the fact that this small book revealed to Mazzini, for the first time, an adequate and eloquent poetic expression of the new world after which he aspired.

Mickiewicz' use of the simplicity and pathos of the Bible must have been regarded by Mazzini as an inspired solution to the problem of discovering the poetic language which the new ideals required. It was necessary to break completely with the classical tradition of a 'poetry intent upon harmonic forms, rich in colouring and imagery', which avoiding recourse to the anarchy of the romantic innovations, capable only of portraying the sufferings and joys of the individual, if an art fully corresponding to the needs and aspirations of the community, as opposed to the individual, was to be created. And Mazzini was all the more likely to approve this Biblical style, in that there was something Biblical in his own way of living and acting.

Another point is noteworthy in connexion with that nocturnal conversation on the shores of Lake Geneva: the association of the names of Byron and Mickiewicz. Mazzini always had a great affection for Byron— an affection, however, tinged with regret. 'Byron was a man of independent judgment, depth of thought, great sensitivity and magnificent spirit, accustomed to long wanderings—Byron, and Mickiewicz whose first works had been influenced by Byron, were both "pilgrims"— but in *The Book of the Polish Pilgrims* the idea of "pilgrim" had already become different from the Byronian conception, and sanctified by misfortune. He would thus have served as a model for the "European poet" if calumny, envy and the indifference of his fellow-men had not driven him to solitude and despair, causing him, in the

main, to depict his own self instead of acting as a spokesman for humanity.'[1]

Consequently, it was not to Byron, as he would have
wished, that Mazzini entrusted the standard of the new
literature—but to Mickiewicz. Byron, withdrawn into
himself, was unable, or did not know how, to transcend
his own individuality. Mickiewicz, on the other hand, had
been led by his country's misfortunes to discover a means
to a union between the individual and the community, and
to the penetration of the individual with universal human
ideals. It was here that the Italian exile met him and
accepted him as the spokesman for what he himself
believed in. Perhaps Mazzini reflected this regret concerning Byron and this less qualified admiration of Mickiewicz,
when, in that conversation with his two friends, he linked
the poet nearest to his heart and the poet nearest to his
own ideals.

Mazzini was not the only Italian to be fascinated by
The Book of the Polish Pilgrims. It was, indeed, even more
appreciated by one of the most distinguished Italians of
that period—Niccolò Tommaseo.

It would be difficult to find, even among Polish
admirers of the work, anyone expressing so moving an
opinion as that delivered by Tommaseo in a letter written
to his friend Gino Capponi in 1835: 'Lamennais (a comparison between *The Book of the Polish Pilgrims* and
Lamennais' *Paroles d'un croyant* suggested itself spontaneously to Italian readers of these works) has returned to
Brittany. . . . A weak thinker, moved only by passion.

---

1. 'D'una letteratura contemporanea', *Scritti*, Vol. I. p. 215.

A mere talker. His *Paroles* are child's play compared
to Mickiewicz' *Book of the Polish Pilgrims*. Yesterday
evening I re-read this, in the Italian translation. . . . The
last prayer, with the litany, brought tears to my eyes.
I recited them aloud towards midnight, yesterday, the
festival of St. Anthony the Thaumaturge; and I felt very
insignificant when reading such simple words of affection
and faith. In Lamennais' book there is not a single word
which comes so directly from the depths of the heart; or
rather there is only one, which he imitated in the chapter,
"Nous crions vers vous, Seigneur". But, that other book
with its "Kyrie Eleison", how much more noble it is! Read
it. Read Montalembert's preface . . . read Mickiewicz, you
will be delighted. . . . You would be equally delighted if
you knew him: simple, frank, eloquent, spontaneously
affectionate: he reveres Italy, religion and beauty; he
makes a show neither of faults, as certain eminent persons
are wont to do, nor of good qualities, like smaller spirits!
To know Mickiewicz in Paris is like plucking a violet in
Siberia.'[1]

Even this opinion, conveyed so spontaneously in a
private letter the very day after Tommaseo had re-read
The Book of the Polish Pilgrims, was due to reasons which
partly coincided with, while partly sharply differing from,
those which had provoked Mazzini's admiration. Both
had an inborn aversion for useless rhetoric and a warm
sympathy for 'simple words of faith and affection'; both
considered that art should not be dissociated from ethics;
both desired that poetry should promote action and be

---

1. N. Tommaseo and G. Capponi. *Carteggio inedito*, per cura di I. Del Lungo and
P. Prunas, Vol I, Bologna, 1911, p. 262–3.

addressed to the greatest possible number of people. However, for Tommaseo, this was an attitude for certain occasions, rather than a general programme; and he never visualized literature as being both a reflection of and a guide to the new epoch.

Again, the two men differed in character and in the degree of sympathy which they had for the Slav world. With Mazzini, this sympathy was due not only to the breadth of his political and cultural horizon but to his carefully thought-out plans for a new world, in which the young nations would have the task of redressing past wrongs and exercising a regenerative influence on the future. But in the case of Tommaseo, who was of Dalmatian origin and of mixed Italo-Slav blood, this sympathy for the Slavs was to some extent spontaneous and inborn; from the south Slavs it ranged with particular warmth to Poland. 'Everything touching unhappy Poland arouses my respect, nay veneration' (*Antologia* di Vieusseux, December 1831).

The two men also differed in their religious outlook. Tommaseo was firmly attached to Catholic doctrine; Mazzini, though deeply religious, was neither a Catholic nor a Christian. This explains their different attitudes towards Lamennais, who was esteemed by Mazzini as a reformer, but despised by Tommaseo for the same reason. Further, it is clear, even from the brief opinions which they both expressed concerning *The Book of the Polish Pilgrims*, that Mazzini was impressed mainly by the faith in justice and fraternity emanating from it, and Tommaseo by its fundamentally Catholic nature.

Neither man was likely to understand the other, and

never in fact did so. It is all the more significant that, with
The Book of the Polish Pilgrims, Mickiewicz had a new
message of comfort and faith for both of them. This
'concordia discors', as well as the great popularity which
The Book of the Polish Pilgrims enjoyed in Italy, at least up
to 1848, clearly shows what a deep impression this work by
the Polish poet made upon the minds of the Italian people.

The year 1834 was thus a memorable date in the history
of the literary relations between Italy and Poland. Until
then, these relations had been purely unilateral. It was not
that Italy had disinterested herself in distant Sarmatia or
had been insensitive to the memorable historical events
and combats which won such glory for Poland in the
eyes of every western country; on the contrary, from this
standpoint Italy had long been a pioneer. But whereas, in
the literary field, Poland had made abundant use of Italian
models, Italy had been more or less completely unaware
of that literature which, more than any other, had undergone Roman and Italian influence. It was reserved for
Mickiewicz—as also and, almost at the same time, for the
music of Chopin—to put an end to this unequal state of
affairs, and to transform what had formerly been a purely
negative situation into something positive, greeted with
enthusiasm.

Tommaseo, like many others, reserved his admiration
for *The Book of the Polish Pilgrims* alone. Voracious
reader that he was, he certainly knew other works by the
Polish poet; but he condemned them because, in his
opinion, Mickiewicz 'had over-imitated the lame Scottish
Titan', 'that spirit withered by its own ardours' *(Diʒio-
nario Estetico)*.

With Mazzini it was quite the opposite. After his memorable discovery of *The Book of the Polish Pilgrims*, he assiduously sought to penetrate ever deeper into the essence of Mickiewicz' work as a whole. In 1836, he translated the poem *To the Polish Mother* and sent it to his own mother, promising her something else by Mickiewicz 'when he should be a little more at peace'. (So far as is known, this promise was never kept.) Two years later, he anonymously contributed to the new Polish review, *The Polish Monthly Magazine*, a very successful short description of Mickiewicz.[1]

The importance of this article was somewhat diminished by the fact that few Italians were able to read it; but it is so necessary for a complete understanding of these fruitful relations between Italy and Poland that it is worth quoting the principal passages.

'For us, Mickiewicz is more than a poet; he is a prophet—like the great poets of Israel, with whom he has so many points of resemblance. He preserves for the Polish people their traditions, which have been violently abused; he vivifies, in his verses, the lamentation of all, the hope of all; his voice is the voice of millions proclaiming by his mouth that their existence, as a people, is not consummated; that Poland has yet a great mission to perform; and that, since she is conscious of her destiny, she wishes and will know how to fulfil it. This voice, we do not admire, we *feel* it; for us it is a guarantee of our future existence—one that is stronger than all the deceitful words of diplomacy, as well as of those who seek the salvation

---

1. The authorship of the article was revealed by A. LEWAK: 'G. Mazzini e l'emigrazione polacca', in *Risorgimento italiano*, 1924.

of their country in cabinet intrigues. . . . It is a new
mission which begins, and it is therefore a new literature
that is required as the expression of that mission. And, as
if to justify foresight and hopes, this literature springs up,
all at once; it is Mickiewicz—be he conscious or not of the
fact—who is its founder. . . .

'He has struggled, we say, and the traces of this
struggle appear here and there like extinct volcanoes, in
his poems, particularly in those which belong to his first
epoch; and it is by those traces themselves that the action
of the poet over us is stronger; for we see therein a mark
of fraternity, we know that if he has raised himself above
us by genius, he has done so by passing through the
same storms which we passed through, either on a grand
or on a small scale. . . . Mickiewicz has traced—has engraved, as we may say—in gigantic characters, the combat
which he has sustained against this proud perception of his
own superiority—a perception which tends to isolate the
poet and to break up the road of art, which is great only
when it is religious, in *Forefathers' Eve*, and particularly in
the second part. . . . The struggle between the man and
the universe . . . which characterizes the first poems of
Mickiewicz, has ceased. . . . The poet, who, when he was
writing his sonnets of the Crimea, cried out " Happy he who
knows how to pray ", prays today. He has understood that
human glory is a mere nothing before Infinity; he has felt
God and his law; he has become convinced that earthly
life would be the most contemptible of all possessions,
were it not a mission; and to that mission he has devoted
himself, with fervour and resignation. A second phase has
commenced for him since then, the first step of which has

been marked by *The Book of the Polish Pilgrims*—a work that we shall perhaps have to speak of some other time. To all his doubts, to all his internal agitation, he has found a solution.

'This solution, we must say, is not ours; but every conviction is sacred for us, and faith is a state of progress from doubt. The faith of Mickiewicz is, moreover, identified to such a point with the future emancipation of our common country—whatever may be the means of effecting its realization—it so sweetly murmurs forth promises of regeneration and elevation, that we cannot abstain from giving our frequent sympathy to it, even when our own reason and our own belief repel it.'

One of the peculiarities of this article—which contains numerous passages translated from the original texts, including some from the *Improvisation* of *Forefathers' Eve*, as well as the whole of *Farys*—is that it seems to have been written by a Pole: this was also the opinion of Mickiewicz, according to his son Władislas. This fact, even if accounted for by the editorial requirements of the review, possibly reflected Mazzini's hesitation to assign to Mickiewicz, openly, the mission for which he considered him pre-destined.

Indeed, in all the articles signed by himself, Mazzini always maintained an attitude of prudent reserve. This was true of the essay, *De l'état actuel de la littérature*, written in 1837: 'Where is the school which, by means of all its works, doubles our power of action and improves our hearts and minds, making us more fervent and readier to exercise our faculties of enthusiasm and devotion? Is there one man, in this whole generation of poets, who reinvigorates us with strong social beliefs and consoles us for our individual hardships and disappointments by placing us face to face with the hardships and sufferings of humanity?' It is equally true of his later study on the two poets, *Byron and Goethe*, whom he prized most of all among the poets of the past: '. . . Today we can catch a glimpse, albeit very vaguely, of that new social poetry which will sing of the destination of man and appease his anguished soul by teaching him to ascend towards God through Humanity.'

However, the idea which became rooted in Mazzini's mind, after he had read *The Book of the Polish Pilgrims* triumphed over all his uncertainties and his differences of opinion with Mickiewicz. When the latter moved to Lausanne and there became an intimate friend of Mazzini's two companions and disciples, Luigi Amedeo Melegari and Giovanni Scovazzi, Mazzini wrote to Melegari: 'By now you will have certainly become acquainted with Mickiewicz, and I can well imagine how each of you has quickened the other's Catholicism. But Catholicism apart, give me your opinion, if you know him, of the man. As to the poet, I love and admire him as the most powerful poetic genius of the present century.' There is no doubt that this lavish praise of Mickiewicz must have been known to Mazzini's friends and, in general, to all cultured Italians of the period (cf. for instance the words of Cavour, quoted further on); but it never became known to the general public.

Only on one occasion did Mazzini decide, without resorting to anonymity, to make known publicly his own personal opinion of Mickiewicz' work. For some unknown reason, however, this opinion, expressed in 1847 and included in the lengthy article entitled *Of the Slavonian National Movement* (the first two parts of which, translated from French into English, appeared in *Lowe's Edinburgh Magazine*), was published in Italy only in 1922.[1] It is not, however, without importance, as it shows that in the meantime Mazzini, always in search of arguments in support of his ideas, had extended his studies, perhaps owing to the influence of Mickiewicz' lectures at the Collège de France, to the other poets of the Polish emigration.

Thus in this article he says that 'Polish poetry, as it appears in the works of Mickiewicz, Garczyński, Zaleski, Goszczyński, Krasiński, and certain others, not only occupies a place in the front rank of contemporary poetry, in everything concerning form and artistic power; it seems to us also to be that which, by its fundamental tendencies, comes nearest to the ideal of poetry; that ideal which we see to be needed, and can already glimpse, for the new Europe in process of development. It is *the only* poetry which lives in the present and can therefore exercise an influence on the future.'

Mazzini thus began to regard other Polish poets, in addition to Mickiewicz, as precursors of the literary revival; partly, perhaps, because the leader himself had been silent for many years and because his last great poetical work, *Pan Tadeusz*, did not correspond to the requirements of Mazzini's aesthetics. There are numerous indications that Mazzini transferred his attention to other Polish poets—particularly in his endless correspondence.

1. *Scritti*, Vol. XXXVI; *Politica*, Vol. XII.

We shall mention only the most interesting of them. The first letter, in 1864: 'You are extremely cruel towards my poor Slavs. They have three great things in their favour. They are in the birth stage; they are about to begin life; we are dying. . . . Secondly, since the death of Goethe and Byron, they are today producing the only spontaneous, living and invigorating poetry that I know of. You mention Mickiewicz, whom I knew; he is not their only poet. They also have Malczeski, Garczyński, Krasiński. There is more poetry in one of Zaleski's lyrics on the Ukraine and its steppes or in certain scenes of Krasiński's drama, in his *Dream of Cesara* and in his *Prisoner*, than in all Lamartine's elegies and all Victor Hugo's bas-reliefs. Life, action, the feeling of a task to be accomplished, characterize all the writings of these men whom you call inept' (letter to Marie d'Agoult). The second letter was written in 1869: 'Krasiński is the most powerful poet of latter times, since Byron and Goethe' (letter to E. A. Venturi). The third dates from 1870: 'Believers in everything that constitutes the eternal religion of the soul, priests of action, Mickiewicz, Zaleski and Goszczyński are, since Byron, the greatest European poets' (letter to G. Uberti).

However, whereas Krasiński, Zaleski and the other poets of the Polish emigration remained almost unknown in Italy ('are unknown in our country', Mazzini wrote regretfully), Mickiewicz' fame spread rapidly. This was largely due to Mickiewicz' lectures at the Collège de France, which were attended by quite a large number of Italians. The philosopher and statesman, Terenzio Mamiani, in a speech delivered in 1877 at the unveiling of a memorial tablet on the house in the Via del Pozzetto (Rome) where

Mickiewicz had lived in 1848, described the deep impression which those lectures made, even upon foreigners: 'I had the opportunity of visiting him in his own house, of taking a meal with him, and of attending, with great profit, his lectures at the Collège de France. Each time I heard his enthusiastically applauded words, I returned to my miserable room strengthened in heart and mind.'

A number of the lectures at the Collège de France had also been attended, in 1842, by Cavour. In the Paris *salons* which he frequented, he had probably heard about the praise that Mazzini had for some time been lavishing in the letters, and in his private conversations, on Mickiewicz' work, and he would have at least read *The Book of the Polish Pilgrims*. Thus, the words used by him in the Turin Chamber of Deputies on 20 October 1848 were not merely sincere but personal in their appeal: 'The great Slav movement has inspired the greatest poet of our century, Adam Mickiewicz; thus we can place full faith in the destinies of these peoples, for history shows that when providence inspires such sublime geniuses as Homer, Shakespeare and Mickiewicz, then the peoples in whose midst they are born are fore-ordained to high destinies.'

In the meantime, after *The Book of the Polish Pilgrims* had been translated, other translations of the Polish poet's works began to appear in Italy, as well as the first studies on him. A biography of Mickiewicz, based on French sources, was published in 1842 by E. Valtancoli Montazio in the Florentine review *Mondo contemporaneo*. A more important and original study was devoted to him, in the *Rivista di Firenze*, 1846, under the title 'Studi sulle letterature straniere: Adamo Mickiewicz', by Napoleone Giotti.

Lastly, at Trieste, in *La Favilla*, which under the direction of the poet Francesco Dall'Ongaro was designed to inform Italians about the Slav world, the Ragusan, Orsato Pozza (known in Croatian literature under the name of Medo Pucić), published, in addition to information on Mickiewicz' life and works, the first Italian translation of the famous *Improvisation* of *Forefathers' Eve*. This translation deserves special mention, not only by reason of its own merits and the fact that it was the first Italian poetic translation of a work by Mickiewicz, but also because this welcome contribution to knowledge about the Polish poet in Italy came from a Dalmatian Slav of predominantly Italian culture. Unfortunately, this good example was not repeated—knowledge of the Polish language was just as rare among the Croats and Serbs as among the Italians—except by Pozza himself, who, in 1860, published at Zara a booklet entitled *Mickiewicz—Le Conferenze parigine. Dei canti popolari illirici. Discorso detto da A. M. nel Collegio di Francia.*

Despite all these tributes, and notwithstanding the appearance of the first translations of Mickiewicz and essays on his work, it cannot really be said that the Italians, before 1848, were familiar with his name, still less that any substantial number of them were acquainted with his main works. But in that year of revolution the Polish bard suddenly attained wide and unexpected fame, and his name became surrounded with a halo of glory.

This fame was based on a strange combination of elements—vague scraps of information about his poetry; rumours about his impressive, priest-like personality; reports in the papers about his founding of the Polish Legion in Rome; and, above all, the courageous and

'Adam Mickiewicz.' Pen-and-ink drawing by Cyprien Camille Norwid (1821–83), 12.5 × 7 cm. (Rome, 1848). The original is in a private collection; there is a copy in the Mickiewicz Museum, Paris. Photograph by L. Sempoliński.

telling contribution of the Poles to the fight for the Italian Risorgimento.

The exciting history of the Legion is known in great detail, thanks to an important book, the *Mémorial de la Légion polonaise de 1848*, written by Adam Mickiewicz' son Władislas.[1] This is not the place to go into details, or to quote from the large quantity of material supplied by this writer, the impassioned speeches made by Mickiewicz in the towns through which the legionaries passed, and the glowing reports appearing in the papers at that time. The main interest lies in discovering what impression this extraordinary politico-military exploit made on the Italians.

The first point to note is Mickiewicz' unusual capacity for adaptation to, and sensitive intuitive understanding of, an atmosphere with which he could not be said to be really familiar: he had been in Italy, off and on, from the end of 1829 until May 1831, but as a tourist interested in Italian culture rather than as an observer of Italian life. Then there was his astonishing command of the Italian language; and, his lofty self-confidence, born of absolute faith in his mission. Thanks to these qualities, he won from the Italians, although his aims and theirs were not always completely identical, a deep affection, such as they rarely vouchsafe to any foreigner.

It is not surprising, in view of the conditions then prevailing, that his plan to undermine from Italy the position of one of the three powers partitioning Poland, and thus pave the way for Poland's salvation, should have come to nought. What is surprising is that, hampered on

1. 3 vols., 1877, 1909, 1910.

the one hand by counsels of excessive though perhaps understandable caution, and on the other hand by not always disinterested intrigues, and amid general ignorance of the ferment of nationalist ideals likewise existing on the eastern frontiers of a still disunited Italy, he should nevertheless have had considerable success. It was no mean achievement to speak of a 'legion' and give it a 'political creed', enunciated in Rome and intended to remodel all social and international relations under the slogan of equality, freedom and Christian charity—and this with a mere handful of followers of most unwarlike mien, whom he none the less succeeded in carrying with him in the fight for the liberation of Poland, of Italy and of all oppressed peoples.

The memory of another Polish legion—Dombrowski's legion of 50 years earlier—lent weight to the tradition; but at the same time, in the more difficult conditions, emphasized the contrast between the exalted aims and the meagre resources for attaining them. Under another leader, this handful of men striving for a new country and a new social order would have provoked ridicule. But Mickiewicz' every gesture, word and act revealed a spiritual force which captured the Italians' imagination, and compelled general admiration.

During the period when Mickiewicz, in Milan, was striving to win over the Government of Lombardy to his cause, Mazzini, who had also been summoned, at last had an opportunity of making the personal acquaintance of a man for whom he had long had the greatest reverence, both as an individual and as a writer. He wasted no time, and only two days after Mickiewicz' arrival sent him the

following note: 'Brother, allow me to address you thus.
I do not share your genius, but I share your aspirations,
your hopes and your faith in the sacred cause of mankind,
and of my country advancing, as part of mankind, towards
that ideal of brotherhood which is God's purpose for man.
I have read and I love your work, and it is my earnest
desire to meet you. . . .'

Of this encounter—which was to be the culmination
of their spiritual alliance and, over and above their personal
destinies, of the relations between Italy and Poland—
practically nothing, however, is known. Were the two able
to discuss what they had in common, and to explain to
one another the points on which they still differed?
Judging by their silence, it appears not. They were probably
too much concerned with urgent practical problems to
have time to dwell on subjects of more intimate, more
personal interest.

Of the very few references to this meeting in Mickiewicz' letters, one, in a letter to Margaret Fuller, appears
to support this theory: 'I have seen Mazzini, the only
man with the political drive required at this hour.'[1] The
silence observed by Mazzini, usually so frank and so eager
to tell his friends about every memorable event in his life,
is even more puzzling. But he may perhaps have been
thinking of these days in Milan when he said later, to
Władislas Mickiewicz: 'If all that remained of the Polish
Legion of 1848 were its political creed, that alone would
be enough to make it glorious.'

Be this as it may, Mickiewicz' reply to Mazzini's

---

1. E. Dotti. *M. Fuller Ossoli e i suoi corrispondenti*, 1942, p. 316.

homage took the form of supporting Mazzini in certain articles in his paper, *La Tribune des peuples* (1849).

Was Mazzini's own work influenced by the ideas and style of Mickiewicz, and if so, to what extent? There are most certainly traces of his influence, not only in *Foi et avenir* but also in *I doveri dell'uomo*, and even in some of Mazzini's shorter works, such as *Prière à Dieu pour les planteurs*. But a detailed study would be needed in order to ascertain how much Mazzini in fact owed to Mickiewicz, and how much to the *Paroles d'un croyant* of Lamennais.

In 1848–49, and indeed as early as 1834, we find Tommaseo mentioned alongside Mazzini in connexion with Mickiewicz' links with Italy. From Venice, Tommaseo was following Mickiewicz' campaign with deep interest and understanding. The paper *Fratellanza dei popoli* which he was publishing at that time 'was permeated with a Messianic spirit, which Tommaseo had inherited to some extent from the Messianic tradition of political romanticism represented by Mickiewicz and Lamennais, the greatest poet of the movement.'[1] Here again, as in his *Dell'Italia* (1835), it is impossible to distinguish between the influence of Mickiewicz and that of the French writer. Apart from the *Litanie dei pelligrini lombardi*—which was written in 1848, before Mickiewicz had arrived in Milan, and is a deliberate and frank imitation of the Litany in *The Book of the Polish Pilgrims*, over which Tommaseo had been moved to tears—other similar works by Italian writers in the next few years also deal with the same

---

1. R. CIAMPINI. *Vita di Niccolò Tommaseo.* 1945, p. 533.

difficult problem, whose importance, incidentally, should not be exaggerated.

On the other hand, the later stages of the consolidation of Mickiewicz' reputation in Italy are worth a brief consideration. The 'new Dante', as he was called, came to be regarded first and foremost as a preacher of patriotic and religious ideals, and of faith in a future ruled by justice and brotherhood. The tendency is to translate mainly those of his works which advocate these ideals and which may in some sense be said to foreshadow his participation in the Italian Risorgimento. The growth of his reputation is due largely to the Italian disciples of Towiański—Tancredi Canonico, Attilio Begey, and Giovanni Scovazzi whom we find planning, but without result, a complete translation of Mickiewicz' works. The fact that many of his Italian admirers were anti-Towiański does not appear to have harmed the Polish poet's reputation.

Until recently the devotees of Mickiewicz, with very few exceptions, knew no Polish; so that most translations of and essays on his work were based on a French version, or made with the help of Polish volunteers.

There have been, however, especially recently, a number of Polish scholars who have given Italy valuable assistance for a correct evaluation and understanding of the work of their greatest national poet.

One of the most interesting studies—also because of the author's personality—which have been written on Mickiewicz, is that by Carlo Cattaneo, who has treated his subject with an independence of judgment not easy for an Italian, since it involved breaking through the aura of myth with which the figure of Mickiewicz had been surrounded in Italy since the exploits of 1848. Cattaneo's method was to take each of Mickiewicz' works in turn and see what lessons they contained for Italian youth. 'It is our desire to make this poet, whose fame is growing steadily outside his own and the other Slavonic-language countries, better known in Italy, since his thought corresponds more closely than that of any great Italian poet, to the high courage and warmth of heart which are the glory of our youth.' After surveying the principal works and emphasizing the Dantean quality of *Forefathers' Eve*, Cattaneo concluded: 'His memory in Poland is sacred. And his name will be held sacred in our country too by all who remember how he gave to a fighting Italy, his blood, his name, and the flag of his comrades.'[1]

Cattaneo was not alone in taking Mickiewicz as a model, and inspiration, for the Italian people. With many others, there was G. Portigliotti in his study 'Un grande centenario polacco: A. Mickiewicz', in *Pensiero italiano*, 1938: 'Into the putrid, decadent atmosphere and negative scepticism of our drab age, this book [*Forefathers' Eve*] brings a breath of mystic faith in political ideals.'

For long the image of Mickiewicz continued, with a few rare exceptions, to be connected only with the romantic movement and the Risorgimento. It is not surprising, therefore, that, even at the beginning of the present century, it should have been thought possible to

---

1. C. CATTANEO. 'Le poesie di A. M.', in *Politecnico*, 1861, reprinted in *Opere edite e inedite*, Vol. I, 1881. For bibliography of Mickiewicz in Italy, see MARIA and MARINA BERSANO BEGEY, *La Polonia in Italia* (1949); a bibliographical study covering 1799–1948.

study his 'spiritual idealism' without any reference to his masterpiece, *Pan Tadeusz*.[1]

This criticism is also to some extent applicable to T. Gallarati Scotti's admirable study on Mickiewicz (1915); and it is not until we come to the monograph *Adam Mickiewicz* by the Polish writer O. Skarbeck Tluchowski (1922) that we get any adequate assessment of Mickiewicz' great poem.

As opposed to the dearth of literary criticism there is, fortunately, no scarcity of translations, some of which are of a high standard. The general tendency is for them to improve as time goes on.

Of the translations published in the last century, the following are worthy of mention: P. Lioy's romantic version of extracts from *Forefathers' Eve* (1862 and onwards), and A. Ungherini's valuable translation of *Forefathers' Eve*, *Konrad Wallenrod* and miscellaneous poems (1875–98), with introduction. The past 30 years have seen C. Agosti Garosci's version of *Pan Tadeusz* (1924), A. Palmieri's *Grazyna* (with a long essay by R. Pollak), a translation of the *Anthology of the Spiritual Life*, also by A. Palmieri (1925), E. Damiani's version of the *Lyrics* (with preface by R. Pollak, 1926), and finally, *The Slavs*, preceded by *The Book of the Polish Pilgrims*, by Marina Bersano Begey (1947).

Add to these an important special number of *Rivista di cultura* (1924), dedicated entirely to Mickiewicz, and numerous lyrics in periodicals and anthologies, including school textbooks, and we shall have a fairly good idea of

---

1. I refer to the essay by P. RAVEGGI: 'Il Dante di Polonia', in *L'idealità spirituale in Dante, Milton, Klopstock, Goethe e Mickiewicz*, 1903.

what has been done in Italy in the course of a century to keep public interest in the Polish poet alive.

Mention should moreover be made of the many tributes which have been paid to Mickiewicz, more or less officially, at various junctures, in Rome, on the occasion of the unveiling of a memorial tablet in the Via del Pozzetto (1877) and of a bust of Mickiewicz on the Capitol; and in Bologna, at the opening of the A. Mickiewicz Academy (1879). The speeches made on these occasions were reported in the press, along with special articles. Władislas Mickiewicz, with untiring filial affection, gives a detailed account of these ceremonies in his book, *Honoration à la mémoire d' Adam Mickiewicz* (1881).

There can be no better illustration of the repercussions caused by celebrations of this kind throughout the whole of Italy than the reaction of an Austrian-subsidized paper, *L'Italie* (1879), published in Italy in the French language, which, dismayed by the proportions the enthusiasm was assuming, expostulated angrily: 'This Pole is becoming a positive nuisance. . . . Who will deliver us from Mickiewicz?'

To show the veneration in which the poet and comrade-at-arms is still held in Italy, another celebration took place in 1948 on the Capitol, to commemorate the centenary of the creation of the Polish Legion; and all kinds of preparations are being made (new translations, articles, lectures, etc.) to pay fitting tribute, on the first centenary of his death, to the great poet and champion of Italo-Polish friendship.

Let us hope that these celebrations will give us a picture of Mickiewicz, at once more precise and more relevant to the present hour, and so revive the warm sympathy felt for him in Italy at the time of the romantic movement and the Risorgimento—the kind of sympathy which, to couple the name of Mickiewicz once again with that of Byron, caused Antonio Fogazzaro to write, as late as 1898: 'At 30, I loved him as much as I had loved Byron at 20—and that, I assure you, is saying a great deal.'[1]

---

1. Letter to M. Zdziechowski in: T. Gallarati Scotti, *La Vita di A. Fogazzaro*, p. 294.

MICKIEWICZ AND THE LITERATURE

OF THE WESTERN

AND SOUTHERN SLAVS

Karel Krejčí

When the first works of the young poet, still unknown but whose name was soon to be celebrated
not only in Polish but in all Slavonic literature,
were published in Vilna, a city far removed from the chief
centres of European culture, the small Slav nations were
passing through a particularly vital phase in their national
history.

With the exception of the Russians, all had lost their
independence during the long centuries of European feudal
development. Some—such as the Slavs of the Elbe, once
so powerful—had been deprived of it at the very beginning
of the feudal system, the Balkan Slavs had lost it at the
time of the Turkish invasion, and those of Central Europe
with the establishment of the absolute monarchies. Poland
had been the last to keep it and, at the time of Mickiewicz,
the loss of its independence was still a fresh and bleeding
wound, painfully felt by those whose fathers had still
been free.

We then observe a complete or partial denationalization
of the ruling classes, the nobility, the rich bourgeoisie and
the intellectuals. National culture fell into decay and lived

143

on only among the unemancipated peasants in the form of a popular traditional literature. The Polish language was looked upon as inferior.

With the collapse of European feudalism under the pressure of the revolutionary middle class, and with the freeing of the peasantry, the awakening of a new national consciousness with particular reference to the mother tongue and historical traditions is noticeable; the renaissance of the Slav nations begins. This renaissance began to develop in the second half of the eighteenth century and continued in the nineteenth. It is distinguished by the disappearance of all inferiority feeling, by the rebirth of national cultures and by the conquest of old and new political and economic positions.

The process was the same for all the Slavonic nations. The new interest in the national language was expressed through philological studies and by its everyday use in all the fields in which it had been supplanted. There was a reawakening of interest in historical and legendary tradition and a rebirth of popular patriotism; consciousness of the right to lead an independent existence grew. These trends were encouraged by the growth of European romantic movements: Rousseau's apology for the simple people, the cloaking of the distant past in heroic garb, and the cult of the popular song which was supposed to be the very essence of spontaneous artistic creation. These trends and currents were guided by the bourgeoisie into channels that led to the winning of independence through revolution.

All the oppressed Slav peoples had, in spite of important differences, a strong consciousness of their common origin and felt the need of combining their efforts in their struggle against their oppressors. The so-called Slav idea, most clearly voiced in the verse and writings of Jan Kollár, a Slovak who wrote in Czech, found profound and swift acceptance among all Slavs.

It was into this setting that the brilliant figure of Adam Mickiewicz entered the scene of Slav life. His enthusiastic verse incited young men to unite into a community or brotherhood in order to give a vigourous impetus to the realization of what seemed impossible. His ballads and stories, harmonious in their simplicity, rekindled the imagination of the peasant people and their unshakeable faith in a higher justice. The chivalrous Grazyna extolled the heroism of a struggle carried on against the enemy and stimulated patriotic devotion. The first part of his *Fore-fathers' Eve* gives passionate expression to the sufferings of unhappy love, such as was lived not only by the Polish poet but also by hundreds of young men of his time, drunk with the *Nouvelle Héloise* and *Werther*. His sonnets are vibrant with souvenirs of love and paint a vivid picture of the colours, sounds and scents of the East. *Konrad Wallenrod* describes the atmosphere of plotting against the powerful enemy and gives the signal for revolutionary combat. The continuation of *Forefathers' Eve* deals with a more recent past and dramatically brings to life the revolutionary struggle and the persecution of the youth of Vilna, while at the same time it makes Messianic prophesies of the future and great mission of the Polish people. In the manner of a Biblical prophet Mickiewicz treats of the same theme in his *Book of the Polish Pilgrims*. Finally, in his masterpiece *Pan Tadeusz*, he paints a balanced and realistic picture of Polish life and people.

Mickiewicz is equally famous for his political activity. Europe had an indication of his genius through the heroic struggle of the Polish insurgents of 1831. It read his propaganda writings and heard him speak on Slavonic literature from his Chair at the Collège de France in Paris. In 1848, it saw him feverishly organizing the Legion, the ambition of which was to be the fountainhead of liberation for all the Slav nations. After the reverse suffered by this legion, it saw him as editor of *La Tribune des peuples,* which fought for the freedom of all nations. Finally, Europe saw him die, still in full activity, during the Crimean War.

These various aspects of the poetic creation and public activity of Mickiewicz have been differently appreciated at different periods. Sometimes it has been the Mickiewicz of the *Ode to Youth* or the ballads and stories who has been dominant, sometimes the Mickiewicz of *Forefathers' Eve* or *Pan Tadeusz,* or perhaps the politician and teacher, the mystic and revolutionary, the patriot, the Slav or opponent of tsarism, the socialist.

Mickiewicz' works first became known to the Slavs of the Austrian Empire, for whom it was the easiest to make contact with Polish literature. In Bohemia, his ballads became popular almost immediately following the publication of the poet's first verse in Vilna. The correspondence of leading figures in the Czech cultural life of this period often bears witness to the live interest aroused by the Polish poet and to the curiosity and enthusiasm he stimulated. In 1829, during his voyage to Western Europe, Mickiewicz stopped at Prague and became friendly with leading figures of Czech literature. His name was also known to the Slovenes under Austrian domination. From 1822 to 1827, there lived at

Lwów, in Galicia, a Slovene professor, Matija Čop, a linguist and keen observer of cultural life, although not a creative writer himself. He witnessed the violent conflicts which animated the literary public on the personality of the new poet and on the romantic trend he represented. With a keen critical eye, he realized the great power of Mickiewicz and when he returned to Ljubljana he introduced his work to his countrymen.

These two nations, then, had the privilege of knowing Mickiewicz before 1831, a date when his activity took a new form. The first phase, where Mickiewicz' work is familiar to all Slav nations, is that of the ballads and stories where Mickiewicz, abandoning the artificial poetry of the *salon*, turned with an ardent love towards the simple people. Through them he sought the elements of sincere art and spiritual health. He tried to understand the obscure forces that govern the destiny of man and of peoples. He then painted patriotic pictures of the nation's past and the heroic struggles of the eastern nations against the powerful expansion of the conquering westerner. He was already the poet, too, of the passionate, heart-rending and romantic love of Gustav in *Forefathers' Eve* and the subtle and delicate artist of the sonnets.

The new school of Czech poetry in course of development, found its true source of inspiration in peasant folklore. Herder's suggestions were received with enthusiasm; collections of popular Russian and southern Slav poetry manifested their rich creative talent. Collections of popular Czech and Slovak songs also began to be made and F. L. Celakovský, J. Kollár, V. Hanka and several other poets interested themselves in this task. At the same time, and in imitation of the epic-historical school of poetry which flourished in Russia, the Ukraine and among the southern Slavs, poetic pictures inspired by ancient legends were written in old Czech, describing the defensive struggles of the Czechs against foreign invaders. By a skilful hoax they were successfully passed off as authentic poems dating back to the distant past by being compared with the manuscripts of Dvur Králové and Zelená Hora.

Under such conditions, it can be understand why Mickiewicz' poems fitted in perfectly with the cultural climate of Czech literary circles and why they were enthusiastically received.

The first wave of interest aroused by Mickiewicz' works among the Slovenes was of a similar nature. M. Čop introduced them to Fr. Préšerer who, drawing his main inspiration from popular traditions and from lyrical poetry on patriotic and love subjects, wrote an epic based on his country's distant past.

But with the appearance of new, richer and more significant works, Mickiewicz' influence became more varied and more complex. Nevertheless, its influence was less strong on the Balkan Slavs, whose popular poetry differs radically from the ballads which are such a characteristic feature of Polish folklore.

On the other hand, Czech literature produced an uninterrupted chain of works influenced by the ballads of Mickiewicz, throughout the whole of the nineteenth century. We mention particularly the creator of the *genre*, F. L. Celakovský, then the greatest of the classic writers, E. J. Erben, and finally Jaroslav Vrchlický, who, in his extremely rich and varied poetical output is sometimes

'Precz z moich oczu' (Far from my eyes). Music by Frederic Chopin, to words by Adam Mickiewicz. Opus 74, no. 6. The manuscript was in the Marie Wodzinska Album (1830), the original of which disappeared in Warsaw during the 1939–45 war. A photostat copy is in the Frederic Chopin Institute, Warsaw. Photograph by F. Myszkowski.

inspired by popular poetry and at other times shows the influence of Mickiewicz. The same influence can be discerned among the Slovaks, the Slovenes and the Lusatian Serbs, whose independent cultural life was the last to be awakened. Their national poet, H. Zejler, was strongly influenced by Mickiewicz.

The Polish poet's influence was considerably strengthened and took on a new character as a result of the events of 1830. All Europe followed with keen interest and deep sympathy the heroic struggle of the Polish revolutionaries. Poets celebrated the heroism of the combatants and mourned the fall of Warsaw. Those who escaped were scattered throughout Europe, filled with nostalgia for their lost country, their revolutionary enthusiasm and the always burning desire to take up again the fight for the freedom of their own and of other oppressed countries. In addition, Mickiewicz was himself the spiritual head of the Polish emigration to Western Europe and devoted new works to the tragic fate of his country.

The wave of emigrants on their way to Western Europe first crossed the Czech countries and there came into contact with a new generation of poets ready to submit to the influence of Mickiewicz' thought and art.

The chief figure of this generation is Hynek Mácha who died young. The notes that he used to append to his works show that he possessed a thorough knowledge of Mickiewicz' writings, including *Pan Tadeusz*, which appeared two years before his death, and in his work numerous traces of the Polish romantic's influence can be noticed.

His friends and disciples reacted in the same way to the

work of Mickiewicz. His revolutionary ardour lived once more in the radical democrats Sańina and Frič and in the sombre, popularly-inspired poetry of Kalina and Erben; while the Lady of the Plague scene from *Konrad Wallenrod* is used as a preamble to V. B. Nebeský's philosophic poem. This group also produced the first translator of Mickiewicz' works, V. Štulc, who, in spite of his stormy youth, achieved a prominent position in the Prague Catholic hierarchy.

The generation of Slovak romantics towards the forties reacted in the same way as the contemporary Czech generation. Their leading figure, K. Štur, although extremely Russophile, was an enthusiastic admirer of Mickiewicz' poetry. The young Slovaks liked reciting his verse at their meetings and, apart from the *Ode to Youth*, it was the ballads and *Konrad Wallenrod* which were the favourites. The poets of the Štur group, especially A. Sladkovič, J. Botta and L. Zello, all show traces of Mickiewicz' influence. His influence can also be seen in Slovak prose and J. Kalinčak, for example, describes Slovak life in a style reminiscent of the author of *Pan Tadeusz*.

Polish refugees also went to Styria where they were warmly welcomed by the group of young Slovene patriots, led by the philologist Fr. Miklosich and the poet Stanko Vraz. These young men were introduced to Mickiewicz' work, which they translated. Stanko Vraz was profoundly impressed by his poetry.

Vraz was of Slovene origin but then began to write in Croat under the influence of the unification movement which, under the name of Illyrism, was being propagated among the southern Slavs and which aimed at unifying the language, culture and politics of the Slavs of southern Austria and the Balkans. In this respect, Mickiewicz' influence can be coupled with that of Kollár, who began to publish his works at roughly the same time. His *Slávy dcera* inspired the Slavs in their fight for national independence and helped them become aware of their unity. Nevertheless the two writers do differ. Kollár, for example, gives the leading role to Russia, Mickiewicz to Poland. The main difference is that Kollár puts Slav unity before the individuality of each nation and shows no understanding for the Polish struggle against tsarism. Mickiewicz did not see eye to eye with Kollár and, at his Paris lectures, while he paid tribute to the work of that poet, he vigorously criticized his apology for tsarist Russia. Kollár's reaction was more violent. He considered the Polish poet as an obstacle to Slav unity and, in the last songs of his *Slávy dcera*, in imitation of Dante, he put his antagonist in hell.

Although the two poets were well aware of the differences of principle which separated them, the greater part of their admirers failed to suspect them. Mickiewicz' influence complemented that of Kollár and the poets of the Illyria movement, whether Croats, Slovenes or Serbs, were inspired by an enthusiasm both for the Slav visions of Kollár and the revolutionary patriotism of Mickiewicz. The same is true for the Czechs, the Slovaks and the Lusatian Serbs.

Slávy dcera is written in the form of sonnets, a form which Mickiewicz, too, employed with classic mastery. At that period, the sonnet was very widely used in Slav literature. It was then that Kollár's sonnets were most frequently copied, while the artistically shaped sonnets of Mickiewicz became generally appreciated only much later.

Mickiewicz was then given the Chair of Slavonic Literature at the Collège de France in Paris, an extremely important event for all the Slav nations. He devoted a large part of his course to Russo-Polish relations, a fact which did not fail to bring him the reproaches of his countrymen who accused him of being Russophile, and even of treason. On the other hand, certain Russophile circles felt that his lectures rather gave the impression of an anti-Russian attitude. It is obvious that all Mickiewicz' opinions on the subject of the other Slav literatures aroused the greatest interest. The teacher-poet paid particular attention to Czech literature and analysed in detail all the so-called old Czech manuscripts, paying tribute to the work of the philologists. To popular songs he devoted a large part of his lectures and aroused considerable interest in them.

During this time Mickiewicz drew close to the Croatian poet Medo Pucić, the son of an old Dubrovnik family, who, desolate at seeing his native town, once so glorious and prosperous, deprived of its liberty, dreamed of a great free Slav nation. He met Mickiewicz in Paris and fell under his influence. When, in 1848, the latter reorganized the Legion to instigate revolution in Austria, Pucić co-operated with him. His poetic story, *Flora*, dated 1864, is reminiscent of Mickiewicz' *Forefathers' Eve*.

Following on the rapid spread of liberation struggles in 1848, reaction won a temporary victory throughout all Central and Southern Europe. As in 1831, Polish missions penetrated into the Czech, Slovene and Croatian provinces. The Polish insurrectionists of this period, particularly those who took part in the Hungarian rebellion, took refuge in the Balkans, where they lived and influenced the Serbs and Bulgars.

At the same time, however, men's ideas were changing, and Kollár's Slavism, which had long been ascendant, was losing ground.

Before 1848, Karel Havliček had already proclaimed the motto, 'Czech first, Slav afterwards'. The Slovaks already felt that they were a completely independent nation, and particularly in the south, the Serbian nationalists spurned efforts toward Illyrian unification. It was then that Mickiewicz' ideas seemed to win the day.

Moreover, the younger generations of all the Slav nations began to distinguish more clearly the differences between the Russian people, whom they continued to love, and the tsarist regime which they realized was the strongest bastion of European reaction. The Russian revolutionary democrats—A. N. Gercen in particular—who carried on an energetic struggle against the despotism that was strangling liberty in their own country from the countries of their exile, were largely responsible for this development. The Polish insurrection of 1863 caused a clean break between the old Slavophiles in the Slav countries who based their nationalistic hopes on the policy of the Tsars, and the young radicals who expressed their solidarity with the Polish and Russian democrats. Its influence was effective and after 1860 profound changes were clearly evident. Literature played a prominent and important part in the movement. In Bohemia, a group of young poets issued an annual almanack called *Mai*, edited by Karel Hynek Mácha. They sought the aid of revolutionary writers of other

countries and manifested sympathy not for Russian abso-
lutism but for the great poet Pushkin, whose works they
translated and imitated. The fourth issue of *Mai*, that
of 1862, included portraits of Kollár and Mickiewicz,
accompanied by a long essay on the latter. As a result of the
1863 insurrection, Mickiewicz' poetry once more became
exceedingly popular among Czech youth. It was translated,
recited, and imitated, particularly the *Ode to Youth*.

The same movement can be observed among the
Serbs, whose new generation called themselves Omladina
(Youth). They established contacts with advanced Russian
thinkers on whom the 1863 Polish insurrection exercised
a profound influence. A large number of the members of
these movements had studied at Bratislava where they had
attended the lectures of the Slovakian patriot L. Štur, who
had introduced them to Mickiewicz and taught them to
love him. Thus it was that Mickiewicz' influence spread
even among the orthodox Balkan Slavs, whose relations
with the Poles had until then been rather distant.

Finally Mickiewicz' influence penetrated deeply into
Bulgaria. During the first half of the century, Bulgarian
literature was still rather primitive and a wide gulf separated
it from Mickiewicz' poetic ideal. It was only during the
second half of the century that it began to develop under
the influence of the liberation battles against the Turks,
in which well-known Bulgarian poets bore arms. Thanks
to the translations made of Mickiewicz' poetry from
Russian into their mother-tongue, the Bulgars became
acquainted with his work. The most famous Bulgarian
poet of the period, Ivan Vazov, translated his sonnets, the
ballad of *Alpenhara*, *Konrad Wallenrod* and extracts of

Pan Tadeusz, while his friend K. Veličkov, a great admirer of Mickiewicz, published the first study on the poet in Bulgarian.

Apart from these political and social reasons, the literary development of these different nations explains the increase of Mickiewicz' influence. Their literature had developed so much during the preceding years that they were more ready to understand and assimilate the Polish poet. Further, since the Slav languages had become subtler and richer, they could now emulate the artistic mastery of Mickiewicz.

The progressive victory of realism over romantic agony was another important factor. All over Europe the prose novel was displacing the epic poem. Although in Slav literature epic poetry still remained prominent for a long time, it was evolving in the direction of the novel and the story in verse. Instead of delighting in the exotic, the poems drew their inspiration from everyday contemporary life, and in their historical poems historical faithfulness and truth displaced wandering fancy. In this connexion, the great Polish romantic had a profound influence. With Goethe's *Hermann and Dorothea*, Byron's *Don Juan* and Pushkin's *Eugene Onegin, Pan Tadeusz* was a most influential work.

It was only in the second half of the nineteenth century, and long after the death of the writer, that this masterpiece was appreciated and understood.

During the second half of the nineteenth century, Mickiewicz' *Short History of the Nobility* was translated either in whole or in part into all the Slav languages. The Czech and Croat translations are especially good. The first which appeared in 1882 was the work of Eliška

Krasnohorska, poetess, writer of opera libretti, and discerning critic, while the latter was the work of an eminent philologist, Tomislav Maretič.

Mickiewicz was the inspiration of a whole literary movement. The Czech author Svatopluk Čech paraphrased almost word for word the verses of the famous poem *Romanticism*, though he changed its spirit a little. In his great epic historical poem, he was inspired by some of the motives of *Konrad Wallenrod*. Two of his other works derive directly from *Pan Tadeusz*. The more important of these is the cyclic poem on the life of a Czech village *In the Shade of the Linden Tree* (1879), which contains an apostrophe to his native land reminiscent of Mickiewicz' celebration of Lithuania in his great poem, as well as certain other themes. Closer still to *Pan Tadeusz* is the great autobiographical poem of *Václav Živsa* (1891).

Pan Tadeusz also influenced Alois Jirásek's historical tale *Maryla* (1885), the great poems of the Slovakian poet P. Országh Hviezdolav and the leading poet of the Lusatian Serbs, J. Barta Čišinski.

The Croat poet Franjo Markovič, in his poem *Dom i svijet* (1865) drew his inspiration from a subject typical of Mickiewicz, that of the student returning from the city to the peace of the countryside where he experiences the idyllic charm of young 'love, and the historical events Markovič mentions—the Bachovian reaction of the eighteen-fifties—were suggestive of the evolution of the Polish nation during the Napoleonic era.

The epic *Karvava piesen* (1813) of Penčo P. Slavejkov, one of the greatest of Bulgarian nationalist poets, is reminiscent of *Pan Tadeusz*.

The meetings of the rebels and the battle scenes remind one of similar scenes in Mickiewicz, with the difference that the poem is not, as is the case in *The Last Foray in Lithuania*, a description of a miniature, half-fantastic battle whose background, the great events of the Napoleonic era, lent it an air of gravity; it is a description of a bloody battle, decisive for the fate of the Bulgarian nation.

Apart from *Pan Tadeusz*, Mickiewicz' other works lost none of their timeliness. *Konrad Wallenrod*, for example, still fascinated because of the exciting picture it gives of the battle against the enemy, and it was not mere chance that it was translated into Czech at that time by J. V. Sládek, a poet hostile to the Hapsburgs and translator of the complete works of Shakespeare.

In Sv. Čech's poem *Václav of Michalovice* (1880) and in that of V. Beneš Třebízský, *Levohradecká povidká*, the characters most resembling Wallenrod are the sons of the leaders of the Czech rebellion of 1620, executed after the defeat of the White Mountain on the spot of the old city of Prague. These sons are brought up by the Jesuits in a spirit hostile to the ideas for which their fathers perished. An old family servant—a parallel character to Mickiewicz' Vajdelot—discloses the secret of their birth and historical background. He succeeds in making them avenge their father's death and serve their country's cause. Also noteworthy is the attempt of Antal Stašek, who, influenced by *Wallenrod*, depicted in verse narrative a Czech government servant in the service of the Austrian government at the period of violent persecution against the Czech national movement.

Among Croatian poets, Fr. Markovič, to whom reference has already been made, drew his inspiration from *Wallenrod* for his poem *Kohan and Vlasta* (1868), depicting the story of the struggle of the Slavs of the Elbe.

Mickiewicz' second Konrad, the hero of *Forefathers' Eve*, was another character who did not die. He came to life again in the work of a great Czech poet of the period, Jaroslav Vrchlický, who combined a wide general knowledge of literature with great technical skill in the writing of verse. He was a prolific writer of original verse and, in addition, translate d a large number of works which enabled Czech readers to fam iliarize themselves with foreign poetry of all times and of all peoples. Among the foreign authors he translated we mention Dante, Petrarch, Tasso, Goethe, Calderon, Camoens, Hugo, Alfred de Vigny, Verlaine, Hafiz, etc. These poets, with whose works he was intimately acquainted as translator, strongly influenced his own writings and he very often developed and paraphrased their ideas. Mickiewicz' name, too, must be added to the list, for Vrchlický also translated his works and made a study of his personality.

Vrchlický lived at a time when the crisis of European thought was becoming more acute; the majority of intellectuals were deeply disappointed with the evolution of society, and doubt and pessimism pervaded their works. Anguished, keen questioning of the meaning of life and of the development of humanity prevailed. Vrchlický was conscious of these problems. For him Goethe's *Faust* and the mythical *Ahasuerus*, in classic form or in different guises, became the symbol of the quest for the meaning of life.

Through his sense of artistic form and the richness of his poetic expression, Vrchlický is close to the last generation of nineteenth-century poets, who were keenly interested in Mickiewicz' sonnets. These were translated into Bulgarian by I. Vazov and K. Christov, into Slovak by Hviezdolav, into Slovene by M. Molé, into Lusatian Serb by J. Mart Cisinski and into Czech by J. Borecký.

Mickiewicz' poetry gained new popularity especially among the young Slovene modernists. Ivan Čankar, leading Slovene writer of the period, expressed his feelings of respect in a poem. The poets, Josip Murn-Aleksandrov, Vojeslav Molé and others were enthusiastic admirers of the work of the great Polish poet.

At the same time, Mickiewicz the politician and publicist enjoyed a return to favour. The socialist movement adopted him. It was as their precursor in this field that Polish radical youth acclaimed him when his ashes were transferred to Cracow in 1890. At his jubilee in 1898, the young Czech historian L. K. Hofman devoted a series of papers to him besides a monograph in which he analysed his relations with utopian socialism. Finally, the Russian Revolution of 1905 brought about a reconciliation of the ideas of Mickiewicz and those of Kollár. The poet Sv. Čech in his fragment poem *Step*, which remained unfinished at his death, hailed this revolution as a purifying storm leading to the resurrection and liberation of all the Slav peoples. The solution of the chronic conflict between the two biggest Slav nations appeared to him as the symbol of the friendship and common destiny of two great poet patriots, Pushkin and Mickiewicz, struggling and suffering under the same despotic rule.

Even after the first world war Mickiewicz' work remained alive and was read, studied and again translated into Bulgarian by Dory Gabe, into Slovene by T. Debeljaka, etc. During the second world war, François Halas, one of the leading Czech modern poets, once more translated, in the stifling atmosphere of Nazi occupation, Mickiewicz' chief works, *Grazyna*, *Forefathers' Eve*, *Konrad Wallenrod*. His early death prevented his being able to crown his work by a new translation of *Pan Tadeusz*.

Now that the hundredth anniversary of Mickiewicz' death is being celebrated for the Slav nations, the great poet's work needs neither to be discovered nor brought back to life. It is enjoying a sustained interest and has exercised a diverse and profound influence for many years. All the Slavs can consider him as their own poet, not only because he is the son of a sister nation, but also because he made a living and beneficial contribution to their own development.

POLAND

IN PAN TADEUSZ

Juliusz Kleiner

Of all poems in Polish literature *Pan Tadeusz* is the
most Polish. Yet strangely enough it is not a
picture of the heart of Poland, but of a class of
nobility in Polish Lithuania. And it was not during the
course of a normal life, amid familiar surroundings on the
author's native soil, that the work saw the light of day—it
is the work of a vagabond poet, torn from his homeland;
it is the enchanting vision of a lost country, of its sufferings
and its longings.

The poem is born of a typically romantic state of mind:
nostalgia. Yet here this has not turned to the realm of
dreams and fiction. The world to which the poet's soul
has flown in desperation is the one which to him was once
the most real of all, and he brings it back to life in concrete
and palpable form. The world of dreams for this Polish
romantic is the cherished reality.

To Mickiewicz the vividness and permanence of
bygone things sometimes appeared as an omen of fate.
One of his sonnets speaks of 'the hydra of memories'
lurking in the depths. But here, for the Paris exile, this
vivid memory has become a blessing.

The reality pictured by that memory is nothing out of the ordinary. Usually the romantics preferred to turn to the exceptional. Mickiewicz' nostalgia, it is true, does not turn its back on splendour; but what he is mainly concerned with is the usual, everyday, things denied to the fugitive, denied to his *émigré* compatriots unable to live a normal life in their own homes, in their own country amid their national customs.

Like the third part of *Forefathers' Eve* a powerful political and religious drama with many ramifications, like *The Book of the Polish Pilgrims*, which comforted while it instructed, the new poem was to be a glorification of 'Polishness'. In the first two works, however, as in nearly all Polish romantic poetry, Polishness was something holy, something sublime, painfully sublime even. Now was to appear something of infinite good humour. The slightest trifles will take on value, for they are of the country, of the home; everything glows in the golden light shed by memory on the years of youth and childhood. The store of adventures and impressions of that age, enriched by the tales of friends and acquaintances, was to form the substance of the work—the old days and their vivid memories.

In spite of this, *Pan Tadeusz* is not, from the literary point of view, a book of memoirs. Though using the greatest artistic realism, the poet has avoided copying. He was not interested in giving his work the stamp of a document as, with revolutionary daring, he had purposely done in the case of *Forefathers' Eve* in which authentic facts and names are quoted. In *Pan Tadeusz* he tends, on the one hand, to amass every possible thing seen, heard or passed on by word of mouth by eye-witnesses and narrators; and on the other hand, he consciously changes objective reality in two ways: through the strength of his feelings and through poetry. By introducing a large number of fictitious names and by pushing the real figures into the background, Mickiewicz reveals the same state of mind as did Goethe when he entitled his own biography *Poetry and Truth*.

It is thus a national epic, not a book of memoirs. And it fulfils the prerequisite of an epic: it depicts on a broad scale a society of men at an important moment in its history. In this way poetry sometimes fixes a collective reality, at times of transition, by rescuing from oblivion and handing down to succeeding generations the picture of a civilization which is drawing to an end.

Mickiewicz has given us a profile of the life of a social class which then formed an integral part of the Polish nation: the nobility. It embraced hundreds of thousands of souls and formed, not as elsewhere a tiny elite, but an important and sharply graduated fraction of society. The poet has done even better. Alongside the living reality of things happening in the present, he has introduced a recent past quite separate from that present and has half opened a window on the future. Of this future he gives us only the briefest glimpse. On the other hand, the period during which the events related occur and the one separated from it by only a few decades are in almost the same relief, and each one reveals its own values. In the reminiscences, so decisive for the genesis and structure of the work, the background of the bygone life of the nation comes to us through the utterances of a few of the principal representatives of the older generation.

So is unfolded this past of nobles and grandees, the oligarchical system of a republic then on the brink of ruin.

There are three important documents for this period: the confession of the real hero of the poem, Hyacinthus Soplica; the confirmatory tale of his adversary; and the long speech on politeness which is delivered at the dinner by the President and which reflects the manners of former days. According to these three documents it is always in the hands of the grandee that human destinies lie. The great nobles hold the small nobility in the hollow of their hands, looking down on them from a very long way above.

In the period brought to life again by the reminiscences it is the grandees who make the nation's history. For them the nobility is sometimes an instrument to be used for patriotic ends; but more often it is a means of bringing their private affairs to a successful conclusion. They govern by conciliating the mass of the nobility, especially its leaders; they fill the leading places. The grandee must accept the noble as his familiar, must lower himself to his level, must open his house to him. He repays the nobility by permitting it to live largely at his expense.

According to the narrators, the rule of the grandees had left memories of an age of abundance and ostentation. Their wealth was displayed in their great banquets and magnificent hunts. They also patronized the theatre, literature and science. They set the tone of intellectual culture. In their courts the young nobles received their schooling, a schooling mainly in that society life which

On me demande une parole pour ce
tombeau illustre. Le généreux fils du grand
poète de la Pologne s'adresse à moi, et
me dit : Parlez de mon père. Parler de son père,
parler de Mickiewicz, c'est parler du
beau, du juste et du vrai, c'est parler du
droit dont il fut le soldat, du devoir dont il
fut le héros, de la liberté dont il fut l'apôtre,
et de la délivrance dont il est le précurseur.

Mickiewicz a été un évocateur de toutes
les vieilles vertus qui ont en elles une
puissance de rajeunissement ; il a été un prêtre
de l'idéal ; son art est le grand art ; le
profond souffle des forêts sacrées est dans
sa poésie ; il a compris l'humanité en même
temps que la nature ; son hymne à
l'infini se complique de la sainte palpitation
révolutionnaire. Banni, proscrit, vaincu, il
a superbement jeté aux quatre vents l'altière
revendication de la patrie. Le diane des peuples,
c'est le génie qui la sonne ; autrefois c'était
le prophète, aujourd'hui c'est le poète ; et
Mickiewicz est un des clairons de l'avenir.

Il y a de la vie dans un tel sépulcre.
L'immortalité est dans le poète, la résurrection est
dans le citoyen. Un jour les Peuples-Amis d'Europe diront
à la Pologne : lève-toi ! et c'est de ce tombeau que s'élèvera
sa grande âme.

Oui, ce sublime fantôme, la Pologne, est couché là avec le
poète. Salut à Mickiewicz ! salut à ce noble endormi qui se
réveillera ! Il m'entend, je le sais, et il me comprend. Nous
sommes, lui et moi, deux absents. Si je n'ai, dans mon isolement
et dans mes ténèbres, aucune couronne à donner au nom de la
gloire, j'ai le droit de fraterniser avec une ombre au nom du
malheur. Je ne suis pas la voix de la France ; mais je suis
la voix de l'exil.

Hauteville-House. 17 mai 1867.   Victor Hugo

Letter from Victor Hugo to Władislas Mickiewicz (1867). In the collection of the Adam Mickiewicz Museum, Paris.

accorded with the deepest inclinations of this group of
Poles. Sometimes there was a streak of the patriarchal idyll
in their lives: 'Father of the peasants and brother of the
nobles' was the description of Pantlet Horeszko given by
his faithful servant Gervais. But this feeling of wealth,
power and impunity also brought with it a contempt for
man, a contempt for the law.

The harmful ways of the caste are embodied in *Pan
Tadeusz* in the 'last turnkey'. He knows how to win over
the nobles, how to stir them up, how to use, for personal
ends, their temperament and their narrow-mindedness.

Despite all this, the poem shows the predominance of
the grandees to be over. The Soplicowo group to which
the principal characters belong welcome two aristocrats;
no one denies them the respect due to their high birth, but
they themselves would no longer dream of claiming the
role of the old grandees. And the idea of the union of a
well-to-do 'small' noble with the heiress of a great family
no longer shocks, whereas in the generation before it
would have led to tragedy.

Such is the social evolution in progress as it appears
in the epic. It is unquestionably somewhat stylized,
shaped to fit the poet's postulates; but he has grasped
exactly the process of the change brought about by the
economic and political factors of Polish and European
history—merely speeding up the completion of that
change.

The evolution towards a lessening of the rigorous
division between grandee and squireen is decidedly
democratic in comparison with the immediate past. For the
time being that democracy is limited to what was, in fact,

the very principle of the traditional Polish system: the equality of the nobles. The Polish 'demos', which was to become one great national body, is the whole of the nobility, ranging from the grandee to the impoverished mass of nobles reduced to peasant status and working their own patch of earth with their own hands. But in the final canto of *Pan Tadeusz* the student of Vilna University, a soldier in Napoleon's army, drinks an enthusiastic toast 'to the free and equal Polish subjects'. For in building up the world of Poland shown in his epic, Mickiewicz takes as his ideal the widest possible extension of the national body, regardless of all class barriers.

Within the body of this nation the poet boldly included the Jew. He endows him with a soul filled with the country's historic splendours, which he taps out on the cords of his dulcimer; he causes him to sing of the liberated homeland with all the ecstasy of the messianic faith of Israel.

But the essential problem of democratization is the fate of the people who work the land. The solution is however left to the future. In *Pan Tadeusz* the peasants are not yet a part of the active community. They appear only as a vague mass, at work, during the religious ceremony, at the public feast. It is true that the feast is crowned by the act of emancipation. Like the Democratic Society founded by the Emigrants, Mickiewicz proclaims that national revolution is inseparable from social revolution.

The presence of the peasant mass and the expressive figure of the Jewish musician do not radically alter the characters of the whole. The poem is entitled *An Account of the Life of the Nobility*; it is the world of the nobles in itself which forms its subject. In literature, class has always been a feature of the epic poem; whether it extolled the Achaeans or the knights of the Middle Ages, or, as in Goethe's poem, promoted in dignity the German provincial bourgeois, it has always been strongly imbued with class consciousness.

Mickiewicz has by no means made this period of change a period of decline for the then ruling class. The society of *Pan Tadeusz* is young and vital, the young people in it are progressive, it withstands the foreign poison and, despite egoism and disagreements, it knows how to stand up to the tsarist usurper; Soplicowo is to prove capable of assimilating new and salutary elements. It is the centre of the old traditions and old virtues; moral strength, physical vigour, order and foresight, kindness to the lowly, solid religious faith, and a national and patriotic conscience prepared for sacrifice. Also full of vitality is the squireen village of Dobrzyn. It represents the continuity, the permanence, the indestructibility of a collective Polish soul whose feeling and will are to rise to the occasion at a great moment in history.

Poland's evolutionary process is thus presented in an optimistic light, though without dulling the sharpness of the critic's view of the shortcomings. But the criticism is indulgent. The poem describes a phase which is over, gone for ever, and on which, at the end, the sun symbolically sets. It is a picture gallery of 'the last' which is unfurled—'the last', that epithet so beloved of the romantics. Mickiewicz, however, has no grudge against this past, which comes to life again in his sunlit memories. On the contrary, he is grateful to it for forming a part of

his happy childhood, for being steeped in the sun and air
of Lithuania, saturated with the purest outflow of that
native soil which knows neither the harshnesses of
foreign lands, nor the anguishes of exile, nor the sterile
bickerings of emigrants. He is grateful to it as we are to
our mothers and fathers for our peaceful childhood, as
we are to the old kinsfolk and old friends for forming part
of those delightful pictures, for belonging to that carefree,
fairylike world which is more 'our own' than anything we
call our own today since there is no danger of it changing,
no danger of it being taken from us. We clearly see the
weaknesses and defects, but we smile at them without
thinking of finding fault with them. We shall avoid those
defects, we may not even copy certain qualities which are
no longer suited to our times, but we should never dream
of quarrelling with them. We love those old times as they
are, without wanting to idealize or rehabilitate anything.
They can do no further harm.

But this affectionate criticism, which emphasizes the
favourable aspects and brings conviction that in Poland
nobody is entirely bad, becomes sterner once the question
of aptitude for collective action arises.

It is a picture of society which an epic must present,
not a collection of individuals. The true nature of the
body stands out sharply, at this time of political, economic
and cultural crisis, against the most brilliant historical
background which the generation of that time knew:
that of the Napoleonic victories. One after another the
general pictures come tumbling out. We see how gregari-
ous Polish life is, how sociable and parliamentarian a
nation the Poles are. Just as, in sixteenth-century poetry,

the originality and Polishness of Kochanowski's classic tragedy, *The Dismissal of the Greek Ambassadors*, lies in the fact that the work pivots around a decision of the Diet; just as, during the French classical period, Felinski, in his tragedy of *Barbe Radziwill*, assigns the decisive role to the Diet; so in *Pan Tadeusz* the action is led by a miniature diet of nobles. But it is a fatal lead, for Mickiewicz, writing after the 1831 disaster amid the arguments as to the causes of the catastrophe, notes the political immaturity of the community. Nevertheless, this community seems to him to contain forces capable of improvement and conquest, and above all that spirit of sacrifice which he was to preach in *The Book of the Polish Pilgrims* and which is incarnated in Robak the monk.

On the whole it is of the average, ordinary human being that the poem tells; the commanding figure of Hyacinthus Soplica, who becomes Robak the monk, towers far above them.

Mickiewicz, as a man and artist, had passed through many phases, and his principal characters are made to pass through them too. Walter, the patriot knight, is made to suffer, triumph and then perish under the tragic mask of Wallenrod, Grand Master of the Teutons. In *Forefathers' Eve*, Gustav, an image of himself, who attaches the highest value in life to sensual love, changes into Konrad, who feels himself to incarnate the suffering and militant nation and who claims command of it.

The Pole is a new Gustav, a new Konrad. From the depths of a wild and criminal youth he climbs by the lowly path of expiation, through the heroism of the soldier and conspirator and through sacrifice, to the very

peaks. But in his changes this hero with the ways of a
soldier-monk, simple, rough and jovial in speech, his
features drawn with so much realism, is in no way like
the Konrad of *Forefathers' Eve*, a romantic, inspired, isolated
individual; he is one with a land, a people, he is of the
crowd, one man, one Pole among so many others. After
the brilliant romantic exploits comes the long and sombre
calvary of effort and struggle which the poet recommends
as the path to the Polish fighters.

The end of the road travelled by Hyacinthus is his
shining death:

> . . . diamond bright
> The sun's rays, piercing through the panes,
> Played on the pillow round his dying head
> And, gilding brow and temple, gave to it
> The shining splendour of a pictured saint
> In lambent glory. . . .

A saintly halo encircles the heroic head of the dying man;
a halo coming not from the angels but from the ordinary
sun of our universe, which makes the wonder all the
greater. The rays also twice encircle the golden tresses of
the young Sophie, the central female character.

In the poetic world of a realist epic he has fused the
two highest values of romanticism, in which man is a giant
and woman a supernatural being.

In like fashion he has been able to fuse together these
two worlds by painting that nature which he loved so
much. In one of the books of *Pan Tadeusz* we are made to
hear the evening concert. At the end, two ponds 'talk to

each other across the fields, like two æolian harps playing
in turn'. The 'evening music', one of the great finds of
romanticism, is here an orchestra of mosquitoes, corn-
crakes, woodcocks and frogs, whose names alone create
an atmosphere of the everyday. Thus once again the
highest values of romanticism are carried into the world
of realism.

In Mickiewicz' epic the romantic tones stem from the
element of history; the realist aspects stem from the
descriptions of customs. Both are harmoniously combined.
The historical poem shows Poland at the time of Napoleon,
throws into relief the struggle for independence; he tells
the story up to the end of the eighteenth century in the
accounts of the older generation and in the concert of
Jankiel who, in the presence of the organizer of the
legions, Henryk Dombrowski, and of the other generals
and officers of the new Polish army, includes in his 'programme' an account of recent great events in our history.
At the beginning of the work, it is the novel of manners
that fills the foreground. Its dominant feature is a picture
of Polish life and customs set against a background of
fields and meadows, gardens and woods, of the bank of
the Niemen, where people work, enjoy themselves and
quarrel. The hunt which crowns the triumphal life of the
old Seneschal, master of the hunt, poet of ancient things
and incomparable story teller, is the culminating point of
this life of landowners and lawsuits. With the romantic
and legal episodes goes the political activity of Robak the
monk, who tries to anticipate the arrival of Napoleon's
armies and pushes Lithuania into insurrection. The
pictures of the customs of the time continue to unfold

before our eyes; next to the wealthy aristocratic manor we see the stirrings of the boisterous squireen village. The action then takes us through the abuses of the unwritten law, the judicial expedition, the carrying out of the court's sentence by force of arms, and the seizure of the property. The intervention of a detachment of Russians then throws light on the methods of the tsarist government and leads to a battle which shows up the passion and truculence of the nobles, who nevertheless end by subordinating their interests and rancours to the public good. Many Polish characteristics are revealed during this battle, including their skilled swordsmanship, yet the attention is focused on the rapid development of events. And while the tragic confession of Hyacinthus, that pattern of moral stature, tenderness of conscience and firmness of expression, takes us back over his life and background, the political upheavals and patriotic struggles, it is the powerful personality of the pentitent which mainly holds the interest. In the last two books, in which Lithuania greets the Polish army marching under the banner of Napoleon, we return to the vast background of nature and society which featured in the early books. The landscape of the Niemen appears again, in yet greater beauty. The old republic of nobles is shown once more against the peaceful, well-to-do background of its pleasant country life, with its qualities, its faults and its absurdities, but also with its dignity and gracefulness. And it is dismissed, in the rays of the setting sun, in the name of a better future.

The completeness with which Polish life is portrayed in this radiant, kaleidoscopic, thrumming poem in which so many colours and voices converge in pictorial and

musical compositions, in which the individuals and
crowds move so rhythmically, in which the most realistic
details abound (though not to excess), is due to the variety
and wealth of literary styles which have been poured into
it. In spite of the modest title of 'narrative', which
emphasizes its simplicity, *Pan Tadeusz* is obviously
designed as an epic. But the poet has deliberately avoided
the traditional 'epos'. The slightness of the characters and
their adventures is amusingly stressed by the poet's mock-
heroic style; he takes pleasure in the eighteenth century's
discovery of the poetry of daily life, thereby showing
himself akin to *Herman and Dorothy*; even the poetry of
gastronomy is not disdained. He accepts the mantle of the
georgic poems which glorified the Poland of his youth.
The gardens and groves of Delille are opened to him; his
architectonics are well suited to the descriptive. His idyll
of nobles, truer than the new pastoral of the English or
Germans or the bourgeois idyll of Goethe, becomes an
elegy for the now dead past. However, there is here no
crying over the past, but an enshrining of national and
regional memories, as Walter Scott did. From Scott, too,
is taken the literary method, current in Europe around
1830, of endowing the historical novel with an enthralling
and sometimes mysterious plot. Though the work has a
note of Walter Scott in its realism, it none the less fully
conforms to the Polish novel of manners, to the satire of
Poland's 'enlightened century', and to the exaltation of
rustic life contained in Krasicki's *Pan Podstoli*.

This realist epic is permeated with lyricism, a quality
basically foreign to the peaceful ways of an epic, and this
intrusion of romanticism has enabled the poet to introduce

many minor details dear to the heart. The moving aspects of the turning points in history, of the tragic fate of an exceptional individual, go hand in hand with a humour which, sometimes close to Cervantes, helps to fuse the heterogeneous elements into one harmonious whole.

Mickiewicz' poetry is essentially synthetic. His masterpiece of realism teems with romanticism. The patrons of Poland's national epic are Homer, Tasso, Goethe, Walter Scott, Kochanowski, Krasicki. The poem, seemingly written to glorify a province, mirrors all the features and all the yearnings of a great people. The Polish patriot becomes a soldier of Napoleon; and Polish society, implacably hostile though it is to tsarism, gives a friendly welcome to the decent, honest Moscovite. An undying love of the past goes hand in hand with prospects of change and hopes for a better future. A deep feeling for the idyllic restfulness and solitude of the country retreat is allied with that revolutionary love of freedom which is characteristic of the Poles.

The storms and sorrows of the nation and its individuals are deeply enshrined in this work; in the hands of a man of genius arrived at full maturity and the height of his artistic powers they have given us this wonderful, and yet simple, pacifying, soothing poem.

SELECTIONS

FROM

MICKIEWICZ'

WRITINGS

SHORTER POEMS[1]

Ode to Youth

Here, heartless, spiritless, throng skeletons in sorry plight!
Youth, give me wings, that I may rise
Above this dead world, cursed and bare,
Into the realm of dreams and light,
For ardour brings forth marvels there,
Strews each new dream with blossoms rare,
And dresses each in golden hope's fair guise.

Let him whom age makes dark of mind,
His stupid brow, care furrowed, bending low,
Only such near horizons know
As he with hopeless, dullard eyes can find.

Above these plains, youth, thou must fly—
As far above as doth the sun—
And with its vast, all-seeing eye
View all humanity as one!

1. These poems have been published in the volume entitled *Poems by A. Mickiewicz*, edited by George Rapall Noyes (New York, Polish Institute of Arts and Sciences in America, 1944), with the exception of 'To M. . . .' and 'To. . . .' which have been translated by Marion Moore Coleman.

Look downward! Where eternal mists make dark
Chaotic wastelands flooded o'er with sloth,
Behold, that is the earth, repulsive, stark!
Look, there upon its stagnant seas
Some shell-clad mollusc takes its ease.
It for itself is ship and sailor both;
Pursuing smaller molluscs for the sport alone,
It rises now, now sinks from sight;
The wave cleaves not to it, it cleaves the ocean's might,
Then, bubblelike, it breaks against a stone:
None knew its life, none cares that it no more exists.

Such are all egoists!
O youth, to me life's ruddy, sparkling wine
Is sweet but when I share its ecstasy:
For joy gives drink to souls inspired and free
When golden threads bind them with love divine.

Young friends, together heed my call!
The aims of all are in the joy of all.
Strong in our unity, mad yet discreet,
On! on! young friends, nor fear to fall!
He too knows joy and gladness, he who fell,
If his prone body at their feet
Aided his friends to mount Fame's citadel.
Together, friends, fear not its towering wall!
Though steep and slippery the path,
Though spineless hatred bar the gate,
Let strength meet strength and wrath fight wrath,
And let us learn while young to spurn the weakling's hate.

Who, yet an infant, crushed the serpent's brow,
In youth will choke the centaur's breath,
Snatch victims forth from hell below,
And win heaven's laurels after death!
Brave youth, reach outward far beyond thy sight,
Crush what mere human reason cannot harm!
For like an eagle's is thy lofty flight,
The strength of thunderbolts is in thine arm.

Arise! United stand! With chains of harmony
Let us encircle the vast world,
Our thoughts into one mighty focus hurled,
Our spirits unified, yet free.
Thou earth-bound human clod, away!
We point thee a more lofty goal,
Till, freed from mouldy bark, thy soul
Recall its long-lost, verdant day.

And as in realms of chaos and of night,
Beset by elemental war,
One 'Let there be' of God's transcendent night
Gave to the universe its form—
Once oceans surged, once roared the storm,
Now stars shall shine forever more;
So in our human realms night rules the skies,
Still war the human passions of desire—
Lo, love will breathe on them with fire!
From chaos will the spirit world arise!
Youth will conceive it in her fertile womb
And friendship nurture it amid the gloom.

Numb, icy hearts are rent by love's decree,
And lifeless, blind beliefs that dim the light.
Hail, hail, thou dawn of man's new liberty!
Salvation's sunrise will disperse the night!

[Translated by George Rapall Noyes and Marjorie Beatrice Peacock, 1944.]

'Adam Mickiewicz.' Head (wood-carving) by Xavier Dunikowski, height 40 cm. (Cracow, 1920). Bronze replica (1948), height 70 cm. Mickiewicz Museum, Warsaw. Photograph by L. Sempoliński.

The Lilies

Monstrous deed: A lady bright
Slays her own, her wedded knight;
Buries him beside a brook
In a grove where none will look.
Lilies on his grave she plants;
As she sows them, thus she chants:
'Lily flowers, grow as high
As my husband deep doth lie;
As my husband deep doth lie,
Do ye, lilies, grow so high!'

Dabbled with his blood the wife,
She who took her husband's life,
Rushes over hill and dale,
Speeds away through wood and vale.
Evening, and the cold winds blow,
All is dark and chill and foul:
Now the cawing of a crow,
Now the hooting of an owl.

She has come to river lands
Where a beech's branches rock
And a hermit's cottage stands:
Knock, knock! Knock, knock!

'What is that?' The metal pin
Falls, the hermit brings a light;
With a shriek she rushes in
Like a vampire of the night.
Blue her lips and wild her eyes,
White her face as linen thread;
Shivering, the lady cries,
'Oh, my husband! He lies dead!'

'God be with thee, woman! What
Dost thou in the wood alone?
What has brought thee to this spot
While the stormy night-winds moan?'

'Over wood and marshy hollow
Shines my castle, but to far
Kiev must my husband follow
King Boleslaw in the war.
Years went on, and still among
Battle's noise he wandered free;
I was young amid the young,
Virtue's path is slippery,
And I broke my vows at last.
Woe upon me and alack!
Stern the laws our king has passed,
And the warriors have come back.

'But my husband shall not know:
See the blood upon this blade!
He is silenced and laid low!
Full confession I have made:
Give me, therefore, holy sage,
Prayers to say and pilgrimage;
Tell me where I am to go!
I would walk to hell, endure
Brand, and scourge that tears the skin,
If I only could be sure
Night would cover up my sin.'

'Woman, dost thou then repent
Of the crime that brought thee here,
Or but dread the punishment?
Go in peace, cast off thy fear,
Clear thy brow, thy secret lies
Safe forever from men's eyes.
Thus the Lord commands us: those
Things thou dost in secret, none
But thy husband can disclose,
And thy husband's life is done.'

With this judgment well content,
As she came, the lady went,
Homeward through the night she stole,
Saying naught to any soul.
At the door her children wait,
'Mother,' eagerly they cry,
'Why does father stay so late?'
'What!' she thinks, 'You wait the dead?'

But at last she makes reply:
'He is in the wood near by,
He will come tonight,' she said.

So the children wait perplexed
All the next day and the next;
All the week they watch the door,
Till at last they watch no more.

But the lady finds it hard
To forget her guilty act;
From her lips the smiles are barred,
And her heart is ever racked.
Sleep will close her eyes no more;
For at night when all is dark
Something knocks upon the door;
Something walks the courtyard. Hark!
'Children, hear me!' comes the cry,
'Tis your father, it is I!'

Through the night she lies awake,
Conscious of her guilty act,
On her lips no smiles will break,
And her heart is ever racked.

'Hurry, Hanka, for I hear
Trampling on the bridge. I see
Clouds of dust now drawing near.
Are they guests to visit me?
Haste through wood and highroad, say
Whether someone rides this way!'

'They ride hither in their might,
All the road a whirling cloud,
And their sharp swords glisten bright
And their black steeds neigh aloud.
They are knights-at-arms who ride,
Brothers of our lord who died.'

'Greetings! And how dost thou fare?
Greet us, sister! Tell us, where
Is our brother?' 'He is dead,
He no longer lives,' she said.
'When?' 'A year ago. He died
In the war,' the wife replied.
'Nay, 'tis false! Be happy, thou,
For the war is over now;
He is well and of good cheer,
Soon thou shalt behold him here.'

In her fright the lady paled,
Swooning, and her senses failed,
While with vacant eyes she gazed
Terror-stricken and amazed.
'Where is he, a man long dead?'
And then, coming back to life
Slowly, like a faithful wife
Who had swooned for joy, she said:
'Where is he, my own true knight?
Will he soon rejoice my sight?'

'He returned with us, but then
Hastened on ahead that he

Might receive us with his men
And the sooner comfort thee.
He will come, if not today,
Then tomorrow; he perhaps
In his haste has lost the way.
We will let a day elapse
And then seek him. Never fear,
One more night will bring him here.'

They sent searchers high and low,
Waiting one day, then another;
When they cannot find their brother,
Weeping, they decide to go.

But the lady's pleas begin:
'Brothers, my beloved kin,
Autumn is no time for travel,
Winds are cold and rains are wet;
You have waited without cavil,
Wait a little longer yet.'

So they waited. Winter came,
But no brother. Just the same
Still they waited, saying then
Spring would bring him back again.
But he lies within his grave,
O'er him flowery branches wave,
And the lilies grow as high
As his body deep doth lie.
So they waited on through spring,
Putting off their journeying.

For their hostess pleased them well
And her youth had cast its spell.
They pretended they would go—
But they tarried even so,
Waiting on; and by another
Summer had forgot their brother.

For the lady pleased them well,
She was young and cast her spell;
And as they were two, they both
Fell in love and sought her troth.
Both their hearts by hope were fanned,
Both were seized with love's alarms;
Neither would renounce her charms,
Both could not possess her hand.
To the lady they agree
To repair and make their plea.

'Take our message in good part,
Lady, once our brother's wife!
He has surely lost his life!
We sit idle here. Thou art
Youthful—far too young, in truth,
To renounce the world and smother
All the impulses of youth:
Take one brother for another!'

So they spoke and paused. In each
Jealousy and anger blazed;
Both in twin burst forth in speech,
Both upon the lady gazed,

Bit their lips till they were blue,
Seized their swords and almost drew.

When the lady saw their wrath
She was doubtful what to say,
So she sought the forest path,
Bidding them to wait a day.
Down she rushed through river lands
Where the beech's branches rock
And the hermit's cottage stands:
Knock, knock! Knock, knock!
All her story she goes through,
Asking what she is to do.

'Tell me how to reconcile them,
Both would have me, I must choose.
Either suits me: how beguile them?
Who shall win and who shall lose?
I have children. I command
Wealth of stores and settled land,
But my wealth will soon have fled
If I stay alone, unwed.
Ah, but there can never be
Any wedded joy for me!
God has sent a cruel blight
And a spectre haunts my night.
Scarcely have I closed my eyes,
Creak! and up the door latch flies;
And I wake and see and hear
How it pants as it draws near,
And its panting and its tread

Tell me that I hear the dead!
Whir! It holds a knife in air,
Wet with blood, above me there.
From its mouth the sparks fly free
And it pulls and pinches me.
Ah, enough of torment! I
Must from my own dwelling fly;
Happiness I shall not see,
Wedded joy is not for me.'

'Daughter,' said the priest, 'no crime
But is punished in due time.
Yet the Lord doth still give ear
When repentance is sincere.
I know secrets hid from men,
And I bring thee words of cheer:
I can raise thy knight again
Though he has been dead a year.'

'What, my father! Do not thou
Raise the dead! 'Tis over now,
And the blade of steel must sever
Me and him it slew forever.
I am worthy punishment,
I will suffer what is sent,
Only let this ghost relent!
I will give up all my goods,
Far within the lonely woods,
In a cloister take the vow,
Only, father, do not thou
Raise the dead! 'Tis over now,

And the blade of steel must sever
Me and him it slew forever!'

 Heavily the old man sighed,
Wrung his hands and hid his face,
Weeping for a little space;
And with sadness he replied:
'Go then, while thou canst, and marry:
Do not fear the spectre form!
In the grave the dead will tarry,
For death's gate is hard to storm,
And thy husband will appear
Only if thou call him here.'

 'How appease the brothers? Who
Shall be favoured of the two?'
'Let God choose, and do thou call
Him on whom the lot shall fall.
Let them both at break of day
Go and gather flowers, and they
From the flowers for thee shall twine
Each a wreath and put a sign
In the garland that shall show
Which is which for all to know;
Then in church will their own hands
Place them where the altar stands.
He whose wreath thou choosest, he
Thine own lord and love shall be.'

 Then the lady, well content,
All her thoughts on marriage bent,

Ceased to fear the phantom; for
She knew very well indeed
Never in the direst need
Would she summon him once more.
So, with spirit confident,
As she entered, so she went.
Homeward hurriedly she stole,
Saying naught to any soul.

Swift she ran through field and wood,
Rushing on, then, halting, stood,
Stood intent and listened. Hark!
Someone softly seemed to follow,
Something whispered through the hollow
Wood, where all was still and dark,
'Tis thy husband, I am here!'
So she halted, caught by stark
Terror, listened, and then fled,
Every hair on end with dread.
Yet she dared not look around
Though she heard the whisper sound,
Echoing ever in her ear,
'Tis thy husband, I am here.'

But the festive Sunday came
When her suitor she might claim.
With the early rays of dawn
Forth the two young men had gone
And the lady fair, attended
By her bridal maids, descended
To the church; nor did she falter,

But, advancing to the altar,
Raised a wreath and bore it round.
'Lo, the wreath of lilies! Whose
Are they, who is it I choose,
Who the true love I have found?'

Up the elder brother springs,
Joy upon his face ashine;
Claps his hands and leaps and sings:
'Mine thou art, those flowers are mine!
There inside the lily wreath
I enwove a ribbon band:
See the token underneath!
It is mine—I win thy hand.'

'Tis a lie!' his brother shouted;
'Not far off there is a plot
In which lily plants have sprouted
And these flowers are from that spot
In a forest opening,
On a grave beside a river.
I will show you grave and spring:
This my wreath and I the giver.'

Wrangling thus with evil hearts
One denies and one upbraids;
From the scabbards fly their blades;
And a bitter combat starts,
And the wreath before the shrine
They both pluck at, shouting, 'Mine!'

Suddenly the church door trembled
And the altar lights were quenched;
There before the host assembled
Rose a form in white: they blenched,
For the bearing was well known
And the arms; a voice malign
Then rang out with hollow moan:
'Tis my wreath, and thou art mine!
From my grave the flowers were broken:
Bind me, father, with thy stole!
Evil wife, by every token
I am thine! Cursed be thy soul!
Cursed be you, my evil brothers,
Who have thus despoiled my grave!

'Cease your struggle for each other's
Life-blood. Mine the wreath you gave!
Wife and brothers, you shall go
With me to the world below!'

Thereupon the church foundation
Shook. The walls and arches slipped
From their lofty elevation,
Sinking down beneath the crypt.
All lie buried underground,
Lilies blossom on the mound,
And the flowers grow as high
As the dead man deep did lie.

[Translated by Dorothea Prall Radin, 1938.]

The Three Budrys Brothers

A Lithuanian Ballad

Doughty Budrys the old, Lithuanian bold,
    He has summoned his lusty sons three.
'Your chargers stand idle, now saddle and bridle
    And out with your broadswords', quoth he.

'For with trumpets loud braying in Vilna they're saying
    That our armies set forth to three goals;
Gallant Olgierd rakes Russia and Kiejstut takes Prussia
    And Skirgiell—our neighbours the Poles.

'Stout of heart and of hand, go, fight for your land
    With the gods of your fathers to guide you;
Though I mount not this year, yet my rede ye shall hear:
    Ye are three and three roads ye shall ride you.

'By Lake Ilmen's broad shores where fair Novgorod towers
    One shall follow 'neath Olgierd's device:
There are sables' black tails, there are silvery veils,
    There are coins shining brightly like ice.

194

'With Kiejstut's hordes ample the next son shall trample
    That dog's breed, the Knights of the Cross;
There lie amber thick-strewn, vestments diamond-sewn,
    And brocades all a marvellous gloss.

'In the barren, stripped land beyond Niemien's wide strand,
    Where goes Skirgiell, the third son shall ride;
Only buckler and sword will he get as reward,
    But from there he shall bring him his bride.

'For 'tis Poland the world over that's the land for a lover:
    All the maids are like kittens at play;
Faces whiter than milk, lashes soft as black silk,
    And their eyes—like the star-shine are they!

'Fifty years are now sped and my bride is long dead,
    The bright Pole I brought home from a raid;
And yet still when I stand and gaze out toward that land,
    I remember the face of that maid.'

So he ends and they turn, he has blessed them their journey;
    They've armed them, they've mounted and fled:
Fall and winter both pass, never word comes, alas,
    And old Budrys had thought his sons dead.

Through the high-piling drift comes a youth riding swift,
    'Neath his mantle rich booty doth hide:
'Ah, a Novgorod kettle full of silver-bright metal!'
    'Nay, my father, a Polish bride!'

Through the high-piling drift comes a youth riding swift,
    'Neath the mantle rich booty doth hide:
'Ah, amber, my son, in the German land won!'
    'Nay, my father, a Polish bride!'

Through the high-piling drift rides the third. Ah, his gift,
    'Tis the pride of the west and the east!
But while yet it is hidden, old Budrys has bidden
    His guests to the third wedding feast.

[Translated by Dorothea Prall Radin, 1925.]

'Adam Mickiewicz the Pilgrim.' Full-length statue, by Antoine Bourdelle (1861–1929). Mickiewicz Memorial, Place de l'Alma, Paris. Date of first model: 1912–14. Memorial erected in 1929. Photograph by Wł. Slawny.

To the Niemen

Where are the waters of those golden years
That oft I dipped, as smoothly we would glide
To some wild solitude where youth might hide
A restless heart beset with childish fears?
Here, Laura, loosening her soft hair, peers
At her reflected face with wondering pride;
Her picture, painted in the silvery tide,
I, ardent lover, marred with bitter tears.

Where are those sources, Niemen, that would fain
Bring me such happiness and hopeful dreams?
Where is my childhood with its varied themes?
Where are my friends? I sigh for them in vain.
Where is my Laura, mirrored by the streams?
Since all are gone, why do my tears remain?

[Translated by George Rapall Noyes and Doris Durst, 1929.]

To M. . . .

Written at Kovno in 1822

'Be off', you tell me. 'Leave my sight!' I go.
Your heart you bid me flee: I do, but still
Wherever flight may lead, shall stay, I know,
Forever in your heart, beyond your will.

As distant objects cast the longer shade,
And sorrow, orbs that widen ever round,
So shall my thoughts your own more deep invade,
The farther off my living self is found.

'Twill be, as lone you muse in yonder bow'r,
That oft your vagrant hand will touch a string
And waken chords to make you cry: 'This hour
It used to be this song with him I'd sing.'

Or, playing chess, if king you sometimes see
Ensnared by an opponent's skilful aim,
You'll think: Is't not the same manoeuvre he
Employed the time we played our final game?

And ever, as you read with tender eye
Of lovers whose delight too quick is flown,
You'll lay the volume down, and with a sigh
Confess: 'The tale's, alas, our very own.'

And if at last, by dint of author's help,
Some happiness befall the luckless pair,
You'll blow the candle out and ask yourself:
'Why could our own romance not end so fair?'

And always, when the skies are rent with flame,
Or when the pear tree murmurs in your ear,
When seems the night-owl's wing to brush the pane,
You'll know it's still my spirit hovering near.

[Translated by Marion Moore Coleman, 1946.]

Wer den Dichter will verstehen
Muss in Dichters Lande gehen.
                                    —Goethe

The Akkerman Steppes

I sail a sea where waters never ran;
My wagon like a boat with plunge and dip
Cuts waves of green and floods of flowers, to slip
Past rosy isles of wild cornelian.
Night falls. No road or hill—my eyes must scan
The stars by which the sailor guides his ship.
That distant cloud, the Dniester's gleaming strip;
That star, the evening lamp of Akkerman.

We halt. How still! I hear the cranes that pass
So high the falcon cannot see. I hear
The butterfly that rocks upon the grass,
The slippery-breasted serpent where it crawls.
So still it is, a voice might reach my ear
From Lithuania—Onward! No one calls.

[Translated by Dorothea Prall Radin, 1929.]

The Calm of the Sea

(from the heights of Tarkankut)

The flag on the pavilion barely stirs,
The water quivers gently in the sun
Like some young promised maiden dreaming on,
Half-waking, of the joy that shall be hers.
The sails upon the masts' bare cylinders
Are furled like banners when the war is done;
The ship rocks, chained on waters halcyon,
With idle sailors, laughing passengers.
O sea, among thy happy creatures, deep
Below, a polyp slumbers through the storm,
Its long arms ever lifted, poised to dart.
O thought, the hydra, memory, asleep
Through evil days, in peace will lift its form
And plunge its talons in thy quiet heart.

[Translated by Dorothea Prall Radin.]

The Rock of Ayudah

I love to lean against Ayudah's face
And watch the frothing waves as on they pour,
Dark ranks close-pressed, then burst like snow and soar
A million silver rainbows arched in space.
They strike the sands, they break and interlace;
Like whales in battle that beset the shore,
They seize the land and then retreat once more,
Shells, pearls, and corals scattered in their race.

And so it is, young poet, in your heart.
There passion raises storms, but when you start
Your strains, the whirlwinds harmlessly depart
And sink deep down in pools of memory. Yet
They leave you songs, which after years will set
As shining jewels in your coronet.

[Translated by Dorothea Prall Radin, 1929.]

Bakhchisaray

Those halls of the Gireys—still vast and great!—
Are galleries where desolation falls;
Those varicoloured domes, those crumbling halls
Where proud pashas upon rich divans sate:
Retreats of love and palaces of state—
Here now the locust leaps, the serpent crawls,
And bindweed RUIN writes, as on the walls
The hand of doom once traced Belshazzar's fate.

Within, the marble fountain made to hold
The harem waters still unbroken stands,
Which, shedding pearly tears, 'neath shattered panes,
Cries: 'Where are ye, O Glory, Love, and Gold?
Ye should endure, while streams waste into sands.
O shame, ye pass—the ageless spring remains!'

[Translated by Benjamin Collins, Woodbury.]

To . . .

Written in the Alps, at Splügen, 1829

Never! No, I never shall be free
Completely from yourself, that land and sea
Canst skim across, to shine from glacier's sheen
And whisper in the hum of Alpine stream!
Ungrateful one! As, yonder soaring peaks
Ascending, my uncertain footstep seeks
Some solid base whereunto it may turn,
So, ever through my tears the magnet firm
Of distant Northern Star I hold in view,
And by it Litwa seek, your home, and you.

E'en though, ungrateful one, you be today
The very Queen of Jest, at banquet gay
Some new-found love be snaring with your glance,
E'en entertaining him with our romance!

Confess it: are you happy to receive
The bow of lowly serfs unto their liege?
Has ecstasy so claimed you for its own
That all the past from memory is flown?

Or would you not be happier far, my fair,
If lot of faithful exile you might share?

Could I but lead you by the hand along
These crags, the journey sweet'ning with a song!
Could I but plunge headlong into some stream
And find you in its bed a stone to gleam
Beneath your little feet, lest any harm
Befall you! If I could but smother warm
Your tender hands with kisses, stand with you
An hour in yonder hut, our love renew!
And if, beside me there, by shepherd's flame,
You could but sleep, and waking, speak my name!

[Translated by Marion Moore Coleman, 1946.]

View of the Mountains from the Steppes of Kozlov

Pilgrim and Mirza

PILGRIM

Did Allah raise a wall of frozen foam?
Or for his angel hosts a cloud throne rear?
Or did the divs lift half a hemisphere
To keep the caravan of stars at home?
The summit flames. Stamboul a fiery dome!
When Night spead out her cloak, did Allah here
Hang up a lantern in the sky to steer
The worlds that through the sea of nature roam?

MIRZA

I know that region—There the winter sits
And streams and rivers drink from its cold bed
Where storm-steeds pause and curb their mania
I've breathed the air which ev'n the eagle quits,
And there with only stars above my head,
Where thunders sleep without their wild holla,
There is Chatyr Dagh!

PILGRIM

Ah!

[Translated by Dorothea Prall Radin.]

'*Spin Love from out Your Heart*'

Spin love from out your heart as silkworms spin their thread,
Pour forth your love as fountains pour waters from within.
Sow it as corn is sown. Let its wide surface spread
Like gold plate from a golden kernel beaten thin.
Nurture its growth as mothers feed their children bread.

   As waters from the fountainhead
Plunge underground, let it dive deep; and then begin
To blow it high to spaces only winds may win.
Sow it like corn, and like a mother feed it bread.
So shall your strength attain to nature's elevation—
It shall increase and gain the strength of propagation—
The strength of men, the strength of angels, till it reach
At last the strength of the Creator of creation.

[Translated by Dorothea Prall Radin.]

To a Polish Mother

O Polish mother, if the radiant eyes
    Of genius kindle in thy darling's face,
If even in his childish aspect rise
    The pride and honour of his ancient race;

If, turning from his playmates' joyous throng,
    He runs to find the bard and hear his lays,
If with bowed head he listens to the song
    Of ancient glory and departed days:

O Polish mother, ill must be his part!
    Before the Mother of Our Sorrows kneel,
Gaze on the sword that cleaves her living heart—
    Such is the craven blow thy breast shall feel!

Though peoples, powers, and schisms a truce declare,
    And though the whole wide world in peace may bloom,
In battle—without glory—must he share;
    In martyrdom—with an eternal tomb.

Soon bid him seek a solitary cave
    And ponder there—on rushes lay his head,
Breathe the foul vapours of a hidden grave,
    And with the envenomed serpent share his bed.

There will he learn to hide his wrath from reach
    To sink his thought as in the abyss profound,
Slyly to poison with miasmic speech,
    And humbly, like the serpent, kiss the ground.

A child in Nazareth, our Saviour mild
    Fondled the cross whereon he saved mankind:
O Polish mother, I would have thy child
    Thus early learn what playthings he will find.

His young arms load with chains, his body frail
    Full soon have harnessed to a barrow, so
Before the headsman's axe he shall not pale,
    Not at the swinging halter crimson grow.

Not his to venture like a plumed knight
    And plant the holy cross on pagan soil,
Nor like a soldier of new faith to fight
    In freedom's cause, and for her sake to toil.

One day an unknown spy will challenge him,
    A perjured court his adversary be,
The jousting-field, a secret dungeon grim;
    A powerful foe the verdict will decree.

And for the vanquished man as monument
   The gallows tree will rear its sullen height:
For glory—but a woman's tears, soon spent,
   And fellow patriots' whispered words by night.

[Translated by Jewell Parish, 1925.]

KONRAD WALLENROD

Part IV

THE SONG OF THE WAJDELOTA

Whene'er the plague toward Lithuania turns,
The wajdelota's eye her doom foresees;
For, if the bard relate his tale aright,
Oft moves o'er empty graveyards and broad leas
The Maid of Pestilence, robed all in white:
About her brow a fiery garland burns;
Taller than Bialowieza's trees she stands,
And waves a bloodstained kerchief in her hands.

On castle walls the sentries on their round
Behind their visors fain would hide their eyes;
In village lanes the dogs, with dismal cries,
Dig, scenting death, their muzzles to the ground.

The maiden paces on with steps of doom
Through many a village, castle, and rich town;
Each time she waves her bloody kerchief, down
Falls a fair palace; and, amid the gloom,
Where'er she steps, arises a fresh tomb.

Ah, devastating phantom!—but a loss
Far deadlier shadows forth the casque that shines,
The plume that waves beyond the German lines,
And the broad mantle, blackened with the cross!

Where such an apparition has stalked by,
None says, 'Here was a castle, there a town';
The whole land in one grave is sunken down.
If there be any who can yet defy
That spectre—if there still be one to keep
A Lithuanian soul—come to me now!
Above the grave of nations let us bow;
There we will ponder, there will sing and weep.

Saga! thou, ark of that most holy plight
Between the years of yore and after years,
In thee the folk lays armour of its knight,
Fabric of thoughts, blossoms of joy and tears.

O ark, no power can break thee, while thine own
Take heed of thee! O folk song! thou dost stand
On guard before the nation's inmost shrine
Of memory, and wings and voice are thine
Of an archangel—but not these alone,
For an archangel's sword is in thy hand.

The flames will gnaw away a painted tale;
The fruits of conquest, vandals will despoil:
But song unscathed springs from the murk and moil
And, if the sordid souls who hear it fail
To give it food of grief and drink of hope,

It cleaves to ruins, seeks the rugged slope,
And thence mourns ever for the ancient days.
Thus flies the nightingale before the blaze
And on the burning gables fain would rest;
When fall the roofs, she flees to wooded hills,
And over graves, from her sonorous breast,
The pilgrim's lonely path with mourning fills.

I have heard songs: a peasant, bent and grey,
His ploughshare turning up forgotten bones,
Has paused, upon his willow flute to play
A requiem, or with impassioned tones
To raise a chant for you, O ancient sires,
Who have no sons to tend your altar fires!
The echoes made responses far and clear:
I grieved the more, that I alone should hear.
As the archangel on the day of doom
Calls forth the dead past from its sunken tomb,
So, at the song, the bones beneath my feet
Fused into giant forms; from heaps of stone
Columns and ceilings rose again complete,
A thousand cars stirred the deserted lake,
Wide open were the doors of castles thrown:
There did the minstrels sing, the maidens dance,
The light from princely crowns and armour glance—
Bravely I dreamt, and cruelly did awake.

Gone are the forests, gone the ancestral peaks;
Thought, flying back, her wonted refuge seeks,
As homes the wearied dove upon spent wings.
In listless hands the lute no longer rings;

Seldom the voice of old can I divine
Through Lithuanian lips, that but repine.
But still the sparks of youthful ardour glow,
Deep in my breast, and often kindle there
The flames that warm my soul and brighter show
The scenes of old. For memory, like a rare,
Crystalline globe of intricate design,
Though filmed with dust and scratches, if one set
A candle in its heart, again will shine
With limpid colour; once again will throw
On palace walls a fair and delicate net,
Though somewhat blurred and darkened, radiant yet.

If only I could pour out mine own fire
Into my hearers' breasts; could I inspire
A second life in phantoms of old time;
Could I but pierce with ringing shafts of rhyme
My brothers' hearts—in that one moment when
Their fathers' song aroused them, they might know
The ancient stirring of the heart, the old
Elation of the soul; one moment then
Might they be lifted up, as free and bold
As lived and died their fathers, long ago.

But why for ages that are vanished yearn?
The bard will not belittle his own day;
A hero liveth yet, not far away:
Of him I sing—ye men of Litwa, learn!

[Translated by Jewell Parish.]

PAN TADEUSZ

THE LAST FORAY IN LITHUANIA [1]

BOOK I

The Farm

Lithuania, my country, thou art like health; how much thou shouldst be prized only he can learn who has lost thee. Today thy beauty in all its splendour I see and describe, for I yearn for thee.

Holy Virgin, who protectest bright Czenstochowa and shinest above the Ostra Gate in Vilna! [2] Thou who dost shelter the castle of Nowogrodek with its faithful folk! As by miracle thou didst restore me to health in my child-hood—when, offered by my weeping mother to thy pro-tection, I raised my dead eyelids, and could straightway walk to the threshold of thy shrine to thank God for the life returned me—so by miracle thou wilt return us to the bosom of our country. Meanwhile bear my grief-stricken soul to those wooded hills, to those green meadows stretched far and wide along the blue Niemen; to those fields painted with various grain, gilded with wheat, silvered with rye; where grows the amber mustard, the buckwheat white as snow, where the clover glows with a maiden's blush, where all is girdled as with a ribbon by

---

1. The figures, here and in the text, refer to the notes on this poem, p. 226-7.

a strip of green turf on which here and there rest quiet pear-trees.

Amid such fields years ago, by the border of a brook, on a low hill, in a grove of birches, stood a gentleman's mansion, of wood, but with a stone foundation; the white walls shone from afar, the whiter since they were relieved against the dark green of the poplars that sheltered it against the winds of autumn. The dwelling-house was not large, but it was spotlessly neat, and it had a mighty barn, and near it were three stacks of hay that could not be contained beneath the roof; one could see that the neighbourhood was rich and fertile. And one could see from the number of sheaves that up and down the meadows shone thick as stars—one could see from the number of ploughs turning up early the immense tracts of black fallow land that evidently belonged to the mansion, and were tilled well like garden beds, that in that house dwelt plenty and order. The gate wide open proclaimed to passers-by that it was hospitable, and invited all to enter as guests.

A young gentleman had just entered in a two-horse carriage, and, after making a turn about the yard, he stopped before the porch and descended; his horses, left to themselves, slowly moved towards the gate, nibbling the grass. The mansion was deserted, for the porch doors were barred and the bar fastened with a pin. The traveller did not run to make inquiries at the farm house but opened the door and ran into the mansion, for he was eager to greet it. It was long since he had seen the house, for he had been studying in a distant city and had at last finished his course. He ran in and gazed with eager emotion upon the ancient walls, his old friends. He sees the same furniture, the same hangings with which he had loved to amuse himself from babyhood, but they seemed less beautiful and not so large as of old. And the same portraits hung upon the walls. Here Kosciuszko,[3] in his Cracow coat,[4] with his eyes raised to heaven, held his two-handed sword; such was he when on the steps of the altar he swore that with this sword he would drive the three powers from Poland or himself would fall upon it. Farther on sat Rejtan,[5] in Polish costume, mourning the loss of liberty; in his hands he held a knife with the point turned against his breast, and before him lay *Phaedo* and *The Life of Cato*. Still farther on Jasinski,[6] a fair and melancholy youth, and his faithful comrade Korsak[7] stand side by side on the entrenchments of Praga, on heaps of Muscovites, hewing down the enemies of their country—but around them Praga is already burning.

He recognized the tall old musical clock in its wooden case near the chamber door, and with childish joy he pulled at the string, in order to hear Dombrowski's old mazurka.[8]

BOOK XI

The Year 1812

Memorable year! Happy is he who beheld thee in our land! The folk still call thee the year of harvest, but the soldiers the year of war; old men still love to tell tales of thee and

poets still dream of thee. Thou hadst long been heralded
by the marvel in the sky and preceded by a vague rumour
among the folk; with the coming of the spring sun the
hearts of the Lithuanians were seized with a certain strange
foreboding, as if the end of the world were approaching—
by a certain yearning and joyous expectation.

In the spring, when the cattle were driven forth for the
first time, men noticed that, though famished and lean, they
did not run to the young corn[9] that already made gay the
fields, but lay down on the ploughed land, and, drooping
their heads, either lowed or chewed the cud of their winter
food.

The villagers too, as they ploughed for the spring grain,
did not show their wonted joy in the end of the long
winter; they did not sing songs, but worked lazily, as
though forgetful of the sowing and the harvest. As they
harrowed, at every step they checked their oxen and their
nags, and gazed anxiously towards the west, as though from
this direction some marvel were about to appear. And they
regarded anxiously the birds, which were returning home;
for already the stork had flown back to its native pine and
had spread its white wings, the early standard of spring;
and after it the swallows, coming on in noisy regiments,
gathered above the waters, and from the frozen earth
collected mud for their tiny houses. At evening in the
thickets one could hear the calling of the woodcocks as
they rose from the earth; and flocks of wild geese honked
over the forest and, wearied, settled noisily down to feed;
and in the depths of the dark heaven the cranes kept up
a continuous clamour. Hearing this, the night watchmen
would ask in dread whence came such disorder in the

winged kingdom, and what storm had driven forth these birds so early.

And now new swarms, like flocks of finches, plover, and starlings, swarms of bright plumes and pennons shone bright upon the hills and came down into the meadows. It was cavalry! In strange array, and arms never seen before, came regiment after regiment; and straight across the country, like melted snows, the ironshod ranks flowed along the roads. From the forests emerged black shakos, a row of bayonets glittered, and the infantry, countless as ants, swarmed forth.

All were turned towards the north; you would have said that at that time, coming from the sunny south[10] and following the birds, men too were entering our land, driven on by the force of some instinct that they could not comprehend.

Steeds, men, cannon, eagles flowed on day and night; here and there fires glowed in the sky; the earth trembled, in the distance one could hear the rolling of thunder.

War! War! There was no corner in the Lithuanian land to which its roar did not reach; amid dark forests, the peasant, whose grandfathers and kinsmen had died without seeing beyond the boundaries of the wood, who understood no other cries in the sky than those of the winds, and none on earth except the roaring of beasts, who had seen no other guests than his fellow-woodsmen, now beheld how a strange glare flamed in the sky—in the forest there was a crash—that was a cannon ball that had wandered from the battlefield and was seeking a path in the wood, tearing up stumps and cutting through boughs. The hoary, bearded bison trembled in his mossy lair and bristled up his long shaggy mane; he half rose, resting on his forelegs, and, shaking his beard, he gazed in amazement at the sparks suddenly glittering amid the brushwood: this was a stray bombshell that twirled and whirled and hissed, and at last broke with a roar like thunder; the bison for the first time in his life was terrified and fled to take refuge in deeper hiding.

'A battle! Where? In what direction?' asked the young men, as they seized their arms. The women raised their hands in prayer to Heaven. All, sure of victory, cried out with tears in their eyes: 'God is with Napoleon and Napoleon is with us!'

O spring! Happy is he who beheld thee then in our country! Memorable spring of war, spring of harvest! O spring, happy is he who beheld how thou didst bloom with corn and grass, but glittered with men; how thou wert rich in events and big with hope! I see thee still, fair phantom of my dream! Born in slavery and chained in my swaddling bands, I have had but one such spring in my whole life.

.   .   .   .

BOOK XII

.   .   .   .

Hardly did the hearers have time to recover from their amazement, when once more the music changed: at first there were once more light and gentle hummings; a few thin strings complained together, like flies striving to free themselves from the spider's web. But more and more strings joined them; now the scattered tones were blended and legions of chords were united; now they advanced measuredly with harmonious notes, forming the mournful melody of that famous song of the wandering soldier who travels through woods and through forests, oft-times fainting with woe and with hunger: at last he falls at the feet of his faithful steed, and the steed with his foot digs a grave for him. A poor old song, yet very dear to the Polish troops! The soldiers recognized it, and the privates crowded about the master; they hearkened, and they remembered that dreadful season when over the grave of their country they had sung this song and departed for the ends of the earth; they called to mind their long years of wandering, over lands and seas, over frosts and burning sands, amid foreign peoples, where often in camp they had been cheered and heartened by this folk song. So thinking, they sadly bowed their heads!

But they raised them straightway, for the master was playing stronger and higher notes; he changed his measure, and proclaimed something quite different from what had preceded. Once more he looked down and measured the strings with his eye; he joined his hands and smote with the two hammers in unison: the blow was so artistic, so powerful, that the strings rang like brazen trumpets, and from the trumpets a well-known song floated to the heavens, a triumphal march, 'Poland has not yet perished; march, Dombrowski, to Poland!' And all clapped their hands, and all shouted in chorus, 'March, Dombrowski!'

The musician seemed amazed at his own song; he dropped the hammers from his hands and raised his arms aloft; his fox-skin cap dropped from his head to his shoulders; his uplifted beard waved majestically; his cheeks glowed with a strange flush; in his glance, full of spirit, shone the fire of youth. At last, when the old man turned his eyes on Dombrowski, he covered them with his hands, and from under his hands gushed a stream of tears.

'General,' said he, 'long has our Lithuania awaited thee—long, even as we Jews have awaited the Messiah; of thee in olden times minstrels prophesied among the folk; thy coming was heralded by a marvel in the sky. Live and wage war, O thou our—'

As he spoke, he sobbed; the honest Jew loved his country like a Pole! Dombrowski extended his hand to him and thanked him; Jankiel, doffing his cap, kissed the leader's hand.

It was time to begin the polonaise. The Chamberlain stepped forward, and, lightly throwing back the flowing sleeves of his *kontusz* and twirling his moustache, he offered his arm to Zosia; with a polite bow he invited her to lead off in the first couple. Behind the Chamberlain a long line of couples formed; the signal was given and the dance began —he was its leader.

Over the greensward glittered his crimson boots, the light gleamed from his sabre and his rich girdle shone. He advanced slowly, with seeming carelessness—yet in every step and every motion one could read the feelings and the thoughts of the dancer. He stopped, as if he wished to question his lady; he bent his head down towards her

as if wishing to whisper in her ear; the lady averted her
head, was bashful, would not listen; he doffed his white cap
and bowed humbly; the lady deigned to gaze upon him,
but still kept a stubborn silence; he slackened his pace,
followed her glances with his eyes, and at last he laughed.
Happy in her reply, he advanced more quickly, gazing
down at his rivals; now he hung his white cap with its
heron's plumes over his brow, now he shook it above his
brow; at last he cocked it over his ear and twirled his
moustache. He strode on; all felt envious of him and pressed
upon him in pursuit; he would have been glad to steal
away from the throng with his lady; at times he stood still,
courteously raised his hand, and humbly begged them to
pass by; sometimes he meditated withdrawing adroitly to
one side; he often changed his course, and would have
been glad to elude his comrades, but they importunately
followed him with swift steps, and encircled him from all
sides in the evolutions of the dance: so he grew angry,
and laid his right hand on his sword hilt, as if to say:
'I care not for you; woe to those who are jealous of me!'
He turned about with a haughty brow and with a challenge
in his eye, and made straight for the throng; the throng
of dancers did not dare withstand him, but retired from
his path—and, changing their formation, they started again
in pursuit of him.

Cries rang out on all sides: 'Ah, perhaps he is the last
—watch, watch, you young men—perhaps he is the last
who can lead the polonaise in such fashion!' And the
couples followed one another merrily and uproariously;
the circle would disperse and then contract once more!
As when an immense serpent twines into a thousand folds,

so there was seen a perpetual change amid the gay, parti-
coloured garments of the ladies, the gentlemen, and the
soldiers, like glittering scales gilded by the beams of the
western sun and relieved against the dark pillows of turf.
Brisk was the dance and loud the music, the applause, and
the drinking of healths.

Corporal Buzzard Dobrzynski alone neither listened
to the band, nor danced, nor made him merry; with his
hands behind him he stood glum and sullen and called
to mind his old-time wooing of Zosia; how he had loved
to bring her flowers, to plait little baskets, to gather birds'
nests, to make little earrings. Ungrateful girl! Though he
had wasted upon her so many lovely gifts, though she had
fled from him, though his father had forbidden him, yet
how many times he had sat on the wall just to see her
through the window, and had stolen into the hemp in
order to watch how she tended her little flower garden,
picked cucumbers, or fed the roosters! Ungrateful girl!
He drooped his head; finally he whistled a mazurka; then
he jammed his casque down over his ears and went to the
camp, where the sentinels were standing by the cannon;
there, to distract his mind, he began a game of cribbage
with the private soldiers, and sweetened his sorrow with
the cup. Such was the constancy of Dobrzynski to
Zosia.

Zosia was dancing merrily: but, though she was in the
first couple, from a distance she could hardly be seen; on
the broad surface of the turf-spread court, in her green
gown and decked with garlands and with flowery wreaths,
she circled amid the grasses and flowers unseen in her
flight, guiding the dance as an angel guides the motion of

the stars by night: you could guess where she was, for
towards her all eyes were turned and all arms stretched
out; towards her the tumult pressed. In vain did the
Chamberlain strive to remain by her side; his envious
rivals had already pressed him out of the first couple: nor
did the happy Dombrowski long enjoy his triumph; he
yielded her to a second, but a third was already hastening
up; and he, too, at once pressed aside, departed without
hope. At last Zosia, by this time wearied, met Thaddeus
as she passed down the line: and fearing further change,
and wishing to remain with him, she brought the dance
to an end. She went to the table to pour wine for the
guests.

The sun was already setting, the evening was warm
and quiet; the circle of the heavens, here and there strewn
with little clouds, was azure on high, but rosy in the west;
the little clouds foretold fine weather, being light and
shining—here like flocks of sheep sleeping on the greensward, there of somewhat smaller size, like coveys of teal.
In the west was a cloud in shape like the drapery curtains
of a couch, transparent and with many folds, pearly at the
summit, gilded on the margin, purple in the centre; it still
burned and glowed with the western gleams; at last it
slowly turned yellow, then pale and grey; the sun dropped
its head, drew the cloud about it, and sighing a single time
with a warm breath—it fell asleep.[11]

But the gentlefolk continued to drink and to pro-
pose the healths of Napoleon, the Generals, Thaddeus,
and Zosia; finally of all three betrothed pairs in turn,
of all the guests present with them, of all those that
had been invited, of all the friends that any one alive

could remember, and of all the dead whose memory had
remained holy.

And I was there among the guests, and there drank wine
and mead; and what I saw and heard I wrote, that all of
you might read.[12]

> [Translated by George Rapall Noyes: *Pan Tadeusz or the Last
> Foray in Lithuania* (J. M. Dent and Sons, Ltd., London and
> Toronto, 1917).]

NOTES

1. In the time of the Polish Commonwealth the carrying out of judicial decrees
was very difficult, in a country where the executive authorities had almost no
police at their disposal, and where powerful citizens maintained household regiments, some of them, for example the Princes Radziwill, even armies of several
thousands. So the plaintiff who had obtained a verdict in his favour had to
apply for its execution to the knightly order, that is to the gentry, with whom
rested also the executive power. Armed kinsmen, friends, and neighbours set
out, verdict in hand, in company with the apparitor, and gained possession,
often not without bloodshed, of the goods adjudged to the plaintiff, which the
apparitor legally made over or gave into his possession. Such an armed execution of a verdict was called a *zajazd* (foray). In ancient times, while laws were
respected, even the most powerful magnates did not dare to resist judicial decrees,
armed attacks rarely took place, and violence almost never went unpunished.
Well known in history is the sad end of Prince Wasil Sanguszko, and of Stadnicki,
called the Devil. The corruption of public morals in the Commonwealth
increased the number of forays, which continually disturbed the peace of
Lithuania. (The rendering of *zajazd* by *foray* is of course inexact and conventional;
but the translator did not wish to use the Polish word and could find no better
English equivalent.)

2. Everyone in Poland knows of the miraculous image of Our Lady at Jasna Gora
in Czenstochowa. In Lithuania there are images of Our Lady, famed for miracles,
at the Ostra (Pointed) Gate in Vilna, the Castle in Novogrodek, and at Zyrowiec
and Boruny.

3. Tadeusz (Thaddeus) Kosciuszko (1746–1817). This most famous Polish patriot
was a native of the same portion of Lithuania as Mickiewicz. He early emigrated
to America and served with distinction in the Revolutionary War. After the
failure of the insurrection of 1794 Kosciuszko was imprisoned for two years in

St. Petersburg; in 1796, on the death of the Empress Catherine, he was released by the Emperor Paul. He thereafter lived in retirement, first in France and then in Switzerland, resisting all the attempts of Napoleon to draw him into his service. At the Congress of Vienna he made fruitless efforts in behalf of Poland. His memory is probably more reverenced by the Polish people than that of any other man. His remains rest in the cathedral at Cracow, and on the outskirts of the city is a mound of earth 150 feet high raised as a monument to him.

4. *Czamarka* (diminutive of *czamara*) in the original; the *czamara* is a long frock-coat, braided on the back and chest like a hussar's uniform, and with tight sleeves.

5. Rejtan had taken part in the Confederacy of Bar. Owing to the disasters to Poland he lost his reason, and in 1780 killed himself.

6. A soldier and poet, of a Vilna family. As a colonel of engineers he fought in the war of 1792. He prepared and led the insurrection in Vilna in 1794, and perished at the siege of Praga in the same year.

7. Korsak was a deputy to the Four Years' Diet, and a leader in Kosciuszko's insurrection. He perished by the side of Jasinski.

8. Dombrowski's march, 'Poland has not yet perished'.

9. *Run* (the Polish word here used) is the winter corn when it comes up green.

10. *Wyraj* (the Polish word here used) in the popular dialect means properly the autumn season, when the migratory birds fly away; to fly to *wyraj* means to fly to warm countries and especially to some fabulous, happy countries, lying beyond the seas.

11. 'Readers who have already observed into what close connexion Mickiewicz loves to bring the phenomena of nature and the affairs of men, will not find it difficult, nor will they regard it as a forced interpretation, to understand the clouds, which at the close of the poem . . . he paints with such disproportionate breadth and with such apparent minuteness, as something quite different from mere external reality. They will have no difficulty in seeing in that western cloud, which was adorned with gold and pearl, but in the centre was blood-red, Napoleon, the great warrior of the west; or, if they prefer, the hopes of Poland that were linked to him. We are in the year 1812: both the aureole of that name, and the hopes and rejoicing that it aroused, we may recognize in the gleaming, but fleeting picture, which "slowly turned yellow, then pale and grey", and behind which the sun fell asleep with a sigh. Thus in this passage, as well as earlier, in the words of Maciek, the poet gives us warning of the great tragedy which was soon to overwhelm not only Lithuania and Poland but the world.'— LIPINER.

12. This concluding couplet imitates the conventional ending of a Polish fairy tale.

THE BOOK OF THE POLISH PILGRIMS

III

Polish pilgrim, thou wast rich, and behold, thou sufferest poverty and need, that thou mayst know what poverty and need are, and, when thou returnest to thy land, that thou mayst say: 'The poor and the needy are joint heirs with me.'

Pilgrim, thou madest laws and hadst a right to the crown, but lo, in a strange land thou art taken out from under the protection of the law, that thou mayst know injustice, and when thou returnest to thy land, that thou mayst say: 'Strangers are joint lawgivers with me.'

Pilgrim, thou wast learned, and behold the knowledge which thou didst value hath become unprofitable for thee, but that which thou didst hold lightly thou now dost value, that thou mayst know what the knowledge of this world is, and when thou returnest to thy land, that thou mayst say: 'The simple are joint learners with me.'

XXII

When on your pilgrimage ye come into a city, bless it, saying: 'Let our freedom be with you.' If they receive you and heed you, then shall they be free: but if they scorn you and heed you not, and drive you away, then shall your blessing return to you.

When ye depart from a city and a district that are godless, slavish, and minister-ridden, shake off the dust from your shoes; and verily I say unto you that it was better for Toulon and Nantes and Lyons in the days of the Convention than it shall be for that city in the days of the Confederation of Europe.

For when Freedom shall have her seat in the capital of the world, she shall judge the nations.

And she shall say to one nation: 'Lo, I was set upon by robbers, and I called to thee, thou nation, for a piece of iron for my defense and a handful of powder; but thou didst give me an article from a newspaper.' And that nation shall answer: 'My lady, when didst thou call unto me?' And Freedom shall answer: 'Behold, I called unto you through the mouths of these pilgrims, and ye heeded me not; depart therefore into slavery, where there shall be the whistling of the knout and the clank of ukases.'

And Freedom shall say to another nation: 'Behold, I was in distress and need, and I besought thee, O nation, for the protection of the law, and for tendance; and thou didst hurl ordinances at me.' And the nation shall answer: 'My lady, when didst thou come to me?' And Freedom shall answer: 'I came to thee in the garb of these pilgrims, and thou didst scorn me: depart thou therefore into slavery, where there shall be the whistling of the knout and the clank of ukases.'

Verily I say unto you that your pilgrimage shall become a stumbling stone for empires.

The empires rejected your stone from the building of

Europe, and lo, that stone shall become the corner-stone and the head of the building that is to be; and on whomsoever it shall fall, him it shall crush, and whosoever shall stumble on it shall fall and he shall not rise.

And of the great political building of Europe there shall not be left one stone upon another.

For the capital of Freedom shall be removed elsewhere.

Jerusalem, thou that killest men speaking of Freedom, thou dost kill thy prophets; and a people that killeth its prophets smiteth itself in its own heart, like a madman who slayeth himself.

There shall come upon Judah and Israel great tribulation.

XXIII

Rulers of France and ye men of France who call yourselves wise, ye who talk of freedom and serve despotism, ye shall lie between your people and foreign despotism as a tire of cold iron between the hammer and the anvil.

And ye shall be beaten, and the dross from you, and the sparks from you, shall fly to the ends of the earth, and the nations shall say: 'Of a truth, the hammering there is as great as in the forge of hell.'

And ye shall cry out to the hammer, to your people: 'O people, forgive thou and cease, for we have talked of freedom.' And the hammer shall say: 'Thou didst talk in one wise, but thou didst act in another.' And it shall fall with new force upon the tire.

And ye shall cry out to foreign despotism, as to a deaf anvil: 'O despotism, we have served thee, soften thyself, make an opening, that we may hide ourselves from the hammer.' And despotism shall say: 'Thou didst act in one wise, thou didst talk in another.' And it shall present to you a back hard and cold, till the tire shall be forged so that none shall know it.

Rulers of England and ye men of England who call yourselves wise, ye pride yourselves on your birth, and say: 'My grandfather was a lord and my great-grandfather a king, let us live therefore in friendship with our kinsmen the lords and kings of Europe'; but lo, the days will come when ye shall cry to the people: 'Grant us our lives, for there hath been in our race neither a single king, nor a single lord, nor a single esquire.'

And ye, merchants and traders of the two nations, who are greedy of gold and of the paper that giveth gold, ye did send money for the suppression of freedom; and lo, the days shall come when ye shall lick your gold and chew your paper, and none will send you bread and water.

Ye have heard of famines such that mothers have eaten their children; but your hunger shall be more grievous, for I say unto you that ye shall cut off the ears of living fellow creatures, and your own ears, and roast them and eat them. For ye have deserved that ye should be without ears as are felons.

THE PRAYER OF THE PILGRIM

Lord God Almighty! The children of a warlike nation lift up to thee their unarmed hands from the various ends of the earth. They call to thee from the depths of the mines of Siberia and from the snows of Kamchatka, from the plains of Algeria, and from France, a stranger land. But in our Fatherland in Poland, faithful to thee, they may not call upon thee! And our old men, our women, and our children pray to thee in secret, by thoughts and tears. God of the Jagiellos! God of the Sobieskis! God of the Kosciuszkos! Have mercy on our Fatherland, and on us. Grant us again to pray to thee according to the custom of our fathers, on the field of battle with our weapons in our hands, before an altar made of drums and cannon, under a baldachin made of our eagles and standards; and grant our kinsfolk to pray to thee in the churches of our cities and of our villages, and our children on our graves. Nevertheless not our will, but thine, be done. Amen.

[Translated by Dorothea Prall Radin: *Poems by A. Mickiewicz*, published by the Polish Institute of Arts and Sciences in America, New York, 1944.]

ARTICLES FROM

'LA TRIBUNE DES PEUPLES'

OUR PROGRAMME

(14 March 1849)

Europe has now reached a stage where any nation proceeding alone along the path of progress risks losing itself
through, by this action, injuring the common cause.

In Europe the enemies of the people have always
presented a united front; their daily acts are proof of this
solidarity.

Since they, essentially, are alive to their common
dangers, they cling together as never before. Their tactics
are to mobilize the whole machinery of government against
each nationality achieving separate emancipation—to set
one against the other, and crush each in turn. Their plans,
of long standing, reveal themselves only in their execution;
they are based on detailed information, permitting an
assessment of all the selfish interests cherished by governments and the individuals behind them, and of the degree
of ambition which actuates them all.

The enemies of the people in Europe have powerful
allies, through whom they influence the centre of popular
action itself; they have allies in France, the chief champion
of Europe's democratic ideals and interests; for friends and
foes alike recognize that France is the moving spirit in

Europe. It is in France that our most loyal friends, but also our most cunning and powerful enemies, are to be found.

France alone knows what this position of 'leader' has cost her; but it is for us to tell her, frankly, what it would cost her to lose it. The France of the February Revolution preserved this leadership through an act of European significance; she established the Republic and, through the voice of the people, invoked the principle of brotherhood at a juncture when the old order imagined that it had recovered all its rights, and was laying claim to an irrevocable victory.

A principle proclaimed by the French people becomes a reality; it commits France for the future; but the other peoples, who have seen it emerge in a concrete, living form and, thanks to France, have been able to greet its advent must labour closely together if they wish to see it established on their native soil.

The great French Revolution, heir to Christianity, had through its leading spokesmen invoked the principle of absolute eternal justice as against the abuses of the old order; but that principle had to be strengthened and expanded afresh if it was to operate among all the other peoples.

The political inertia of all French governments since the Restoration is due, not merely to their pusillanimity, but to their profound ignorance of European affairs and events—an ignorance that has more than once been pleaded by French statesmen themselves, both in official papers and in public pronouncements.

A fortiori, the common people—those who have hitherto had no opportunity of schooling or book reading—have even less means of knowing what is really happening abroad; yet foreign events have always in-fluenced, and will never cease to influence, their own fate. It will be our task to tell the people the truth, and nothing but the truth, about foreign affairs; the true facts have too often been concealed from them, even more by design than by ignorance.

The immediate purpose of the People's Party—the only genuinely progressive party in this country—is to estab-lish, between France which is seeking to build its future and Europe which is striving to cast off the skin of its past, relations that are true and therefore new; for 'political truth' has hitherto been conspicuous by its absence.

This aim, pursued in the interests of the common cause, presupposes a knowledge of the *terrain* on which new interests are astir, and of all the factors—religious, social, national, political and industrial—that are favourable to or militate against action by the people.

The task we are undertaking—inspired as it is by the spirit that has been present in the building of a new Europe, with due regard to its duties and its needs—has its main-springs in France, yet cannot be accomplished solely with French resources.

We are founding an organ for the European peoples, *La Tribune des peuples*. Resolved to proclaim and defend the rights of France, in so far as they harmonize with the interests of the people's cause throughout Europe, we call upon all nations to speak from this tribune, each with its own free voice.

Several friends from abroad, who have won popularity at home by speaking out from a life of toil and sacrifice, are giving us their support. Through them we shall obtain exact and detailed intelligence on matters concerning their countries.

We—men of the February Revolution—are no less sons of the Great Revolution, whose general principles we support, just as we support what was creative in the Napoleonic period. Napoleon put into practice the revolutionary ideals when, as an armed missionary, he passed through the republican phase of his life. But when the First Consul cast those ideals aside, to compromise with the old order and place a crown upon his head, he let loose that series of misfortunes from which the nations are suffering today. Yet for the French people it is still Napoleon the Republican who represents the Great Revolution, since it was he who defended its ideals with the greatest and most fruitful determination. His successors, on the other hand, all betrayed those ideals, from the moment when they acceded to power.

We, for our part, shall set the limits of the Republic beyond those conceived of by Napoleon; we shall regard as retrograde all who, while accepting the republican principle, measure its impact abroad in terms of their own selfish interests, or who, admiring the energy and force characteristic of the Napoleonic era, would nevertheless discount the need for a spirit of self-sacrifice and republican expansion.

France, as we conceive her, is this very spirit embodied in a people and incarnated in a republic.

We shall therefore defend the present Constitution and co-operate, with all our strength, to develop it in a republican sense, with all that this implies.

So much for France itself.

Abroad, we shall deal first and foremost with issues of

immediate concern—those affecting Italy, Poland, Germany, Denmark, Spain, the Slav countries, Hungary and the Danubian provinces.

At home and abroad alike, our platform will be a Christian policy and the brotherhood of the peoples. As for the parties contending for power in Europe, in France and in the National Assembly, we shall always be found on the side of men who, faithful to the progressive instincts of the masses, work for a social order corresponding to the people's new needs. On that condition alone shall we recognize in them the true political representatives of the people's interests throughout the world, which in turn are the only true interests of France.

SOCIALISM

Part II
(17 April 1849)

Everything that has been said of the present social disorder is accepted without question by even the most hardened enemies of Socialism. All agree when it comes to condemning the abuses of the old social system.

But how can these abuses be remedied? Everyone expects a remedy and, in the hope of discovering it, is quite willing to note the existence and progress of the disease. The right to deny the legitimacy of the old social order is already recognized; the National Assembly even concedes this right to the socialists. Yet both the Assembly and the public continue to regard Socialism as a negative doctrine.

The thinkers and theologians of the Assembly are perpetually recalling the heresiarchs, the schismatists and the leaders of the Paris mobs. Listening patiently to expositions of socialist doctrines, they counter every new proposal with some recollection of the past, and say to themselves: 'The Gnostics made the same claims; Luther and Calvin rejected the existing order in their day more forcefully and effectively than Saint-Simon and Fourier; Luther and Calvin set peoples and armies on the move; they succeeded in interesting heads of governments in their cause; they made city march against city, and prince against prince; they brought about the dissolution of that greatest of empires, the Universal Church. But what did they put in its place? The molecular Church of Geneva and innumerable Protestant chapels, devouring one another and constantly changing like so many infusoria. They diverted our attention from the great phenomena stirring up the ocean of Catholicism, to their minute observations of what was going on in such drops of water as a Father Chatel chapel, the "Mômiers" of Lausanne or the official Church in Geneva.[1] All the founders of these variegated

---

1 Father François-Fernand Chatel founded, on 15 January 1831, a 'French Church'. His doctrine resembled most closely that of the English and American Unitarians. He styled himself 'Primate' and published a series of papers: *Le Bon Pasteur*, *Le Catholique français*, *Le Réformateur*, *L'Église française*, *La Religion naturelle*, *Le Réformateur religieux*. This movement seems to have come to an end in 1844, the year in which the last paper published by this sect was discontinued.

The 'Mômiers', similar to the Methodists, were active in the cantons of Vaud and Geneva around 1828; they were proscribed for a time, but subsequently tolerated. Their numbers decreased rapidly, and statistics showed that there were no more than two hundred in the whole of French-speaking Switzerland. [Editor's note.]

bodies claimed to found new societies; each of them posed
as a prophet of the "new Socialism". But although they
were forceful agents of destruction, none of them has so
far produced anything positive. In order to produce an
idea, one must have productive soil; productive soil means
capital, which is positive; it involves a group which
exploits, a head who receives profits, an administration
whose employees are paid, and lastly, laws to protect the
capital, those who exploit it, and the administration. No
system of Socialism so far heard of, from that of Plato to
that of Citizen Considérant, has been capable of setting up
a legal system, a police force, or a militia; thus these
systems do not exist, they are merely negations of existing
systems. Strong in "denying" and attacking, they are
completely impotent when it comes to constructing and
preserving.'

This, we repeat, is the argument of the thinkers and
theologians of the Assembly.

The plea consistently made against any socialist system
is that it is negative.

Socialism must answer this first charge. We will answer
on its behalf.

No, Socialism is not a negative system. You may say
that the idea in which it is rooted has not yet acquired
sufficient strength to overcome the resistance of its native
soil, the earth's atmosphere or the malice of official gar-
deners. You may say that the basic thought of Socialism
does not yet glow brightly enough to be visible to the eyes
of those in power, the representatives of an anti-socialist
society. But you have no right to say that Socialism is a
mere negation.

Modern Socialism is but the expression of a feeling which is as old as life itself—the feeling that our existence is somehow incomplete, truncated, abnormal, and hence unhappy. The socialist idea is an aspiration to a better life—a life no longer individualist, but one of community and brotherhood. We must admit that this feeling has acquired a new force; intellectual man has discovered a new path, a new source of enthusiasm. In ancient times men waxed enthusiastic over their native cities, or over purely political states. These sentiments were doubtless noble when compared to the passionate interest of a cannibal in a meal made off his enemy's flesh, or to the purely financial interest of a Swiss mercenary of a Pope or King of Naples. But nowadays they are regarded as being on a level with a child's taste for toys and sweet-meats, as something holding out the prospect of immediate enjoyment. The same may be said of the deputy's love of well-paid appointments—a proclivity justifiable in the past, a legitimate passion under the Restoration and in the time of Louis Philippe, but one that no longer holds any attraction for men impressed with Socialism.

Socialism, a new movement, creates new desires and new passions, which cannot be grasped by men of the old order, any more than the aspirations of a young man can be understood by a child or by an old man in second childhood. Desires and passions are never negative; they are the soul asserting itself, as the intellect asserts itself with problems. A dogma is an 'affirmation of the soul' in the past; an axiom is an 'affirmation of the mind', like-wise in the past. A problem and a desire are affirmations of a mind and a soul looking towards the future. Society buries itself beneath dogmas and axioms; desires and problems resuscitate it.

A moribund society clings to dogmas and axioms. This is the kind of society that accepts nothing and denies everything; it is this society that is a negation. All those who have resisted the Church or the law have been merely negative; servants of authority or of the Church, ministers of monarchy or of heresy, they have never 'affirmed', only protested. Luther and Calvin protested against the Church, as Mr. Guizot and Mr. Thiers protest against the Republic.

In this lies the great difference between the modern socialists and the schismatics and heresiarchs of the past. The latter sought to defend themselves against a dogma, and its implications, which threatened their legitimate rights as individuals. Socialism calls on all individuals and states to sacrifice their rights to an idea which contains the seed of a universal dogma. Schismatics and heresiarchs have so far succeeded in retaining their place in the world. Today their true character stands revealed; for all of them, schismatics and heresiarchs alike, are already united against Socialism. They are all, confessedly, anti-social.

TRIBUTES BY CONTEMPORARIES OF MICKIEWICZ

ALEXANDER PUSHKIN

Sonnet[1]

Stern Dante did not scorn the sonnet; in it Petrarch
poured forth the fire of love; Macbeth's creator loved its
play; Camões clothed in it his sorrowful thought. In our
day too it captivates the poet; Wordsworth has chosen it
as his instrument when, far from the bustling world, he
depicts ideal nature. In the shade of distant Tauris'
mountains the singer of Lithuania for a moment confined
his dreams in its cramped frame. In our land maidens did
not yet know it when for its sake Delvig already was
forgetting the sacred melodies of the hexameter.

To Mickiewicz[2]

He lived among us, amid a race that was foreign to him.
He cherished in his soul no bitterness against us, and we
loved him. Peaceful, kindly, he visited our gatherings. We

1. Published in May 1830 in the *Moskovsky Vestnik* (Moscow Herald).
2. This poem, dated 10 August 1834, was not published in Pushkin's lifetime.

shared with him pure dreams and song (his inspiration came from on high, and it was from on high that he looked on life). He spoke not seldom of the time that was coming, when the peoples, forgetting their feuds, would be united in one great family. We listened eagerly to the poet. He departed westward and our blessing attended him on his way. But now our peaceful guest has become our enemy, and, to flatter an unruly mob, he infuses poison into his poetry. From afar the voice of the embittered poet reaches us, a voice we knew! . . . O God, sanctify his heart with Thy truth and with peace.

CHARLES DE MONTALEMBERT

Introduction to the translation into French of
The Book of the Polish Pilgrims, 1834

Since then, Mickiewicz' soul, wedded to the destiny of his
country, appears to have grown greater with its advers-
ities. The admirable drama *Dziady* [*Forefathers' Eve*], part
of which was written since the latest catastrophe, is destined
to save from oblivion the Vilna persecution of which he
himself was among the victims. We know nothing superior
to this work in modern literature. In it a genius which is
both intensely Catholic and intensely national has ranged
through the entire realm of poetry, from the bitter,
vengeful vigour of satire to so ardent and sublime a
piety that it might have been drawn from the legends
of the early Church or from the concerts of the heavenly
spirits.

Yet, at the same time, still under the guidance of his
grief and his patriotism, he has not feared to grapple with
the vastest problems of the future.

The *Book of the Polish Pilgrims* is the first revelation of
this new course which his genius has taken. Never, it
seems to us, has a bolder and firmer hand unveiled the
destiny which awaits the political and social organization
of our days, apart from any question of nationality or party.

His poetical imagination is at home amid the symbolism, as national as it is evangelical, which he has employed to render his work accessible, so far as the form is concerned, to the most simple minds, as he has placed it, in the matter of content, on the level of the loftiest thought which has ever honoured mankind. To achieve this end he has made use of the Biblical language which has been stabilized and popularized in Poland, as it has been in Germany and England, by translations of the Scriptures made about the end of the sixteenth century.

JULES MICHELET

Speech delivered at the Collège de France, in Paris,
23 December 1847

Our illustrious colleague and friend Mickiewicz once
spoke to me of the impression he received as a child when
those masses of men on their return from Moscow reached
Lithuania, where he was then at school, and of the relations
which he had with them. It was the time of the year when
the intense cold was beginning to set in; the Poles were
in a state of intense uneasiness, of extraordinary suspense
and anxiety. Every morning people went to consult the
thermometer and were alarmed to see it steadily falling.
Then, gradually, men began to arrive in ever greater
numbers until the city was full of them: houses, public
buildings, the college where Mickiewicz then was—all
without exception were crowded. The cold was growing
sharper, and the people lighted fires everywhere for them.
In the halls, in the corridors, everywhere were soldiers,
Frenchmen. Mickiewicz, who was then 14 years of age,
went from time to time to gaze at these phantoms. Numbers of them had marched until long after their strength
was spent, by virtue of some inner energy which found
no explanation in their external appearance. The great poet
at once observed a thing which no one else has related:

these old soldiers did not lie down to sleep; at night, around the fire, there they were always, musing, with their heads resting on their elbows. They had lost the faculty of sleep, being so well used to hardship and fatigue, so unaccustomed to rest. They were brooding over the great story they had lived. It was too much, you will appreciate, for the same men to have begun in 1792 and, in 1812, to find themselves there; the thing was excessive, beyond the capacities of men. And so the story kept returning to their minds and they remained there, musing around the fire.

The great poet of the dead (this is the title of Mickiewicz' first work) after gazing long at them with a gravity beyond his years, ventured to ask a question of these old men: 'You are well on in years; how did you come to leave your country at your age, and, this time, to go so far from home?' And then these old grenadiers, twirling their long white moustaches, replied simply: 'We couldn't leave him, couldn't let him go all alone.'

Here was the profound voice of the Grande Armée: 'We couldn't let him go!' And the last phrase is sublime: 'Let him go alone!' So then, these old soldiers counted as nothing the new generations and the 50 nations whom Napoleon swept along with him. Without them Napoleon would have been alone.

A great reply, the profound voice of the heart of France. The heart had survived the sacrifice. This was the most precious treasure of the rout, and it was saved in this way, preserved by a Polish child. And he has kept this treasure. It is this that has sustained him through so many ordeals. By this force of memory, at a time when France has forgotten so much, Mickiewicz has remained, if I could venture to say it in this place, almost more French than France.

GEORGE SAND

Essay on the Drama of Fantasy
Goethe—Byron—Mickiewicz[1]

． ． ． ． ． ． ． ． ． ． ． ． ． ． ． ． ．

The real name for these strange, daring works, the product
of an age of philosophical scrutiny, to which nothing in
the past can be compared, is that of metaphysical drama.
From among a number of more or less noteworthy
attempts in this field, three take their place in the front
rank: *Faust*, which Goethe styles a tragedy, *Manfred*,
which Byron calls a dramatic poem, and the third part
of the *Dziady* [*Forefathers' Eve*], to which Mickiewicz
gives the more unassuming title of act.

These three works are, I venture to say, very little
known in France. *Faust* is really understood only by what
is called the intellectual aristocracy; *Manfred* has contributed little, even in England, to the glory of Byron,
although it is perhaps the most magnificent flight of his
genius. Included as a make-weight in his collected works,
if it has been read at all it has been proclaimed inferior to
The Corsair, *The Giaour* and *Childe Harold*, all of which,
however, are only either reflections of his genius, adapted
to the requirements of the ordinary run of readers, or

---

1. *Revue des deux mondes*, December 1839.

incomplete sketches of the poet's thought. As for this act of the *Dziady*, by Adam Mickiewicz, I venture to assert that it has not found a hundred readers in France, and I know of fine minds which have been unable or unwilling to understand it.

.   .   .   .

He [Mickiewicz] does not confuse the framework with the idea, as Goethe does in *Faust*. Neither does he separate the frame from the idea, as Byron does in *Manfred*. Real life is in itself a vigorous, arresting, terrible picture, and the idea is in the heart of it. The world of fantasy is not outside or above or beneath; it is in the core of everything, it moves everything, it is the soul of all reality, it resides in all the facts. Every character, every group, carries it within itself and manifests it after its own fashion. All Hell is unchained, but the host of Heaven is also present; and, while the demons triumph on the material plane, they are vanquished on the intellectual plane. To the temporal power belong the ukazes of the *knutopotent* Tsar, the tortures, the hangmen's arms, exile, the fetters, the instruments of torment; to the angels belong the spiritual kingdom, the heroic soul, the pious aspirations, the holy indignation, the prophetic dreams, the divine ecstasy of the victims. But these heavenly rewards are won through martyrdom, and it is scenes of martyrdom which the sombre brush of Mickiewicz brings before our eyes. These paintings are such as neither Byron nor Goethe nor Dante could have created. Perhaps even in the life of Mickiewicz himself has there been only one moment when this truly supernatural inspiration was vouchsafed to him. At all events, persecution, torture and exile have developed in him potentialities which were unknown to him before; nothing in his first productions, admirable as they already were, although in a less austere style, gave any indication that there existed within the poet this chord of malediction and grief which the ruin of his country has made simultaneously to quiver, to thunder and to groan. Since the tears and the imprecations of the prophets of Zion no voice had been raised with such power to sing so vast a theme as that of the fall of a nation. But, if the lyricism and splendour of the sacred chants have never in any epoch been surpassed, the human spirit has in our day revealed an aspect which was not displayed in the time of the Hebrew prophets and which casts an immense radiance upon modern poetry. It is the philosophical feeling which extends to infinity the narrow horizon of the people of God. Jew and Gentile exist no longer; all the inhabitants of the globe are the people of God and the earth is the holy city which, through the mouth of the poet, invokes the justice and the mercy of Heaven.

.   .   .   .

But what matters the language in which genius pronounces its oracles? The language of Mickiewicz is Catholicism, true. I cannot believe that, for the great minds which still remain under this veil, the formulas have not a wider sense than the mere words imply. The Catholicism of Mickiewicz, sincere as it may be, lends itself to allegory as readily as the mocking catholicism of *Faust* and *Manfred*'s pagan fantasy.

This vigorous and menacing Catholicism is far removed from the apathetic resignation of Silvio Pellico. Konrad is the antithesis of that kind of ecstatic submissiveness which

is worthy of India, perhaps, but which is certainly un-
worthy of Europe. His burning energy breaks out in
accents which would make God himself grow pale, if God
were the miserable Jehovah who plays with the peoples
on earth as a chess-player does with the kings and pawns
on the chess-board. Accordingly, the silence of this divinity
whose merciless laws Konrad cannot understand enrages
and bewilders him—a remarkable protest on the part of
the Catholic poet against the God whom his dogma pro-
poses to him, a protest to which Catholicism can find no
reply and which Mickiewicz himself cannot refute when
he has launched it! Oh great poet! Philosopher in spite of
yourself! You are right to curse this God whom the
Church has given you! But to us who conceive of a greater
and a juster God your blasphemy appears as the most
religious outburst of your generous soul!

The angel reminds Konrad of his past revolts, of his
disregard of Heaven.

This monologue of the angel, a gracious, charming
peristyle set at the entrance to an abyss, is followed by the
attacks of the demons.

The devils offer a furious opposition, and to anyone
who reads the little volume of the *Dziady* right through,
they will at first sight appear to have been borrowed from
Callot or from the legends of the Middle Ages, much more
than from poetic allegory. But, if one considers the matter,
one perceives that this hell is appropriate to the subject
and contains a biting satire. Within the innumerable hosts
of wicked spirits which are for religious poetry the symbol
of every vice and every evil, there are several hierarchies.
Goethe's mocking demon is a Voltairean Frenchman.

Byron's dark genius is the romantic spirit of the nineteenth century. Mickiewicz' Beelzebub is brutal despotism, the patron spirit of the Tsar; he is a base, bloody, gross monster, ferocious and stupid.

.   .   .   .

To sum up, we would say that we see in *Faust* the urge to poetize Spinoza's deified nature; in *Manfred*, the desire to give man a part worthy of his faculties and aspirations within this divinized nature; in *Konrad*, an attempt to justify the work of creation in the thought of man by justifying the lot of man upon the earth. None of these poems completely attained its goal. But to how many valiant and tragic works will the fever of poetic inspiration yet give rise before mankind can produce the singer of hope and certainty!

ERNEST RENAN

Speech delivered in the name of the Collège de France
on the occasion of the exhumation of the ashes of Adam
Mickiewicz in the cemetery of Montmorency, 28 June 1890

Not all of Adam Mickiewicz is leaving us. We shall still
possess his spirit, his memory. Our old halls will keep the
distant echo of his voice. A few survivors of those heroic
times can still tell us of the intoxication, the magic, the
enchanting power that lay in his words. Associated in a
glorious trinity with two other names that are dear to us,
those of Michelet and Quinet, the name of Mickiewicz has
become for us a symbol, an inseparable part of our old
glories and our old joys.

For your illustrious compatriot, gentlemen, had the
master quality through which men dominate their age—
sincerity, disinterested enthusiasm, selflessness, which
creates a spiritual state in which a man does not do or
say or write what he wishes, but in which he does, says
and writes what is dictated by a spirit existing outside of
himself. This spirit is nearly always the age, the eternal
invalid who desires that we caress his wounds and calm
his fever with sonorous words. It is, still more, the race,
the inner voice of ancestors and blood. Mickiewicz possessed these two great sources of inspiration.

When George Sand comprehended his genius at the

first word it uttered, it was because she understood that that heart had suffered all of our wounds, that it had throbbed at all of our convulsions. The glory of our age is to have aspired to achieve the impossible, to solve the insoluble. Glory to it!

Men of action who may endeavour to carry out this programme in all its immensity, will all prove impotent; men of reason will attain only contradictions. But the poet, he who does not doubt, who after each defeat sets to work again, stronger and more ardent, is never dismayed. Such a one was Mickiewicz. He had within him the sources of resurrection without number. He experienced the cruellest anguish, but despair never; his unshakable faith in the future derived from a profound instinct, from something which exists within us and which speaks to us more loudly than dismal reality can do—the spirit of the past, the feeling of fellowship with that which does not die. The strong man is he in whom a form of the universal consciousness is thus incarnated, who accomplishes his human destiny as the ant works, as the bee makes its honey.

Sprung from that family of the Aryan race which has most carefully husbanded the original gifts, from Lithuania, which, by its language, its calm, its moral earnestness, is the best representative of our upright, grave ancestors, Mickiewicz was attached to past centuries by links of secret communication which made of him a seer of the past. And at the same time he was a seer of the future. He believed in his race; but he believed above all things in the divine spirit which animates all things that contain the breath of life and, through all the clouds, he perceived a brilliant future in which poor mankind will receive consolation for its sufferings. This great idealist was a great patriot; but he was above all a believer; and, as the true reason for belief in immortality are the martyrs, his prophetic imagination convinced him that it was not in vain that mankind had toiled so long and the victims suffered so much.

It was for this reason that enlightened French society so gladly welcomed this great and noble mind, associated him with the dearest of its possessions, appointed him, readily and almost without consulting him, member of a triumvirate to defend liberty and to resist perverted religion. The day when Slavonic culture had won its place among those national cultures which are the object of scientific study, when the creation of a Chair of Slavonic Languages and Literatures was decided, the men who at that time directed the intellectual life of France conceived the eminently liberal idea of entrusting the post to Mickiewicz. The poet, the man who represents the soul of a people, who is the repository of its legends, who intuitively understands its earliest history, was preferred for the task of profound analysis of a race, to the scholarly recluse who operates only with books. They were right. The living meadow with its flowers is superior to the dried-up herbarium which offers only a pale memory of life. The volumes which comprise Mickiewicz' first courses of lectures are a treasure-house of original material on the early history of the Slavonic race, material which the professor expounded as a scholar and felt like a man of the people.

He was accused of ranging beyond his curriculum. Ah! How difficult it is to restrict oneself to the limits of a curriculum when one is intoxicated with the infinite.

Such as he was, with his bold divinations, his overflowing aspirations, his noble, prophetic illusions, we are proud of him, and, although political scruple has retarded the decree announcing his official nomination, we have inscribed his name upon the marble tablets which carry the names of our predecessors. He had for him the best of decrees, that which is countersigned by public enthusiasm.

From the hospitable land where he has rested for 35 years you are about to transport him to your Saint-Denis, to those vaults of Wawel, where your ancient sovereigns rest. He will be there beside Kosciuszko and Poniatowski, the only members of that noble assemblage of the dead who were not kings. Beside those who drew the sword you have been pleased to lay the inspired poet who gave a voice to your ardent, strong genius, to your exquisite legends, to everything which, in your national heritage, transports and consoles, arouses tears and smiles. Thereby you give a great lesson in idealism: you proclaim that a nation is a spiritual thing, that it possesses a soul which may not be subdued with the weapons which subdue the body.

Great and illustrious colleague, from the royal tomb which the admiration of your compatriots has prepared for you, remember France. Poor France, she does not forget, be sure of it. What she has once loved she loves for ever. What she applauded in your words she would still applaud. The tribune which she offered you she would offer you in greater freedom today. From that tribune you would hesitate now to recall so often the memory of victories, but you would find heartfelt words to teach the duties of the vanquished. Go to the glory which you have earned, return, amid the homage of the peoples, to that country which you loved so well. We limit our ambition to one thing alone: it is, that your tomb proclaim that you were once one of us, that men may know, in the Poland of the future, that there was, in the days of ordeal, a liberal France which welcomed you, applauded you, loved you.

PRINCIPAL

TRANSLATIONS OF

MICKIEWICZ'

WORKS

The poetry of Mickiewicz is very much alive. Whilst in Poland numerous new editions of his works are constantly appearing, and his books, in accordance with his own dearest wish, are 'finding their way into the cottages', the number of translations of his works into foreign languages is continually increasing, side by side with the interest of the reading public and of writers of biography. This new interest in Mickiewicz is concerned as much with his extraordinary personality as his literary works.

Translations of Mickiewicz have appeared in almost every European language and many Oriental ones. Approximately 1,000 translations—in thirty-three different languages—have reproduced the spirit of his poetry, an arduous task since Mickiewicz, like every poet, is very difficult to translate.

Amongst the works that have been translated are to be found those gems of lyric poetry, the *Crimean Sonnets*, poetic prose of a rare spiritual quality, historical and epic poems, a mystery play, his remarkable lectures on Slavonic literature given at the Collège de France, a volume of courageous and revolutionary political articles, and, in particular, the outstanding epic poem of the nineteenth century, *Pan Tadeusz*, a poem of almost 10,000 lines which has been translated in all twenty-eight times.

The real reputation of Mickiewicz and the beginning of his fame in Europe can be dated from 1834, the year which saw the publication of the French translation of *The Book of the Polish Pilgrims*, by Montalembert and Lemaître simultaneously, as well as English, German, and Lithuanian versions of the same poem, while an Italian translation running into five editions appeared in the following year. *The Book of the Polish Pilgrims* was a small volume whose aim and nature were frankly political, written in a New Testament style, and denouncing Europe, with a fearful logic, for the crime of the partition of Poland. The accusations contained in this little book threw European opinion into turmoil. Everybody read it. 'The thing above all that makes the Polish cause undying', wrote Montalembert in the preface to his translation, 'is that it is the cause of all countries, of all peoples of the world.'

This little book was welcomed with particular enthusiasm by youthful idealists, dreaming of freedom, as well as by underground revolutionary organizations such as the Carbonari, which found in it a spirit akin to their own. It aroused the same enthusiasm in Germany as in Italy, where close ties linked Mickiewicz to the patriotic revolutionary movement.

Mickiewicz condemned despotism and advocated the brotherhood and common loyalty of peoples, calling on them to help one another in the struggle for freedom. In all the most frequently translated works of Mickiewicz at this period we find the same ideas: in the *Ode to Freedom* and in *Konrad Wallenrod*, and in a third poem, the most popular of all, which, even when translated into prose, could not fail to stir the consciences of its readers—the moving appeal entitled *To a Polish Mother*. These poems appeared in newspapers and also in pamphlet form.

French translations of Mickiewicz, although relatively numerous, do not reveal, unfortunately, a very thorough knowledge of the poet's work. Most of these translations were made by Poles who, in spite of their long acquaintance with the French language, lacked the necessary gifts for translating poetry. Inspired by a purely political enthusiasm, and lacking literary talent, it must be confessed that they have done no service to the genius and reputation of their fellow-countryman.

Fortunately there were also many gifted French writers who, in their prose translations, in the French tradition, reconstituted perfectly the beauty of the original. Amongst these, the greatest praise is due to the eminent French man of letters and student of Poland and of Polish literature, Paul Cazin, to whom we owe a new translation, the third, of *Messire Thadée* (1934), published on the occasion of the hundredth anniversary of this epic.

Mickiewicz also wrote in French, in which language he is the author of literary and historical sketches, of lectures delivered at the University of Lausanne and the Collège de France, of historical plays and political articles, written in 1849, of which seventy-six are published in the revolutionary Paris paper *La Tribune des peuples*. These articles, although originally written in French, have been published in volumes of translations and in this way have been made available to large numbers of readers throughout Europe.

The Italian translations, less numerous—approximately 100 —have appeared chiefly in the centres formed in several Italian cities for the cult of the Polish poet. The followers of Towiański's mystic theory, which for a time had influenced Mickiewicz, created an atmosphere of interest around the poet's work in Turin. Three eminent Italian scholars, Aurelio Palmieri, Enrico Damiani and Giovanni Maver, have contributed greatly by their translations and publications to spreading a knowledge of Mickiewicz in modern Italy. In 1924 Clotilda Garosci had already made a new and very fine translation (the second in Italian) of *Pan Tadeusz*. A magnificent collectors' edition of the translation of the *Crimean Sonnets* was published in Florence in 1929 by Tyszkiewicz. The translations of Mickiewicz into Italian are remarkable on the whole for their fidelity and their high literary standard.

Unfortunately it cannot be said that translations into other Latin languages achieve more than a pale reflection of the poet's genius. The Spanish translation of *Pan Tadeusz* is incapable of reproducing the beauty of this epic. In Rumania it is only recently that interest in Mickiewicz has been aroused.

Germany took an early interest in Mickiewicz. The attitude of sympathy with Poland which prevailed in certain European circles after the suppression of the 1831 rising, had also spread to Germany. To this favourable attitude must be ascribed the numerous pamphlets and political poems dedicated to the Polish cause. Entire volumes of these writings in English, French and especially in German could be collected, and in fact this work has already been begun. Amongst the authors are some of the greatest poets and publicists of the day.

The relatively high number of German translations (approximately 150) was further increased by Polish translators, though in this case with better results than in France. These translations are characterized on the whole by their great fidelity; they had a wide circulation and were usually the first in existence. As early as 1834, the Germans had a translation of *Konrad Wallenrod*, and they were the first to translate *Pan Tadeusz* in 1836. In the same year, a translation of all the lyric poems was published. The famous German composer, Karl Loewe, set five of them to music. The Germans were also the first to publish, in four volumes, the translation of the Paris lectures: *Vorlesungen über slavische Literatur und Zustände* (1843).

Very early too, Germany had an excellent translation of the sonnets by Cornelius (1869). *Pan Tadeusz* was translated twice more, and one of these translations, by Lipiner, who also

produced an excellent version of *Forefathers' Eve* is particularly
remarkable. Germany has improved on old translations and
produced new ones (Rutra, 1919) and lastly, under the Democratic Republic an important volume of entirely new translations has been published (1953). A new translation by C. von
Pentz is scheduled for publication in the German Federal
Republic in the near future.

Amongst the English translations, about seventy in
number, a small proportion of which were the work of Poles,
the interest in the poem *Konrad Wallenrod* is most notable.
There are also two complete translations and one partial
translation of *Pan Tadeusz*. The merit of translating Mickiewicz
and making him popular in the Anglo-Saxon world belongs
to two women, fervent admirers of his poetry: M. A. Biggs,
the translator of *Konrad Wallenrod* and of *Pan Tadeusz* (1885),
and Monica Gardner, the author of a monograph in English
on Mickiewicz (1911), who was killed during the bombing of
London in the last war.

After 1914, interest in the Polish poet moves from England
to the United States. At Berkeley, California, thanks to the
efforts of Professor George Rapall Noyes, an important
University Centre for the translation and study of the works
of Mickiewicz was set up. This centre produced a new translation of *Pan Tadeusz* (1917, three editions) by Noyes, and
later a long series of other works, faithfully re-translated by a
team of his students and collaborators, with the effective help
and criticism of the Professor himself. Thus, in the space of
thirty years of collective work, in an atmosphere of profound
admiration for the poet and knowledge of his work, and thanks
also to the development of real poetic gifts in several of the
translators, a new Mickiewicz, in English, and much more
accessible to the contemporary reader of 1944, made its
appearance. We owe this achievement to Noyes who, in his
introductions and commentaries, has made an original and

valuable contribution to our knowledge of the poet. A second Research Centre devoted to the study of Mickiewicz has been set up in the United States at the University of New York, by the specialist in Slavonic studies, Arthur Prudden Coleman, the promoter of many translations and of much research on this subject.

Swedish translations of Mickiewicz are not numerous (fourteen only); but amongst them are two of *Pan Tadeusz* which have received high praise from the critics, the first by Alfred Jensen (1898) who had also adapted the *Ballads and Romances* and the second by the Swedish poetess Ellen Wester, writing under the name of E. Weer (1926).

The Lithuanians have always shown a keen interest in Mickiewicz. About 100 translations show this, though most of them are of little significance. However, two complete versions of *Pan Tadeusz* exist in Lithuanian (1924).

In Hungary, with the exception of two editions of the translation of the *Crimean Sonnets*, there are no important translations. It was only in 1950 that a new volume of translations was published. The complete translation of *Pan Tadeusz* by J. Sziklay, is still awaiting a publisher. Finland is able to boast complete translations of *Pan Tadeusz* (1921), *Grażyna* and *Konrad Wallenrod*.

Amongst translations into other languages, we must mention the Hebrew version of *Pan Tadeusz* by Joseph Lichtenbaum (Tel Aviv, 1953) and the Yiddish translation by David Königsberger (Lwów, 1939), a victim of the Nazis.

It is into the Slavonic languages that Mickiewicz has been the most frequently and faithfully translated. The Slavonic versions of his works constitute more than half the total number of translations, a fact which explains the profound influence of Mickiewicz on the Slavonic peoples. His poetry awakened national consciousness, raised the banner of revolt against tyranny, introduced ideas of freedom, a new vision of the world, and above all a beauty of poetic expression hitherto unknown.

The Russian translations are the most numerous (approximately 200), and this in spite of the Russian censorship, which prevented the publication of several works and made disastrous cuts in others. Mickiewicz has been translated by the following great Russian poets: Pushkin, Lermontov, Fet, Ivan Bunin, Constantin Balmont and others. The edition of his complete (or almost complete) works, a collective work, ran into five editions and, with the exception of the Polish one, was the most important and the best edition brought out in the Slavonic countries in the nineteenth century.

After the October Revolution, a new era began in Russia for the reputation of Mickiewicz. It was marked by the completion of new translations of a high literary value, unabridged and faithful to the original, and printed in large editions. Several important volumes of selected works appeared, as well as three volumes out of five of the complete works, and several de luxe editions. New versions of *Pan Tadeusz* (the fourth), the *Crimean Sonnets* (which had already been translated eight times), *Konrad Wallenrod* (also previously translated several times) and *Grażyna*, as well as most of the other poems of Mickiewicz, constitute an unforeseen profusion of production requiring critical study.

In the Ukraine, there are several dozen translations of Mickiewicz. The Ukrainians can be justly proud of their version of *Pan Tadeusz* written in 1927 by their greatest contemporary poet Maxime Rylski, translated into Byelorussian by a Pole, W. Marcinkiewicz, it was the first translation of this poem into a Slavic language; unfortunately only the first chapters still exist (second edition, 1907).

The Czechs have developed an extraordinary cult of Mickiewicz and possess more than a hundred translations, of which many are excellent, including that of *Pan Tadeusz* and two versions of *Forefathers' Eve*, by the greatest contemporary Czech poets, J. Vrchlický, and Halas who died recently. Mickiewicz, as the Czech critics insist, had a profound influence on the development of literature and the awakening of national consciousness in the first half of the nineteenth century.

Amongst the other Slav peoples, the Serbs and the Croats (eighty translations) possess a classic translation of *Pan Tadeusz* by Maretic (1893) and a new and excellent version of *Forefathers' Eve* by Benesic (1948). The Bulgarians have translated short works of Mickiewicz as well as *Konrad Wallenrod*. In addition, a translation of *Pan Tadeusz* (1901) will in the near future be replaced by a new verse translation.

The history of the spread of the knowledge of the works of Mickiewicz in Europe and America requires much more study and analysis. The basic guide for such study will be the *Detailed Bibliography of Translations of Mickiewicz into all Languages*, collected by Alexander Semkowicz (1885–1954), which is to be published in Warsaw, as the second volume of a *Bibliography of the Works of Mickiewicz*. This work will show the exact number and variety of the translations of the poet's works.

The translations into English, French, German, Italian, Russian and Spanish, grouped below in chronological order, and with brief analyses, constitute a selection of the principal translations of the works of Mickiewicz, most of them published separately. This selection does not take into account the quality of the translations. Insignificant and ephemeral versions of the poet's works that have appeared in the daily press have been omitted.

TRANSLATIONS INTO ENGLISH

SONGS OF THE PEOPLE. *The Metropolitan*, London, November 1831.
O pieśni gminna. First work of the poet to be translated into English.

PHARIS. Translated by Henry Reeve. *The Metropolitan*, London, 1833, no. 7.
Farys.

THE BOOKS AND THE PILGRIMAGE OF THE POLISH NATION. Translated
from the Polish. London, J. Ridgway, 1833, v+95 p.
Księgi narodu i pielgrzymstwa polskiego, an anonymous publication translated by a Pole, Lech Szyrma.

CONRAD WALLENROD. An historical poem, founded on events in the annals
of Lithuania and Prussia. Translated from the Polish of Adam Mickiewicz
by Leon Jabłoński. Edinburgh, F. A. Crawford, 1841, xviii+123 p.
Konrad Wallenrod, inept prose translation.

CONRAD WALLENROD. An historical tale from the Prussian and Lithuanian
annals, translated from the Polish of Adam Mickiewicz by H. Cattley.
London, Smith, 1841, xiv+163 p.

CONRAD WALLENROD. An historical poem, translated from the Polish into
English verse by Maude Ashurst Biggs. London, Trübner, 1882, 99 p.

CONRAD WALLENROD. An historical poem. By Adam Mitskievitch (spelt
in Polish, Mickiewicz). Translated from the Polish by Michael H. Dzie-
wicki. London, Richardson, 1883, xxxii+128 p.

MASTER THADDEUS, OR THE LAST FORAY IN LITHUANIA. Translated from
the original by Maude Ashurst Biggs. With a preface by W. R. Morfill,
M.A. London, 1885, 2 vol., xxiv+316, 268 p.
Pan Tadeusz, translation in blank verse, well received by the English
critics.

PAN TADEUSZ, OR THE LAST FORAY IN LITHUANIA. A story of life among

Polish gentlefolk in the years 1811 and 1812. Translated from the Polish by George Rapall Noyes. London and Toronto, Dent, 1917, xxiv+354 p. 2nd ed. 1920; 3rd ed. 1930.

Prose translation: the third edition was slightly revised.

GEMS OF POLISH POETRY. Selections from Mickiewicz. Translated by Frank H. Fortey. With an introduction by R. Dyboski. Warsaw, published under the auspices of the Polish Government, 1923, 99 p.

Contains a selection of 15 short texts: ballads, sonnets, an improvisation and 'The Vision of Father Peter', from *Dziady*.

KONRAD WALLENROD AND OTHER WRITINGS. Translated by Jewell Parish, Dorothea Prall Radin, George Rapall Noyes and others. Berkeley, California, University of California Press, 1925, 209 p.

Contains: Introduction (G. Rapall Noyes); *Konrad Wallenrod* (J. Parish), as well as 11 other works, including: *Forefathers' Eve (Dziady)*, part II, and *The Book of the Polish Nation and of the Polish Pilgrims (Księgi narodu i pielgrzymstwa polskiego)* (D. Prall Radin), and a selection of ballads and poems.

FOREFATHERS' EVE. Part III, scenes 2–5. Translated from the Polish by Dorothea Prall Radin. Edited by George Rapall Noyes. London, 1926. Reprinted from the *Slavonic Review*, 1925, vol. IV, no. 9–10.

CRIMEAN SONNETS. Translated by Edna Wothley Underwood. *The Slav Anthology*. Portland, Maine, Mosher Press, 1931, 346 p.

POEMS. Translated from the Polish of Adam Mickiewicz by Marjorie Beatrice Peacock and George Rapall Noyes. London, 1935. Reprinted from the *Slavonic Review*, 1935, vol. XIII, no. 39.

From the *Forefathers' Eve*, part III: 'The Road to Russia' (Droga do Rosji); 'The Suburbs of the Capital' (Przedmieścia stolicy); 'St. Petersburg'.

CRIMEAN SONNETS. Translated from the Polish by Dorothea Prall Radin, Benjamin Collins Woodbury, George Rapall Noyes and Doris Durst. London, 1938. Reprinted from the *Slavonic Review*, 1938, vol. XVI, no. 48.

THE LILIES. TWARDOWSKI'S WIFE AND RELIGIOUS POEMS. Translated by Dorothea Prall Radin. London, 1938. Reprinted from the *Slavonic Review*, 1938, vol. XVII, no. 49.

Contains: *The Lilies (Lilie)*; *Twardowski's Wife (Pani Twardowska)* *Reason and Faith (Rozum i wiara)*; *Protect me from Thyself (Broń mnie przed sobą...)*; *A Vision (Widzenie)*; *Spin Love (Snuć miłość)*; *Fragment of Improvisation (Fragment Improwizacji)*; *To Bogdan Zaleski (Do Bogdana Zaleskiego)*.

THE SAGES. Translated by G. Rapall Noyes. TO A POLISH MOTHER. Translated by G. Rapall Noyes and J. Parish. *The World's Great Catholic Poetry*. 1940, p. 16–18.

PAN TADEUSZ. Translated by Oliver Elton. *Slavonic Year Book 1939–1940*, p. 1–13.

Fragments from chapters I, II, IV, VIII, XI and Epilogue.

GRAŻYNA. Translated by Dorothea Prall Radin. *Poet Lore*. Boston, 1940, vol. XLVI, p. 3–43.

POEMS BY ADAM MICKIEWICZ. Translated by various hands and edited by George Rapall Noyes, Professor of Slavic Language in the University of California. Published by the Polish Institute of Arts and Sciences in America. New York, Herald Square Press, 1944, ix+486 p.

Contains: Introduction (G. R. Noyes); Collection of 64 works translated by nine translators: *Ballads* and various other poems; *Forefathers' Eve*, Part II; *Grażyna; Crimean Sonnets; Konrad Wallenrod; Faris; Forefathers' Eve*, Part III; *The Book of the Polish Nation and of the Polish Pilgrims;* Notes.

FOREFATHERS. Parts I and II in one volume. Translated from the Polish by Count Potocki of Montalk. London, *The Right Review*, 1944, 66 p.

MICKIEWICZANA. By A. P. and M. M. Coleman. New York, 1946.

Contains among other translations of seven works of Mickiewicz, made largely by Marion M. Coleman, in particular: *Forefathers' Eve*, part IV, autobiographical portions adapted by M. M. Coleman and Alvina Kruszewska; the beginning of *Pan Tadeusz* and other prose poems.

TRANSLATIONS INTO FRENCH

LE ROMANTISME. Traduit par Burgaud des Marets. *Le Figaro*, Paris, 1830, no. 1241.
Romantyczność, first prose translation in France of a poem of Mickiewicz.

KONRAD WALLENROD. Récit historique tiré des annales de Lithuanie et de Prusse. LE FARIS. SONNETS DE CRIMÉE. Traduits du polonais par MM. Felix Miaskowski et G. Fulgencé. Ornée du portrait de l'auteur. Paris, Librairie de Sédillot, 1830, 75 p.; 2ᵉ éd. 1830, 80 p.
First volume published in a French translation with the engraved portrait of the author by Croutelle. Contains the translation of *Faris* made by Mickiewicz for David d'Angers.

KONRAD WALLENROD. Roman historique traduit du polonais d'Adam Mickiewicz. Paris, Gagniard, 1830, xi + 163 p.
Anonymous translation—prose version by Henri Burgaud des Marets.

DITHYRAMBE À LA JEUNESSE. Traduit du poète polonais Adam Mickiewicz par M. Boyer-Nioche. Paris, 1831, typographie de I. Pinard, 4 p.
Oda do młodości.

LIVRE DES PÈLERINS POLONAIS. Traduit du polonais d'Adam Mickiewicz par le comte Ch. de Montalembert; suivi d'un *Hymne à la Pologne*, par F. de Lamennais. Paris, E. Renduel, 1833, lxxv + 176 p.; 2ᵉ éd. 1834.
Księgi narodu i pielgrzymstwa polskiego. Preface by Ch. de Montalembert.

KSIENGUI *(sic)* NARODU POLSKIEGO. Evangile de la nation polonaise pendant son pèlerinage. Traduit par L. Lemaître. Paris, Impr. de Brun, 1833, 124 p.; 2ᵉ éd. 1833, 31 p.
Translator's note: 'This translation is not complete. The original is reduced by half.'

LE FARIS. Poème d'Adam Mickiewicz; suivi de deux fragments de KONRAD WALLENROD par le même auteur, traduit du polonais par le comte Michel Borch. St-Pétersbourg, F. Bellizard, 1833, 47 p.

The translation is preceded by a poem by the translator dedicated to A. Mickiewicz.

DZIADY OU LA FÊTE DES MORTS. Poème traduit du polonais d'Adam Mickiewicz, 2e et 3e parties. Paris, Clétienne, 1834, vii + 174.

Prose translation by J. H. Burgaud des Marets, with an introduction by the translator to the text of Mickiewicz.

KONRAD WALLENROD. Poème traduit du polonais d'Adam Mickiewicz par A. R. Loison. Paris, Ledoyen, 1836, 193 p.

LA POLOGNE LITTÉRAIRE. Traduction et imitation en vers de Krasicki, Niemcewicz, Brodziński, Mickiewicz, etc. par Boyer-Nioche. Paris, Paulin, 1839, iv + 270 p.

Contains seven poems of Mickiewicz badly translated.

LES PRÉLUDES. Par Mme Caroline Pawlof, née Jaenisch. Paris, 1839.

Contains the following translations: *Le Faris*, *Chant du Waydelote lithuanien*, *Alpuhara*, *Chant lithuanien*, fragments from *Conrad Wallenrod*.

ŒUVRES D'ADAM MICKIEWICZ, professeur de littérature slave au Collège de France. Traduction nouvelle par Christien Ostrowski. Paris, H. L. Delloye, 1841, xii + 552.

Contains: *Les Aïeux* (*Dziady*, parts II, III, IV); 'Voyage en Russie' (part III of *Dziady*); *Grajina*; *Konrad Wallenrod*; *Les Pèlerins* (*Księgi narodu*).

ŒUVRES POÉTIQUES COMPLÈTES de Adam Mickiewicz, professeur de littérature et de langue slave au Collège de France. Traduction nouvelle d'après l'édition originale de 1844 par Christien Ostrowski. 2e éd., Paris, Charpentier, 1845, vol. I: xii + 552; vol. II: 423 p.; 3e éd. 1849; 4e éd. 1859; 5e éd. 1859.

Contains: Vol. I: reproducing the 1841 edition, with title-page changed. Vol. II: Sonnets, ballads and other poems, as well as *Zdania i uwagi*, Maxims. These translations by Ostrowski are in prose, with occasional passages in verse. They were badly received by the Polish critics.

L'ÉGLISE OFFICIELLE ET LE MESSIANISME. Par Adam Mickiewicz (cours de littérature slave du Collège de France, 1842–1844). Paris, 1845, vol. I: xii+548 p., 1 pl., vol. II: xv+304 p.

Title of vol. II: *L'Eglise et le Messie*.

LES SLAVES. Cours professé au Collège de France par Adam Mickiewicz et publié d'après les notes sténographiées. Tome premier: *Les pays slaves et la Pologne. Histoire et littérature (1840–41)*; Tome deuxième: *Les pays slaves et la Pologne (1841–42)*; Tome troisième: *La Pologne et le messianisme. Histoire, littérature et philosophie (1842)*. Paris, 1849, vol. I: iii+419 p.; vol. II: 450 p.; vol. III: 374 p.; 2e éd. Paris, 1866.

LA TRIBUNE DES PEUPLES. Journal quotidien. Paris, 1849 (15 mars–10 novembre).

Contains 76 political articles by Mickiewicz, partially reprinted in the collection *La Politique du XIXe siècle*, Paris, 1870: see below.

KONRAD WALLENROD ET GRAJINA. Traduction française par Christien Ostrowski. Traduction anglaise par Léon Jabłoński. Edition illustrée par Jean Tysiewicz. Paris, Impr. Benard, 1851, 268 p., 23 pl.

Text in Polish, French and English.

LES AÏEUX. 'Le Presbytère', IVe partie du poème de Mickiewicz. Traduit en vers par P. Dubois, précédée d'une préface par N. David. Paris, G. Jeune, 1851, 72 p.

Dziady, part IV.

EXTRAITS DES POÉSIES D'ADAM MICKIEWICZ. Traduits par Paul de Saint-Vincent (Wincenty Budzyński): 'Ecrivains et poètes modernes de la Pologne. Mickiewicz', *La Revue Contemporaine*, Paris, 15 novembre 1859, p. 126–55; 29 février 1860, p. 720–68.

Consists chiefly of fragments from nine works.

LES MANES. Poème d'Adam Mickiewicz. Suivi de quelques poésies du même auteur, traduites par le comte Michel Borch. Vilna, Zawadzki, 1859, 176 p., 2 pl.

Dziady, parts II and IV (incorrectly labelled I and II), as well as 13 lyric poems.

LE LIVRE DE LA NATION POLONAISE ET DES PÈLERINS POLONAIS d'Adam
Mickiewicz. Traduction nouvelle par Armand Lévy, avec introduction
et commentaires de Władislas Mickiewicz. Paris, E. Dentu, 1864, xxiv
+480 p.
Księgi narodu i pielgrzymstwa polskiego.

CONRAD WALLENROD. Légende historique, d'après les chroniques de
Lithuanie et de Prusse, par Adam Mickiewicz. Traduction de l'un des
fils de l'auteur avec introduction d'Armand Lévy et gravures sur acier
d'après Antoine Zalewski. Paris, Librairie du Luxembourg, 1866, viii+79 p.,
9 pl.
Translation by Jan Mickiewicz, the poet's son, who died young.

ZYWILA. Légende lithuanienne par Adam Mickiewicz, retrouvée et
publiée, texte et traduction en regard, par Władislas Mickiewicz. Avec une
eau-forte. Paris, Librairie du Luxembourg, 1866, 31 p., 1 pl.
Żywila, Polish and French texts.

DRAMES POLONAIS D'ADAM MICKIEWICZ. *Les Confédérés de Bar. Jacques
Jasiński ou les deux Polognes.* Publiés pour la première fois avec préface de
Władislas Mickiewicz. Paris, Librairie du Luxembourg, 1867, xvi+85 p.,
1 pl.

HISTOIRE POPULAIRE DE POLOGNE. Par Adam Mickiewicz. Publiée avec
préface, notes et chapitre complémentaire par Władislas Mickiewicz.
Paris, Hetzel, 1867, xxiv+617 p.
Contains an extract from the course of lectures given at the Collège
de France, prepared in 1850 in the presence of the poet and completed
by his son.

LA POLITIQUE DU DIX-NEUVIÈME SIÈCLE. Par Adam Mickiewicz. Publiée
avec préface et annotations par Władislas Mickiewicz. Paris, Librairie du
Luxembourg, 1870, lxxxi+505 p.
Contains: I. 'Polish politics' (articles from *Le Pèlerin polonais*);
II. 'French and universal politics' (articles from *La Tribune des peuples*);
III. 'Tsarism, Poland and Napoleon'.

MONSIEUR THADÉE DE SOPLICA, OU LE DERNIER PROCÈS EN LITHUANIE
'SUI GENERIS'. Récit historique en douze chants par Adam Mickiewicz.
Paris, 1876–77, vol. I: 307 p., vol. II: 318 p.

Pan Tadeusz, verse translation of poor quality, made by a Pole, Karol
Przeździecki (Charles de Noire-Isle).

MÉLANGES POSTHUMES D'ADAM MICKIEWICZ. Publiés avec introduction,
préfaces et notes par Władislas Mickiewicz. Deuxième série. Paris, Librairie
du Luxembourg, 1879, cxl+569 p.

Contains: I. Lithuanian legends: *Żywila, Korylla*. II. *Ce que femme
préfère*, a proverb. III. Literary articles: 'Examination of the libraries and
museums of Poland', 'The death of Garczyński'; 'Glance at the *Dziady*
and fragment from the first part'. IV. 'Apologetics for romanticism:
concerning romantic poetry. Reply to the Warsaw critics'. Translations
by Władisłas Mickiewicz. Part of these works were written in French
by the poet.

CYCLE LITHUANIEN. Première partie. *Adam Mickiewicz. Edouard Odyniec.*
Nice, Visconti, 1880, 319 p.

Contains: 33 inept translations of poems of Mickiewicz, by Karol
Przeździecki (Charles de Noire-Isle).

CHEFS D'ŒUVRE POÉTIQUES D'ADAM MICKIEWICZ (1798–1855). Traduits
par lui-même et par ses fils et suivis du *Livre de la nation polonaise et des
pèlerins polonais*, avec une notice sur la vie de l'auteur par Władislas Mickiewicz. Paris, G. Charpentier, 1882, 391 p.; 5ᵉ éd. 1924, 445 p.

Contains prose translations from: *Konrad Wallenrod*, a selection of
ballads, *Crimean Sonnets*; two sonnets, political poems, fragments from
Dziady, The Book of the Polish Nation and the Polish Pilgrims. The fifth
edition (1924) also contains *Grażyna*.

LA REDOUTE D'ORDON. D'après Adam Mickiewicz par Jules Perrin.
Paris, 1887, 8 p.

Reduta Ordona.

KONRAD WALLENROD. Poème polonais, traduit en vers français par
Venceslas Gasztowtt. Paris, C. Lévy, 1889, xi+103 p.

THADÉE SOPLITZA, OU LA LITHUANIE EN 1812. Poème traduit en vers français par V. Gasztowtt. Paris, Impr. A. Reiff, 1899, 256 p.
Pan Tadeusz, verse translation.

LE FARIS. Casside traduite en français par l'auteur et en arabe par M. Jamali. Paris, Le Caire, 1910, xiii+23 p.
Farys, French and Arabic texts.

CORRESPONDANCE (1820–1855). Publiée par Władislas Mickiewicz. Paris, Les Belles Lettres, 1924, 370 p.

PAGES CHOISIES. Paris, Ed. des Amis de la Pologne, 1927, 31 p. 2ᵉ éd. 1929.
Contains six short translations and fragments by various translators.

ADAM MICKIEWICZ (1798–1855). *Les Cent chefs d'œuvre étrangers*. Paris, 1928, p. 100–70.
Contains 15 translations of short works and several fragments of longer works.

L'HOMME ÉTERNEL. Pages choisies en prose, avec préface de M. André Maron et introduction de M. Joseph André Teslar. Paris, Gebethner et Wolff, 1929, xvi+261 p., 1 pl.
Contains five fragments from the correspondence selected from the *Livre des pèlerins*, from the Course in Slavic Literature, from the article in *La Tribune des peuples*, and from the contribution of Mickiewicz to the defence of Towiański.

POÉSIE. Choix de plus anciennes traductions, faites par les écrivains français, contemporains du poète. Paris, Société polonaise des amis du livre, 1929, 64 p.
Contains: 12 works and fragments: *Konrad Wallenrod* (Burgaud des Marets); *Dithyrambe à la jeunesse* (Boyer-Nioche); *Livre des pèlerins polonais* (Montalembert); *A une mère polonaise* (Baze); *Dziady* (Burgaud des Marets); *La Switezianka* (Burgaud des Marets); *La Tempête, Les Steppes d'Akerman* (Boyer-Nioche); *Le Faris* (Jaenisch-Pawlof); *La Mort du colonel* (Cassin); *Do Matki Polki* (P. N. Bonaparte); *Les trois fils de Boudrys* (Mérimée); Introduction and Notes (S. P. Koczorowski).

CHOIX DE POÈMES LYRIQUES. Adaptation de Thérèse Kœrner. Varsovie, Gebethner et Wolff, 1929, 31 p.

Contains 20 short works.

LES AÏEUX. Fragments. Traduction de Christien Ostrowksi. (Illustrations et gravures sur bois de Janusz Tłomakowski.) Paris, Les Amis de la Pologne, 1929, 43 p.

Preface by Rose Bailly.

MONSIEUR THADÉE. Quelques pages traduites en vers français par V. Gasztowtt et illustrées par Xavier Koźmiński. Paris, éd. par les Anciens élèves de l'Ecole polonaise de Batignolles et les Amis de la Pologne, 1929, 64 p.

Preface by S. Szpotański: 'V. Gasztowtt, Translator of Mickiewicz', by Ch. Brzezicki.

PAN TADEUSZ. Traduction de Paul Cazin. Préface de MM. Louis Barthou de l'Académie Française, Juliusz Kaden-Bandrowski de l'Académie de Pologne et Manfred Kridl, professeur de l'Université de Wilno. Paris, Alcan, 1934, xliii+398 p., 2e éd. Paris, Garnier, 1936, xvii+368 p.

LE LIVRE DES PÈLERINS POLONAIS. Texte présenté par Charles Journet. Paris, Fribourg, 1947, 146 p. (*Les Classiques de la politique*, no. 4.)

TRANSLATIONS INTO GERMAN

DAS MÄDCHEN VOM ŚWITEŹ. Übersetzt von Franz Pohl von Pollenburg. *Mnemosyne*, Lemberg, 1824, nr. 84.

Świtezianka, first German translation of a work by Mickiewicz; published in the German newspaper issued at Lwów in which several dozen poems by Mickiewicz had appeared by 1832, chiefly made by Poles.

DIE BÜCHER DES POLNISCHEN VOLKES UND DER POLNISCHEN PILGER-SCHAFT. Aus dem Polnischen des Mickiewicz übersetzt, von P.-J.–B. Gauger, Deutschland. Im Jahr der Gnade 1833, 122 S.

Księgi narodu i pielgrzymstwa polskiego. Anonymous translators. Printed at Paris. Following the title page, a dedication by the author in the following terms: 'Diese Bücher des Polnischen Volkes unter den Augen des Verfassers getreu ins Deutsche übertragen, widmet derselbe dem Deutschen Volke als Zeichen seiner aufrichtigsten Achtung und Dankbarkeit für die brüderliche Aufnahme, die ihm und seinen unglücklichen Landsleuten bei demselben auf ihrer Pilgerschaft zuteil geworden sind. Mickiewicz.'

BILDER AUS DER KRIM. Frei nach dem Polnischen des Mickiewicz von Gustav Schwab. *Deutscher Musenalmanach für das Jahr 1834*. Leipzig, 1833, S. 182–211.
Sonety krymskie.

RUSSLAND. EINE SCHILDERUNG VON ADAM MICKIEWICZ. Aus dem Polnischen von P. L. und F. N. Paris, 1833, 43 S.
'Ustęp' from *Dziady*, part III. One of the translators was the Pole Paweł Lewicki, of Zürich. Unsatisfactory translation, accompanied by erroneous commentaries.

DER POLNISCHE PARNASS ODER EINE AUSWAHL DER SCHÖNSTEN GEDICHTE aus vorzüglichsten polnischen Dichtern ins Deutsche übersetzt und herausgegeben von Juliusz Mendelson. Erste Lieferung. Kurze Gedichte von Adam Mickiewicz. Heidelberg, 1834, Winter, vii+124 S., 2. Aufl. Leipzig, Koehler, 1835.
Contains 25 translations including a choice of ballads, sonnets and various other poems.

NORDLICHTER. Eine Sammlung polnischer Dichtungen, ins Deutsche übertragen von Ludwik Nabielak und J. B. Werner. Mit Bildern von F. Fellner. Erstes Bändchen: *Farys, Konrad Wallenrod, Grażyna*. Stuttgart, Fr. Brodhag, 1834, 158 S., 3 Abb.

KONRAD WALLENROD. Geschichtliche Erzählung aus Lithauens und Preussens Vorzeit. Übersetzt von Karl Ludwig Kannegiesser. Leipzig, 1834, xviii+111 S.
Conscientious verse translation which had a favourable reception.

ADAM MICKIEWICZ SÄMMTLICHE WERKE. Erster Theil. Gedichte. Aus dem Polnischen übertragen von Carl Blankensee. Berlin, Naucksch, 1836, lxiv+343 S., 2 Abb.

Contains 88 successful translations: *Ballady i romanse*, various poems, sonnets and *Sonety krymskie*.

HERR THADDÄUS ODER DER LETZTE SAJASD IN LITHAUEN. Eine Schlecht-schitz-Geschichte aus den Jahren 1811 und 1812. Aus dem Polnischen des Adam Mickiewicz, in Gemeinschaft mit dem Dichter von R. O. Spazier. Leipzig, Weber, 1836, Bd. I: xv+348 S., 1 Abb., Bd. II: 288 S.

Mickiewicz later declared that he had taken no part in this translation, which was favourably received by the German critics.

VORLESUNGEN ÜBER SLAVISCHE LITERATUR UND ZUSTÄNDE. Gehalten im Collège de France in den Jahren von 1840–42 von Adam Mickiewicz. Deutsche, mit einer Vorrede des Verfassers versehene Ausgabe. Leipzig und Paris, Brockhaus, 1843, Bd. I: xxx+651 S., Bd. II: xiv+447 S., Bd. III: Leipzig, 1844, xxvii+357 S., Bd. IV: Leipzig, 1845, xiv+229 S. Neue Ausgabe, Bd. I–IV, ib. 1849.

Translated by Zygfryd Kunaszowski with the collaboration of K. Kunaszowski, N. Rembowski and Dr. Herman Everbeck.

BLÜTHEN SLAWISCHER POESIE. Herausgegeben von A. Bahn. I. Band: Die Polen. I. Abteilung: *Konrad Wallenrod*. Ein episches Gedicht von Adam Mickiewicz. Im Versmasse des Originals übersetzt von Otto Koniecki. Berlin, A. Faudel, 1855, xvi+103 S.

GRAŻYNA, DIE SCHÖNE FÜRSTIN, EINE LITHAUISCHE SAGE. *Farys*, ein beschreibendes Gedicht. *Alpuhara*, eine Ballade. Übersetzt von A. J. Bolek. Teschen, 1860, 78 S.

DIE SONETTE VON ADAM MICKIEWICZ. Deutsch von Peter Cornelius. Leipzig, Reclam, 1869, 46 S. (Reclam's *Universal-Bibliothek*, Bd. 76.)

One of the best German translations of Mickiewicz.

KONRAD WALLENROD von Adam Mickiewicz. Aus dem Polnischen metrisch übertragen von Dr. Albert Weiss. Bremen, Kühtmann, 1871, xiii+104 S., 2. Aufl. Norden, 1888.

BALLADEN UND ROMANZEN VON ADAM MICKIEWICZ. Aus dem Polnischen
metrisch übertragen von Dr. Albert Weiss. Leipzig, Reclam, 1874, 96 S.
(Reclam's *Universal Bibliothek*, Bd. 549.)

DER POLNISCHE PARNASS. Ausgewählte Dichtungen der Polen. Übersetzt
von Heinrich Nitschmann. Vierte sehr vermehrte Auflage. Leipzig,
Brockhaus, 1875.
Contains the biography of the poet and translations of 12 poems.

GRAŻYNA. LITHUANISCHE ERZÄHLUNG. Aus dem Polnischen übertragen
von Dr. Albert Weiss. Prag, Urbanek, 1876, x+58 S.

PETERSBURG VON ADAM MICKIEWICZ. Deutsch von Albert Zipper.
Hamburg, Günig, 1878, 51 S.
Fragment of 'Ustęp', from *Dziady*, part III.

MICKIEWICZ' POETISCHE MEISTERWERKE. Übersetzt von Gothilf Kohn.
Sanok, 1880, 275 S., 1 Abb.
Contains: the biography, *Ballady i romanse*, *Grażyna*, *Konrad Wallenrod*
and 21 poems.

HERR THADDÄUS ODER DER LETZTE EINTRITT IN LITHAUEN. Übersetzt von
Siegfried Lipiner. Leipzig, Breitkopf und Härtel, 1882, xvi+313 S.,
2. Aufl. 1898. (*Poetische Werke von Adam Mickiewicz*, Bd. I.)
This translation was considered excellent by the German critics.

HERR THADDÄUS ODER DER LETZTE EINTRITT IN LITHAUEN. Aus dem
Polnischen metrisch übertragen von Dr. Albert Weiss. Leipzig, W.
Friedrich, 1882, 281 S.
This translation has been superseded by Lipiner's superior version.

TOTENFEIER VON ADAM MICKIEWICZ. Übersetzt und mit erklärender
Einleitung versehen von Siegfried Lipiner. Leipzig, Breitkopf und Härtel,
1887, xxxii+284 S. (*Poetische Werke von Adam Mickiewicz*, Bd. II.)
The German critics considered this translation of *Dziady* as a classic
version.

JUNKER THADDÄUS. Schauspiel in 5 Aufzügen. Nach dem Epos *Pan Tadeusz* des Adam Mickiewicz, von Engelbert Rehbronn. Posen, Decker, 1891, 195 S.

GRAŻYNA (DIE SCHÖNE FÜRSTIN). Ein lithauisches Epos vom polnischen Weissage-Dichter Adam Mickiewicz, übersetzt von Johan Kuk. Milwaukee, Wis., 1894, 32 S., 1 Abb.

POETISCHE WERKE. I. Band. Eingeleitet von Prof. Dr. Brückner. Übertragen von Arthur Ernst Rutra. München, G. Müller, 1919, lii+281 S., 1 Abb. (*Polnische Bibliothek*, 2 Bd.)
    Contains: 'Der Dichter und sein Werk', by Alexander Brückner. Translations of: *Ballady i romanse*, a selection from various poems, *Sonety krymskie*, *Grażyna*, *Konrad Wallenrod*. Part of the poems are given in the translation of K. von Blankensee, modernized by A. E. Rutra.

SONETTE AUS DER KRIM. Nachdichtung und Vorwort von Arthur Ernst Rutra. München, Roland-Verlag, 1919, 44 S.

HERR THADDÄUS ODER DER LETZTE EINTRITT IN LITHAUEN. Übersetzt von Siegfried Lipiner. Freiburg i/B., F. Goerlich, 1952, 272 S. (*Deus et Anima*, 10 Bd.)

MICKIEWICZ. EIN LESEBUCH FÜR UNSERE ZEIT. Weimar, Thüringer Volksverlag, 1953, vii+439 S., 8 Abb.
    Contains: by 13 new translators, 43 translations of various poems, *Sonety krymskie*, extracts from *Dziady* and *Pan Tadeusz*, *Konrad Wallenrod* and a selection of the newspaper articles on revolutionary themes. As preface: 'Mickiewicz' von Ludwig Uhland; 'Die deutsch-polnische Freundschaft in der deutschen Literatur' von Jürgen Kuczyński; 'Leben und Grösse Adam Mickiewicz's' von Nikolaj Tichonov; 'Der feurige Kämpfer für die Freiheit der Völker' von Wanda Wasilewska; 'Das grösste Erbe des alten Polen' von Rosa Luxemburg; 'Die Begegnung mit Goethe'.

TRANSLATIONS INTO ITALIAN

GUIDA DEI PELLEGRINI POLACCHI. Italia, 1834.

Księgi narodu i pielgrzymstwa polskiego. At the same date and under the same title, two other editions were published at Rome and at Lugano.

IL LIBRO DEI PELLEGRINI POLACCHI. Versione italiana. Italia, 1835, 208 p.

IL LIBRO DEI PELLEGRINI POLACCHI DI ADAMO MICKIEWICZ. Con un proemio di Montalembert ed Inno alla Polonia di Lamennais. S.l., 1835, 162 p.

IL LIBRO DELLA NAZIONE POLACCA DAL PRINCIPIO DEL MONDO, FINO AL MARTIRIO DELLA POLONIA. MADRE POLACCA. ODE ALLA GIOVINEZZA. Traduzione di Alberto Redenti. *Annotatore*, Parma, 1860.

DEI CANTI POPOLARI ILLIRICI. Discorso detto da Adamo Mickiewicz nel Collegio di Francia a Parigi, e tradotto da Orsatto Pozza (Medo Pucić). Zara, 1860, 287 p.

Lectures by the poet on Serbian popular songs.

I PELLEGRINI POLACCHI. *Il Museo di Famiglia*, Milano, 1861, 270 p. Ed. 2: 1862.

In addition to selections from *Dziady*.

LA VEGLIA DEI MORTI, FRAMMENTO DEGLI AVI. Volgarizzato da Paolo Lioy. Rovigo, 1862, 39 p.

Dziady, part II, selections.

ALLA MADRE POLACCA. Traduzione di Emilio Teza. Bologna, 1863, 4 p.

IL DELIRIO DELL'ORGOGLIO, CARME TITANICO. Traduzione di Paolo Lioy. Vicenza, 1863, 21 p.

Improvisation, from *Dziady*, part III.

I MARTIRI, frammenti del drama nazionale *Gli Avi*. Una conversazione a Varsavia. Traduzione in versi di Paolo Lioy, con introduzione. *Il Museo di Famiglia*, Milano, 1863.

Selections from *Dziady*, part III.

CORRADO WALLENROD. Versione italiana di Archimede Bottesini. *Annotatore*, Parma, 1865.

TADDEO SOPLITZA O L'ULTIMO PROCESSO IN LITUANIA. Milano, 1871, 142 p.

Pan Tadeusz, prose translation by Arrigo Boïto.

I LITUANI OVVERO CORRADO WALLENROD. Novella storica. Traduzione di F. Fontana. Milano, Treves, 1874, 93 p. (*Biblioteca Amena*, vol. CXVI.)

Prose translation.

CORRADO WALLENROD. Legenda storica lituana. Traduzione dal polacco par Aglauro Ungherini. Assisi, 1876, 60 p.

IL LIBRO DELLA NAZIONE POLACCA E DEI PELLEGRINI POLACCHI. Traduzione di Aglauro Ungherini, Assisi, 1878, 64 p.

ALL'ACCADEMIA DI ADAMO MICKIEWICZ FONDATA IN BOLOGNA dall'Illustre Professore Domenico Santagata. Bologna, 1879, 15 p.

Contains the following translations: *Ode alla gioventù*; *Alla madre polacca*; *Il ridotto d'Ordon*, made by Curzio Antonelli, Andrea Maffei and Ettore Mercucci. The aim of the Mickiewicz Academy was the dissemination of information concerning Poland and its cultural activities.

IL LIBRO DELLA NAZIONE POLACCA E DEI PELLEGRINI POLACCHI. Versione italiana con prefazione e note di Cezare Bragalia. Milano, 1885, 94 p. (*Biblioteca Universale*, n. 137.)

GLI DZIADY, IL CORRADO WALLENROD E POESIE VARIE. Traduzione dal polacco di Aglauro Ungherini. Torino, 1898, xxviii+306 p. Ed. 2, 1902.

Prose translations. In addition to the works mentioned, translations of other poems are included. Preface by Władisłas Mickiewicz.

Russia e Polonia dal dramma Gli Avi. Frammenti, traduzione di Paolo Lioy. Vicenza, 1905.
Dziady, part III, selections.

Pagine scelte dalle opere di Adamo Mickiewicz. Tommaso Gallarati Scotti: Adamo Mickiewicz. Milano, 1915, p. 69–126.
Selections from *Dziady*, part III, *Ode to Youth*, *To a Polish Mother*, *The Prayer of the Pilgrim*, *The Books of the Polish Nation*, selected lectures on Slavic literature.

Gli Slavi. Pagine scelte dalle conferenze di A. Mickiewicz al College de France. Prefazione di W. Lutosławski. Milano, 1918, 79 p. (*La Nostra Scuola*. Quaderni, n. 2.)

Pagine scelte dalle opere di Mickiewicz. *Rivista di Cultura*, Roma, 1924, vol. X, fasc. 6/7, p. 191–292+xii, 1 pl.
Issue dedicated to the poet, and containing 12 translations of works by Mickiewicz, chiefly short stories, as well as several studies on Mickiewicz.

Grażyna. Novella lituana. Traduzione dal polacco, con proemio e note di Aurelio Palmieri, ed uno studio di Roman Pollak. Napoli, publicazioni dell'Istituto per l'Europa Orientale in Roma, 1924, 135 p.

Pan Taddeo Soplitza. Traduzione di Clotilde Garosci, introduzione di Cristina Agosti Garosci. Lanciano, 1924, vol. I: xvi+160 p., vol. II: 193 p. (*Scrittori Italiani e stranieri*, n. 151–2.)
Pan Tadeusz, prose translation.

Antologia della vita spirituale. Con proemio sull'Evoluzione mistica di Mickiewicz. Traduzione di Aurelio Palmieri. Roma, 1925, 209 p. (*Scrittori stranieri*, vol. I. Ed. 2, 1930. *Scrittori classici*.)
Contains several dozen translations of regional poems, extracts from *Dziady*, from letters and from his Paris lectures. Preface: 'La religiosità di Adamo Mickiewicz', by A. Palmieri.

Adamo Mickiewicz: Scritti e traduzioni di: A. Begey, M. Bersano-Begey, E. Damiani, E. de Andreis, C. Garosci, L. Kociemski, M. A. Kulczycka,

A. Lewak, A. Palmieri, P. E. Pavolini, R. Pollak, etc. Roma, 1925, 102 p., 1 pl. (Quaderni della *Rivista di Cultura*. Collezione di *Scritti di Letterature straniere a cura di Enrico Damiani*, n. 1.)

Reprint of issue no. 6/7 of the *Rivista di Cultura* of 1924. The bibliography is enlarged.

CANTI. *Switez, I Sonetti di Crimea, Il Farys, L'Episodio*. Tradotti dal testo polacco da Enrico Damiani con prefazione di Roman Pollak. Seguiti da uno studio del traduttore. Firenze, 1926, 162 p. (*Classici Moderni*.)

L'Episodio is a translation of 'Ustęp' from *Dziady*, part III.

SONETTI DI CRIMEA. Traduzione di Oscar Skarbek-Tłuchowski. Firenze, Tyszkiewicz, 1929, 70 p., 10 pl.

Edition limited to 144 copies. Folio with engravings by Maria Tyszkiewicz.

GLI SLAVI di Adamo Mickiewicz, preceduto dal *Libro della nazione e dei Pellegrini polacchi*. Coi documenti della Legione Polacca del '48 e gli articoli sulla questione italiana del '49. A cure di Marina Bersano-Begey. Torino, 1947, 367 p., 5 pl. (*Classici Politici*, vol. 1.)

TRANSLATIONS INTO RUSSIAN

SVITEZH. BALLADA. *Novosti literatury*. Moskva, 1825, Sentjabr', 168–173 str.
First Russian translation of a work by Mickiewicz.

KONRAD WALLENROD. Perevod S. Sevireva. *Moskovskij Vestnik*. 1828.

STIKHOTVORENIJA ADAMA MICKIEWICZA. Perevod V.R. (V. Lubič-Romanovič). St. Peterburg, 1829, 42 str.
Contains: *Sonety krymskie* and other poems.

KRYMSKIE SONETY. Perevody i podrazhanija Ivana Kozlova. St. Peterburg, 1829, xii+36 str.; Izd. 2, 1833; Izd. 3, 1840 (Sobranie stikhotvorenij I. I. Kozlova); Izd. 4, 1906 (Stikhotvorenija I. Kozlova).

PRAOTTSY. Perevod M. Vročenki. *Nevskij Al'manakh*. St. Peterburg, 1829.
Dziady, part II.

KONRAD WALLENROD. Perevod Afanasija Spigotskogo. Moskva, 1832,
vi+96 str.

STRAŠNYJ GOST'. Litovskaja poema. Varšava, 1844, 193 str.
Dziady, part IV, without the name of the author or the translator.

MICKIEWICZ V PEREVODE OMULEVSKOGO. SONETY. St. Peterburg, 1857,
34 str.

KRYMSKIE SONETY. Perevod N. Lugovskogo. Odessa, 1858, 46 str.

KONRAD WALLENROD. Perevod A. Gorbunova. *Svetoc*, St. Peterburg, 1860.

PEREVODY I PODRAZHANIJA N. V. BERGA. St. Peterburg, 1860, vi+271 str.
   Contains: Fragments from *Pan Tadeusz*, *Konrad Wallenrod*, *Sonety
krymskie*, and 12 other poems.

KONRAD WALLENROD. Perevod F. B. Millera. *Stikhotvorenija*. Moskva,
1860, II, str. 145–224.

KORČMA V UPITE I GRAŽYNA. Dve povesti v stikhakh. Perevod V. Lubiča-
Romanoviča. St. Peterburg, 1862, 216 str.
   Popas w Upicie and *Grażyna*.

KONRAD WALLENROD. GRAŻYNA. Perevod V. Benediktova. S risunkami
I. Tysieviča. St. Peterburg 1863, 191 str.

PEREVODY IZ MICKIEWICZA N. BERGA. Varšava, 1865, 230 str.
   Contains: large fragments of *Pan Tadeusz*, *Konrad Wallenrod*, sonnets
and 11 other poems.

POMINKI. Perevod V. Benediktova. St. Peterburg, 1865, 98 str.
   Dziady, parts II and IV.

PAN TADEUSZ. Perevod N. Berga. Varšava, 1875, xxxii+312 str., Izd. 2, St. Peterburg, 1907, xvi+301 str.

First complete Russian translation of *Pan Tadeusz*, with deletions imposed by the Tsarist censorship and a certain number of omissions made by the translator. 2nd edition, 1907: without deletions.

KRYMSKIE SONETY. Perevod V. A. Petrova. St. Peterburg, 1877, str. 87–112.

SOČINENIJA A. MICKIEWICZA. Russkij perevod V. Benediktova, N. Semenova i drugikh pisatelej pod redaktsiej P. N. Polevogo. St. Peterburg, 1882–1883, Volf, tom I, xx+348 str.; tom II, 416 str.; tom III, 396 str.; tom IV, 409 str.; tom V, 402 str.; Izd. 2, tom I–IV, 1902; Izd. 3, tom I–IV, 1913.

First complete edition, containing nearly all the works of Mickiewicz, with the exception of *Dziady*, part III, translated by 19 different translators. This edition also contains a selection from the Correspondence and from the lectures on Slavic literatures. In the second edition, the translation of *Pan Tadeusz* by D. Minaev was replaced by a new translation by V. Benediktov.

IZ MICKIEWICZA. Perevody N. P. Semenova. St. Peterburg, 1883, xvi + 169 str.

Contains: *Konrad Wallenrod*, *Pan Tadeusz*, chapter IV, fragments, *Farys*, *Sonety krymskie*, and 13 other poems.

KONRAD WALLENROD. Perevod N. Semenova. St. Peterburg, 1883, 69 str.

KRYMSKIE SONETY. S perevodami na russkij i frantsuskij jazyky J. O. Romanskogo, na češskij jazyk J. Kollara i na nemetskij Petra Korneliusa. Lvov, 1888, xi+60 str.

Edition containing the Polish text and translations in Russian, French, Czech and German.

KRYMSKIE SONETY. Perevod L. M. Medvedeva. Moskva, 1895, 21 str.

KRYMSKIE SONETY. Perevod A. Kuguševa. *Vestnik Evropy*. Moskva, 1898, aprel'.

KRYMSKIE SONETY. *Motivy Kryma*. Stikhotvorenija i perevody Ivana Kuklina. Sevastopol, 1900.

ILLUSTRIROVANNOE SOBRANIE SOČINENIJ ADAMA MICKIEWICZA v 4 tomakh. St. Peterburg, 1902.
Change in title of the complete edition: *Sobranie sočinenij*, izd. 2 (2nd ed.) with supplementary illustrations taken from the Polish edition of Lwów. From this illustrated Russian edition the following five volumes were published separately, with illustrations: 1. *Poems. Ballads and Romances;* 2. *Grażyna;* 3. *Konrad Wallenrod;* 4. *Dziady, parts I, II and IV;* V. *Pan Tadeusz* (translated by V. C. Benediktova) 1902. Illustrated by Polish painters.

KONRAD WALLENROD. Vstuplenie D. N. Ovsjaniko-Kulikovskogo. Perevod M. Slavinskogo. Petrograd, 1915, ix+99 str.

KNIGI NARODA POL'SKOGO I POL'SKOGO PILIGRIMSTVA. Perevod Anatolija Vinogradova. Moskva, 1917, 114–70 str.; Izd. 2, 1918.
First Russian translation of *Księgi narodu i pielgrzymstwa polskiego* with a commentary by the translator, Professor Vinogradov, on the messianism of the poet.

IZBRANNYE PROIZVEDENIJA. Vstupitel'nye stat'i A. V. Lunačarskogo i A. K. Vinogradova. Moskva-Leningrad, 1929, 316 str.
Contains a selection of poetic works translated by nine different translators; also translations by Ivan Bunin and S. Solov'ev.

KRYMSKIE SONETY. Perevod Boleslava Petra Vittoviča Svenčitskogo (Gord). S predisloviem A. Millera. Vil'no, 1935, 20 str.

IZBRANNOE. Vstupitel'naja stat'ja, podbor stikhov i kommentarii Marka Zhivova. Moskva, 1940, 63 str.
Contains a selection of poetic translations made by 21 translators.

IZBRANNOE. Moskva, 1943, 117 str.
Contains a selection of poetic works and several political articles translated by 10 translators.

GRAŻYNA. Poema. Perevod A. Kovalenskogo. Moskva, 1944, 45 str.

IZBRANNOE. Lirika, ballady, poemy. Perevod pod redaktsiej M. F. Rylskogo i B. Turganova. Moskva, 1946, 601 str.

Contains, translated by 38 translators, a selection of lyric poems: *Grażyna, Konrad Wallenrod, Dziady* (fragments), *Pan Tadeusz* in a new and abridged translation by Suzanne Mar. Preface by Rylski and Nivov.

IZBRANNOE. Moskva, 1946, 102 str. (*Škol'naja biblioteka.*)

Contains a selection for classroom use, with a preface by M. Rylski.

IZBRANNOE. Redaktsija i vstupitel'naja stat'ja M. Rylskogo. Moskva-Leningrad, 1948, 286 str.

Contains a selection for children, illustrated with wood-cuts.

IZBRANNOE. Perevod s Pol'skogo. Moskva, 1948, 46 str.

Contains a small selection of poems translated by 12 translators.

SOBRANIE SOČINENIJ v 5 tomakh. Pod redaktsiej D. D. Blagogo, F. M. Golovenčenki, A. S. Gundorova, M. S. Zhivova, M. F. Rylskogo (glavnyj redaktor), N. A. Slavjatinskogo, B. A. Turganova. Moskva, 1948-1952, tom I, 526 str.; tom II, 1949, 348 str.; tom III, 1952, 313 str.

The first three volumes of the complete edition contain, translated by 25 translators almost all of the poetical works of Mickiewicz. Vol. I: *Various poems, Ballads, Sonnets* (V. Levik), *Sonety krymskie* (O. Rumer), *Grażyna* (new translation by A. Tarkovski), *Konrad Wallenrod* (N. Aseev); Vol. II: *Pan Tadeusz* (Suzanne Mar Akjenova); Vol. III: *Dziady* (L. Martynov, W. Levik).

BALLADY. Perevod pod redaktsiej M. F. Rylskogo i B. A. Turganova. Khudozhnik V. Domagatskij. Moskva, 1948, 133 str.

Translations reprinted from the first volume of the complete edition, with 16 original sketches in the text.

KRYMSKIE SONETY. Perevod O. Rumera. Pod redaktsiej M. Rylskogo. Posleslovie M. Zhivova. Khudozhnik F. Konstantinov. Moskva, 1948, 53 str.

Polish and Russian texts. Special edition for bibliophiles.

GRAŻINA. LITOVSKAJA POVEST'. Perevod s pol'skogo N. A. Slavjatinskogo.
Pod redaktsiej M. Zhivova i M. Rylskogo. Khudozhnik V. Tauber.
Moskva, 1948, 62 str.
New translation of *Grażyna*, embellished with wood-cuts by Tauber.

TRANSLATIONS INTO SPANISH

TADEO SOPLICA O EL ULTIMO PROCESO EN LITUANIA. Narración histórica.
Primera traducción española por León Medina. Madrid, 1887.

KONRAD WALLENROD. Primera traducción española. Cuba. Musée Adam
Mickiewicz, Paris, Quai d'Orléans.

UNESCO PUBLICATIONS:

NATIONAL DISTRIBUTORS

ALGERIA: Éditions de l'Empire, 28 rue Michelet, Algiers; ARGENTINA: Editorial Sud-americana, S.A., Alsina 500, Buenos Aires; AUSTRALIA: Oxford University Press, 346 Little Collins St., Melbourne; AUSTRIA: Wilhelm Frick Verlag, 27 Graben, Vienna I.; BELGIUM: Librairie Encyclopédique, 7 rue du Luxembourg, Brussels IV; N.V. Stand-ard-Boekhandel, Belgiëlei 151, Antwerp; BOLIVIA: Librería Selecciones, Avenida Camacho 369, Casilla 972, La Paz; BRAZIL: Livraría Agir Editora, rua México 98-B, Caixa postal 3291, Rio de Janeiro; CAMBODIA: Librairie Albert Portail, 14 avenue Boulloche, Phnom-penh; CANADA: University of Toronto Press, Toronto; Periodica Inc., 5112 avenue Papineau, Montreal 34; CEYLON: Lake House Bookshop, The Associated Newspapers of Ceylon Ltd., P.O. Box 244, Colombo I; CHILE: Libreria Universitaria, Alameda B. O'Higgins 1059, Santiago de Chile; COLOMBIA: Hans Otto Ungar, Libreria Central, Carrera 6d. A. No. 14-32, Bogota; COSTA RICA; Trejos Hermanos, Apartado 1313, San José; CUBA: Unesco Centro Regional en el Hemisfero Occidental, Calle 5 No. 306 Vedado, Apartado 1358, Havana; CYPRUS: M. E. Con-stantinides, P.O. Box 473, Nicosia; CZECHOSLOVAKIA: Artia Ltd., 30 Ve smeckách, Prague 2; DENMARK: Ejnar Munksgaard, Ltd., 6 Norregade, Copenhagen K; DOMINICAN REPUBLIC: Libreria Dominicana, Calle Mercedes 49, Apartados de Correos 656, Ciudad Trujillo, R.D.; ECUADOR: Libreria Científica, Luque 233, Casilla 362, Guyaquil; EGYPT: La Renaissance d'Égypte, 9 Adly Pasha Street, Cairo; ETHIOPIA: International Press Agency, P.O. Box 120, Addis Ababa; FINLAND: Akateeminen Kirjakauppa, 2 Keskuskatu, Helsinki; FORMOSA: The World Book Co., Ltd., 99 Chung King Rd., Section I, Taipeh; FRANCE: Unesco Bookshop, 19 avenue Kléber, Paris-16e; FRENCH WEST INDIES: Librairie J. Bocage, rue Lavoir, Fort de France (Martinique); GERMANY: R. Oldenbourg K.G., Unesco Vertrieb für Deutsch-land, Rosenheimerstrasse 145, Munich 8; GREECE: Librairie H. Kauffmann, 28 rue du Stade, Athens; HAITI: Librairie 'A la Caravelle', 36 rue Roux, Boîte postale III-B, Port-au-Prince; HONG KONG: Swindon Book Co., 25 Nathan Road, Kowloon; HUNGARY: Kultura, P.O.B. 149, Budapest 62; INDIA: Orient Longmans Ltd., Indian Mercantile Chamber, Nicol Road, Bombay; 17 Chittaranjan Ave., Calcutta; 36-A Mount Road, Madras; *Sub-depots:* Oxford Book and Stationery Co., Scindia House, New Delhi. Rajkamal Publications Ltd., Himalaya House, Hornby Road, Bombay I; INDONESIA: G.C.T. van Dorp and Co., Djalan Nusantara 22, Jakarta;

IRAN: Iranian National Commission for Unesco, Avenue du Musée, Teheran; IRAQ: McKenzie's Bookshop, Baghdad; ISRAEL: Blumstein's Bookstores, Ltd., 35 Allenby Road, P.O.B. 5154, Tel Aviv; ITALY: Libreria Commissionaria G. C. Sansoni, via Gino Capponi 26, Casella postale 552, Florence; JAMAICA: Sangster's Book Room, 99 Harbour Street, Kingston. Knox Educational Services, Spaldings; JAPAN: Maruzen Co., Inc., 6 Tori-Nichome, Nihonbashi, Tokyo; JORDAN: Joseph I. Bahous and Co., Dar-ul-Kutub, Salt Road, Amman; KOREA: Korean National Commission for Unesco, Ministry of Education, Seoul; LAOS (See Viet-Nam); LEBANON: Librairie Universelle, Avenue des Français, Beirut; LIBERIA: J. Momolu Kamara, 69 Front and Gurley Streets, Monrovia; LUXEMBOURG: Librairie Paul Bruck, 33, Grand-Rue; MALAYAN FEDERATION AND SINGAPORE: Peter Chong and Co., P.O. Box 135, Singapore; MALTA: Sapienza's Library, 26 Kingsway, Valletta; MEXICO: Librería y Ediciones Emilio Obregón, Avenida Juárez 30, Mexico, D.F; NETHERLANDS: N. V. Martinus Nijhoff, Lange Voorhout 9, The Hague; NEW ZEA-LAND: Unesco Publications Centre, 100 Hackthorne Road, Christchurch; NIGERIA: C.M.S. Bookshop, P.O. Box 174, Lagos; NORWAY: A/S Bokhjornet, Stortingsplass 7, Oslo; PAKISTAN: Ferozsons, 60 The Mall, Lahore; Bunder Road, Karachi; 35 The Mall, Peshawar; PANAMA: Agencia Internacional de Publicaciones, Apartado 2052, Plaza de Arango No. 8, Panama, R.P.; PARAGUAY: Agencia de Librerias de Salvador Nizza, Calle Pte. Franco No. 39/43, Asunción; PERU: Librería Mejia Baca, Azangaro 722, Lima; PHILIPPINES: Philippine Education Co., 1104 Castillejos, Quiapo, Manila; PORTUGAL: Publicaçoes Európa-America, Ltda., Rua das Flores 45, 1°., Lisbon; PUERTO RICO: Pan-American Book Co., San Juan 12; SPAIN: Libreria científica Medinaceli, Duque de Medinaceli 4, Madrid; SURINAM: Radhakishun and Co., Ltd. (Book Dept.), Watermolenstraat 36, Paramaribo; SWEDEN: A/B C.E. Fritzes-Kungl., Hovbokhandel, Fredsgatan 2, Stockholm 16; SWITZERLAND: Librairie Antoine Dousse, ancienne librairie de l'Université, Case postale 72, Fribourg. Europa Verlag, 5 Rämistrasse, Zürich. *Sub-depots:* Librairie Payot, place Molard, Geneva; Librairie Barblan et Saladin, 10 rue Romont, Fribourg; SYRIA: Librairie Universelle, Damascus; THAILAND: Suksapan Panit, Arkarn 9, Rajdamnern Ave., Bangkok; TUNISIA: Victor Boukhors, 4 rue Nocard, Tunis; TURKEY: Librairie Hachette, 469 Istiklal Caddesi, Beyoglu, Istanbul; UNION OF BURMA: Burma Educational Bookshop, 551-3 Merchant Street, P.O. Box 222, Rangoon; UNION OF SOUTH AFRICA: Van Schaik's Bookstore (Pty) Ltd., P.O. Box 724, Pretoria; UNITED KINGDOM: H.M. Stationery Office, P.O. Box 569, London, S.E.1; UNITED STATES OF AMERICA: Columbia University Press, 2960 Broadway, New York 27, N.Y.; URUGUAY: Oficina de Representación de Editoriales, 18 de Julio 1333, Unesco Centro de Cooperacion Cientifica para America Latina, Bulevar Artigas, 1320-24, Montevideo; VENEZUELA: Librería Villegas Venezolana, Madrices a Marrón N. 35, Pasaje Urdaneta, Local B, Caracas; VIET-NAM: Librairie Nouvelle, Albert Portail, B.P. 283, Saigon; YUGOSLAVIA: Jugoslovenska Knjiga, Terazijc 27/11, Belgrade.

Unesco Book Coupons

Unesco Book Coupons can be used to purchase all books and periodicals of an educational, scientific or cultural character. For full information please write to: Unesco Coupon Office, 19 avenue Kléber, Paris-16e, France.